NEW PERSPECTIVES ON THE SOUTH

Charles P. Roland, General Editor

Black
Southerners
1619-1869

John B. Boles

THE UNIVERSITY PRESS OF KENTUCKY

Library of Congress Cataloging in Publication Data
Boles, John B., 1943-
    Black southerners, 1619-1869.

    (New perspectives on the South)
    Bibliography: p.
    Includes index.
    1. Slavery—Southern States—History. 2. Afro-
Americans—Southern States—History. 3. Southern States—
History. 4. Southern States—Race relations. 5. Planta-
tion life—Southern States—History. I. Title. II. Series.
E441.B67   1983   975'.00496073   83-10177
ISBN: 0-8131-0303-7 cloth; -0161-1 paper

Scholarly publisher for the Commonwealth,
serving Bellarmine College, Berea College, Centre
College of Kentucky, Eastern Kentucky University,
The Filson Club, Georgetown College, Kentucky
Historical Society, Kentucky State University,
Morehead State University, Murray State University,
Northern Kentucky University, Transylvania University,
University of Kentucky, University of Louisville,
and Western Kentucky University.

Editorial and Sales Offices: Lexington, Kentucky 40506-0024

Contents

Editor's Preface

Of all the institutions and practices that have contributed to the distinctiveness of the South, slavery is the most clearly identifiable. It is the one thing that, beyond question, distinguished the Old South legally, socially, culturally, psychologically, and symbolically from the rest of the country. Its effects have persisted in countless ways to the present day.

John Boles has produced an able and balanced account of southern slavery, its destruction in the Civil War, and its immediate aftermath during Reconstruction. He has wisely avoided making the slaves into angels or supermen, or the owners into demons or monsters. Instead, he has drawn upon a wealth of recent scholarship to show that the relations between masters and chattels were such that the blacks were able to retain both their humanity and significant elements of their African heritage, thus preserving the core of a black community within the embrace of the dominant white society.

Because the story of slavery is central to that of the region, and because of the author's knowledge and insights, this work is an essential volume in "New Perspectives on the South." The series is designed to give a fresh and comprehensive view of the South's history, as seen in the light of the striking developments it has undergone since World War II. Each volume is expected to be a complete essay representing both a synthesis of the best research on the topic and an interpretive analysis derived from the author's own reflections. Twenty or more volumes are planned.

CHARLES P. ROLAND

Preface

Some years ago, having already written a book on the religion of antebellum white southerners, I was asked to write one on religion in Kentucky before the Civil War. In the course of preparing that volume, I realized the need for a chapter on the faith of black people, and hence I was drawn to a fascinating topic of immense complexity. Subsequently I decided to make a major study of slave religion. But as I began to read about religion, I found I had to enlarge my focus to include all of black culture. Soon my reading forced me to consider topics as varied as the rise and influence of the black family and the nature of the antebellum economy. Almost before I realized it, my narrow, manageable topic grew to include the total black experience, from the African background through Reconstruction.

I wanted to emphasize how the institution of slavery changed over time, and I wanted to show the diversity of the antebellum black experience—urban and industrial as well as agricultural slavery—and the development of the free black population. I came to see that one must know the seventeenth- and eighteenth-century background to understand slavery at its height, 1820-60, and that the way slavery ended and evolved into sharecropping after the Civil War illuminated the prewar experience. While I have tried in the present book to discuss a wide range of topics, no one is more aware than I of how much I have left unsaid. I wanted to compress as much of the history of black southerners as I could into relatively few pages, making accessible to readers the fruit of the remarkably rich scholarship on blacks that has appeared during the last two decades.

Writing is just another way of teaching, the major difference being that the students are not sitting in the room with the writer as they are with the classroom teacher. The teacher, having read the literature on a topic that has captivated him, tries to distill the work of others, synthesize it, and present it in as interesting and comprehensible a format as possible. This is what I try to do in this book.

Anyone teaching or talking about slavery is faced with an unusual problem. The scholarship on the subject has been so extensive, and of such high quality, that one does not know which books to assign, or rather, not to assign. This embarrassment of riches is further complicated by the chronological and topical limits of most of the work. There are marvelous books on colonial slavery, on mid-nineteenth-century slavery, on industrial and urban slaves, on free blacks, and on slave religion, but there exists no one brief, interpretative volume that attempts to include all these subjects. This book is offered as a distillation of a distinguished body of scholarship, a synthesis that is more than a summary, more than an introduction. I hope it will lead others to read the books and articles upon which it is based.

My title, of course, makes the point that blacks have been southerners for almost as long as whites have. Indeed, neither the South nor white southerners can be understood without taking into consideration the experience and contributions of those other southerners, the blacks. The South is the blacks' land too, and many of them identify with it and love it. Properly speaking, *southerner* is a biracial term. The blacks' passage toward freedom has been long and arduous, and to a profound degree their experience in the New World constitutes a Middle Passage writ large. With roots in Africa, involuntarily brought to America, they were to find liberty only after two and a half centuries of bondage. Even then, the freedom of the freedmen was circumscribed by habit and racism. Their story consists of equal parts of tragedy and courage but ultimately proclaims that the human spirit is unquenchable.

A number of individuals have assisted me in preparing this book, which has preoccupied me during much of my tenure at three different universities. In addition to the students in my graduate seminars at Towson State, Tulane, and Rice, I would like to thank the following persons, who read the manuscript in various drafts and made helpful suggestions: Cathy M. Azzi, Charles B. Dew,

Irma F. Garlick, Michele K. Gillespie, Thomas L. Haskell, Sanford W. Higginbotham, Allen J. Matusow, Evelyn T. Nolen, Lawrence N. Powell, and Bennett H. Wall. While none of them may be completely satisfied with the final result, I know how much the manuscript profited from their efforts. Of course, I am ultimately responsible for the views and interpretations contained herein, and I absolve them from any possible blame. Elizabeth H. Turner helped with checking the bibliography and proofreading. A series of secretaries have typed versions of the manuscript: Valeria Palo, Elaine Severio, Kelly Kane, Darlene U. Collins, and Kathy Tomasic-Carrazedo. Linda Quaidy rescued me from one major typing emergency. To all of them, thanks.

This book took longer to complete than I originally expected, and throughout, my wife, Nancy (who helped in a variety of ways), and our two boys, David and Matthew, have sustained my energy and spirit.

For Matthew Thomas

Introduction

The fateful relationship between Africa and the American South—indeed, the entire Western Hemisphere—has a history that antedates the initial voyages of Christopher Columbus. Southern and Western Europeans before the fourteenth century were aware of a mysterious continent to their south, and though they considered it backward, heathenish, and darkly exotic, rumors of great riches suggested European opportunities. For countless centuries internal trade routes had facilitated the commerce of Africa, and the long caravans snaking across the vast Sahara from the western Gold Coast to the Arab empires at the eastern end of the Mediterranean had exchanged precious minerals, "teeth" (ivory), cloth, spices, and slaves. In the early fifteenth century enterprising Portuguese merchants, dreaming of the profits to be made from capturing a portion of this carrying trade, began cautiously to explore the western coasts of Africa. Local merchants along the seashore were pleased to trade with the Europeans, exchanging gold, ivory, and some slaves for simple manufactured goods at first. The Portuguese vessels then struggled up-current back to the Mediterranean to markets in North Africa and the Arab end of the sea.

Limited European entry into an ongoing African commercial system was slowed for a number of reasons, among which was the difficulty of making the return sailing voyage against both wind and current from the West African ports. During the early decades of the 1400s, Portuguese shipbuilders, experimenting with sleeker hulls borrowed from northern Europe and the lateen sail from Arab vessels in the Indian Ocean, came upon a combination that greatly eased the return voyage. The triangular lateen sail, hung from a long yard attached at an angle to a short mast, could be maneuvered according to the wind's direction. The resulting ship design, the caravel, could, by shifting the sail, be propelled by winds coming from either side, while the older, flat-bottom ships with one large mainsail were stalled unless the wind blew directly from behind. By being able economically to tack against the breeze, the caravel opened up to Portuguese navigators the possibility of exploring the entire African coast, and with such success that by 1486 Bartholomeu Diaz rounded the Cape of Good Hope, and in 1497-98 Vasco da Gama reached India.

More important for our story, anonymous Portuguese pilots by the 1440s had discovered—probably by accident—that if they let the prevailing trade winds push them far offshore from Africa and to the northwest, they eventually, out north and beyond the Azores, would catch the prevailing westerlies, and the wind and current would steadily carry them back to the Iberian Peninsula. Here was a momentous discovery, for, by unlocking the mysteries of the trade winds and ocean currents, navigators now could reach any place in the world. The Atlantic was thus opened; one followed the trade winds south and, on the return voyage, followed them west, inched north past the trade-wind belt, then rode the westerlies home in a large loop fraught with possibilities for the future. It was on this navigational scheme that Columbus and the early voyagers explored the Western Hemisphere and returned to familiar ports. In seeking to capitalize on the indigenous African commerce, Europeans discovered their way to the New World, thus intertwining the histories of Africa and America.

1. A Tentative Beginning

Part of the mythology every schoolchild in the United States learns, along with the Pilgrims and Thanksgiving and the poignant story of Pocahontas and Captain John Smith, is that the colony of Virginia achieved quick prosperity upon the basis of slaves and tobacco. Thus, "the South"—complete with images of grand plantation mansions and swarms of servile blacks—is assumed to have existed almost from initial settlement, with little change until the cataclysm of the Civil War in 1861. Yet the path to large-scale slavery in Virginia and Maryland, the other Chesapeake colony, was slow, uncertain, and in no way predetermined from the beginning. And South Carolina, where the transition to a slave economy occurred relatively quickly, was in many ways more a colony of the West Indian island of Barbados than of England. There were few blacks in the seventeenth-century mainland colonies, and their relationships with whites were perhaps more harmonious than they would again be for nearly three centuries. Not all blacks were slaves; in fact, the status of all Africans evolved—and for most, declined—over the course of the century. Change in their numbers, in their legal status, in the crops they raised and the chores assigned them, in their ability to have families, in the relative Africanness of their culture, was a constant in the experience of the African people in the South.

Some present-day readers believe slavery began at Jamestown in 1619 when the first blacks were landed, or, if such readers are aware of slavery's existence in the ancient world, they assume it had become extinct until New World plantations arose with their greed for cheap labor. Of course, neither viewpoint is correct, and in order to understand why slavery was introduced in the New

World colonies, its status in fifteenth-century Europe and even earlier must be studied. As the most casual reader of the Bible knows, there were slaves in the ancient Near East and in Greece and Rome. Usually they were not racially distinct but rather were war captives, though there were black—or Ethiopian, as they were called—slaves in antiquity. While most black slaves served in domestic capacities, some were musicians, clerks, tutors, or soldiers. Having been captured from the highly developed kingdom of Nubia (Ethiopia) or descended from the Kushites who for almost a century (c. 1650-1567 B.C.) had ruled Egypt, black slaves in antiquity were not discriminated against as blacks. Theirs was a lesser legal status, not a position of racial inferiority. The same was true for African slaves in the Arabian Peninsula before the rise of Islam. After all, those Africans with whom the Arabians came into contact had a culture relatively equivalent technologically to their own.

Then, during and after the seventh century, as the Islamic Empire was created and swept westward around the perimeter of the northern half of Africa, pushed into the Iberian Peninsula, and marched eastward to the Persian Gulf, Arab attitudes toward blacks changed. By meeting fairer-skinned peoples in Europe and Persia whose heritage if not present civilization seemed more advanced than their own, and at the same time encountering sub-Saharan and eastern African peoples with vastly more primitive cultures, the Arabs subtly transmuted blackness into an indicator of racial inferiority. With the expansion of the Islamic Empire, and with the enslavement of fellow Muslims prohibited, the demand for black laborers grew. By the ninth century thousands were being exported from East African ports into the lands surrounding the Persian Gulf—slaves in the Middle East were even called *Zenj*, the word for East Africa. Still other slaves were imported from West Africa via the overland caravan routes across the Sahara. Black slaves were increasingly forced into more menial tasks, serving not simply as domestics but being pressed into back-breaking labor in the salt and copper mines of North Africa and the sugarcane plantations of Egypt and southern Iraq. Blackness now came to be synonymous with slavery as the original Arabic word for slave, *'abd*, evolved to mean simply a black man. A substantial market for African slaves outside Africa, one far more demeaning than indigenous African slavery, had arisen, and concurrently the African had acquired the image of the natural slave. Both developments were to prove significant for initial European encounters with Africa and subsequently for the New World slave systems.

The onset of the Middle Ages found most of Europe moving toward feudalism and away from slavery. The exceptions were southern Europe and the Iberian Peninsula, where the older forms of forced labor had continued since antiquity. As in the ancient system, slaves were usually captives of war directly or indirectly, with religion, not race, being the crucial factor in Spain and Portugal. Christians used Muslim slaves, and Muslims enslaved Christians. A sprinkling of blacks were purchased from Arab middlemen to serve in harems or as palace guards, or, like dwarfs and jugglers, as court exotics. In regions where a sort of reciprocal Christian-Muslim supply of slaves was unavailable, Europeans imported Eurasians purchased from dealers operating slave factories or bases in the region of the Black Sea. Circassians (from the northeastern shore of the Black Sea, in Russia) and Dalmatians (from the eastern region of Yugoslavia) were traded to the East for the fabled spices and silks.

The flourishing European-Middle East slave trade was at first largely independent of the Arab-African trade in blacks. But borrowing from the Arabs, alert Genoese merchants by the fourteenth century had developed thriving sugarcane plantations on Cyprus worked by black slaves employed in gang labor. Where the Genoese were, the Portuguese were soon to follow. Within a century the plantation system, with its careful organization and ability to control labor at the crucial harvest time, was ensconced in southern Portugal, and by the 1450s the Portuguese were establishing Genoese-like sugar plantations on Madeira and the Canary Islands. Just as the labor shortage on these sugar islands was reaching a crisis because European diseases had killed the native peoples and there were too few Muslim prisoners of war, the Portuguese were making their first successful intrusions into the traditional African slave trade.

With the Black Sea markets for Eurasian slaves closed by the Turkish capture of Constantinople after the mid-fifteenth century and with the convenient acceptance by Europeans of the Arabic conception of Africans as natural slaves, the turning of Portuguese shippers from almost exclusive cargoes of gold and ivory to an emphasis on slaves seems quite understandable. The use of black slaves on the Iberian Peninsula—Seville came to have a sub-stantial African population—and on the sugar islands became extensive. The Portuguese capture just before 1500 of the island of São Thomé, on the equator 200 miles off the coast of Africa, and its conversion into an agricultural factory for the production of sugar employing slaves imported directly from Africa, proved to be both the climax of the European-African slavery system and the perfect model for what was to occur thousands of miles to the west in the Caribbean. Large-scale plantation agriculture with slave labor existed as the prototype for colonial development before Columbus made his vaunted discovery in 1492.

Even though the seeds of black slavery were to be planted very early in the Americas, the full-blown system was slower to develop than one might suppose. On his second voyage to the New World, Columbus introduced sugarcane to Hispaniola, and by 1502 African slaves were being delivered to the Caribbean. The Spanish government subsidized the emigration of a number of Canary Islanders who had mastered the growing and manufacturing of sugar, and by about 1515 samples of the sweet residue were sent to Spain. Shortly a prosperous sugar industry developed on Hispaniola, but it did not appear very glamorous to metropolitan eyes. With the discovery of more glittering sources of wealth in Mexico and Peru, Spanish interests shifted to the mainland, and the Caribbean islands became a virtual backwater for almost a century, though they remained a provisioning stop for vessels en route between the Americas and Europe. The African slave population grew only slowly on the islands, and in the Spanish mainland colonies the indigenous Indian peoples survived the ravages of newly introduced Old World diseases better than the Caribbean islanders (almost all the Carib Indians died) only to be enslaved by their Spanish conquerors. The result was a slower rate of importation for African slaves on the South and Central American mainland than would have been the case otherwise. The Portuguese, confined to Brazil by the terms of the Treaty of Tordesillas (1494) which, with the Pope's approval, divided the world between Spain and Portugal, in the latter half of the sixteenth century developed the kind of large-scale sugar industry there that pointed toward the future. Financed and provisioned largely by the Dutch, Portuguese Brazil by 1600 was the world's sugar bowl.

When, in the early decades of the 1600s, England and France began casting envious glances at the semitropical islands spilled like jewels across the Caribbean, Spain was just economically and politically weak enough, and sufficiently preoccupied in Europe with wars and internal problems, to let them establish toehold colonies. Because the high death rate on the islands had practically destroyed the native peoples and made large-scale English or French settlement unattractive, because Dutch capital and sugar know-how was available, and because the European demand for sugar was on a steady ascent, suddenly conditions were ripe for the sugar revolution that was to change the whole course of New World history. The revolution occurred with astounding rapidity. Permanent British settlers first set foot on Barbados in 1627; by 1643 the population included 6,000 slaves, and in another forty years the number of black slaves (40,000) was almost double the number of resident whites. The other Caribbean islands, controlled by various European powers, followed the lead of Barbados and all became known as the sugar islands: Guadeloupe, Jamaica, San Domingo, St. Croix. By the final quarter of the seventeenth century, the great boom in sugar and slaves was in full swing, European interests switched from the mainland to the islands, and great riches were reaped in sugar and slaves for the next two centuries. Not only did the sugar islands in the West Indies become the centerpieces of Europe's various worldwide imperial systems, but they also received a remarkable one-half of the total of all Africans imported to the New World in the three and a half centuries after 1500. It was in the backwash of this dynamic Caribbean sugar boom that slavery developed on the North American mainland— the present-day United States.

Yet it was by no means predetermined in 1607, when England planted her first permanent settlement in the New World at Jamestown, that slavery would inevitably follow in the mainland colonies. African bondage was already a century old in the Western Hemisphere, but it was under the auspices of the Spanish and Portuguese. Plantation organization and the technological understanding of sugar manufacture had likewise taken root in the New World, but in semitropical islands. Along the western coasts of

Africa the far-flung Dutch maritime interests had supplanted the
pioneering Portuguese traders, and African chieftains were as eager
to deal in human beings in exchange for Dutch bars of iron, cloth,
and simple manufactures as for those of the Portuguese. The
ravenous labor demands of the sugar regions consumed the human
cargoes. The whole transatlantic system was in place, primed to
flourish as the seventeenth century unfolded. Yet this was essentially a Mediterranean-Caribbean cultural development, with roots in
a whole series of Iberian and Genoese (and even earlier Arab) legal
and economic traditions quite alien to the English historical experience. In Europe slavery had survived to the south while
England had moved down another path; there was no evidence that
in the New World the English experience was to be any different.
The indices for the future were mixed as the Elizabethan era in
England drew to a close at the beginning of the seventeenth
century.

The English before Jamestown were certainly aware of the existence of slavery. As part of their preening pride in being
Englishmen, they valued their own liberty and looked down their
collective noses at those southern Europeans who not only were
Catholic but also stooped to enslave with brutal consequences both
American Indians and imported Africans. The crown even en-
couraged English adventurers to raid the trading vessels of the competing nations. The English perception of being set apart from, and
better than, the Spanish and Portuguese included a tendency to
downgrade slavery as something foreign and backward, though on
several occasions English adventurers like John Hawkins overcame
their scruples and traded in slaves when the opportunity presented
itself. In addition to being aware that slavery existed, the English
also were prepared to accept that in certain circumstances it could
be legal—when those in servitude, for example, were war captives
or convicted criminals. Their choice was a bit ethnocentric, but
they simply preferred the English system of modified serfdom that
included temporary ownership of the labor—not the person—of individuals who bartered their service for a certain price, in this case
passage to America.

This system of indentured servitude was similar to apprenticeship, whereby servant and master had reciprocal responsibilities.
When the English began establishing settlements in the New World,

they brought their traditional labor systems with them. Feeling superior to the Spanish anyway and intending to avoid the genocidal horrors attributed to the Spanish in the West Indies, they felt no necessity to throw aside English practices and adopt instead the ways of their European rival. Virginia was to be peopled with and developed by Englishmen, and perhaps willing Indians and such others as wanted to escape the rigors of Spanish authority, but it was intended to be a transplanted England with only minimal concessions to imagined New World conditions. Within a century, however, English mainland colonies, especially those to the south, had made such crucial adaptations that they were unlike anything in the presettlement English experience. The history of those adaptations is the story of the emergence and evolution of a slave society in the American South.

Although there is a slight hint in some of the sources that one or more Africans arrived in Virginia several years earlier, 1619 is the date generally accepted for the introduction of blacks to the English mainland colonies. In an offhand manner John Rolfe wrote to Sir Edwin Sandys, treasurer of the Virginia Company, that five months previously a Dutch man-of-war had arrived at Point Comfort, where the James River emptied into the Chesapeake, and in exchange for badly needed provisions had paid the colony officials with "20. and odd Negroes," meaning evidently a number greater than twenty. With those four words begins the documented history of Africans in what is now the United States (except for one or more blacks who accompanied Spanish explorers in the early 1500s). Yet we know frustratingly little about that initial score of blacks—neither their immediate past before being unceremoniously introduced to Virginia nor their subsequent history. The Dutch captain no doubt sold them without a flicker of conscience, so hardened did those in the slave trade come to be; still, one wonders what thoughts occurred to the Virginia officials as they made that first ill-starred purchase. Did they simply see themselves as buying the labor of the Africans, who would thus be differentiated from countless other servants only by their complexion, or did they purposely acquire them as slaves for life, possibly justifying themselves on the grounds that the Dutch—or the Africans' original captors— had already enslaved them, and thus the Virginians were making a perfectly unexceptional commercial transaction? Did the Virginia

officials harbor deep doubts about the propriety of their actions but
feel that the Dutch captain's "great need" justified their selling him
provisions in exchange for the only currency he had available?
These questions will probably never be answered. The only sure
point that can be made is that the system of black slavery did not
emerge full-blown with the fateful transaction off Point Comfort in
1619.

Certainly one of the reasons Englishmen did not instantly in-
troduce slavery to their mainland colony was their prejudice
against non-English ways of doing things. In the West Indian
islands, where the native populations had essentially died out as a
result of exposure to Old World diseases, where the climate favored sugar cultivation, which, because of the labor demands of
harvesting and processing, seemed to necessitate slave workers,
and where the climate seemed to offer little hope of large-scale
English settlement, the British quickly accepted what they perceived as the reality of the situation and hence began their prosperous sugar-slave empire. None of these precipitating factors
worked to change their expectations for Virginia. True enough,
mineral riches proved nonexistent, but John Rolfe's early discovery
that West Indian tobacco grown in Virginia was sweet to the palates
of English smokers changed only the source, not the prospect, of riches from Virginia. And tobacco, unlike sugar, required
little capital expenditure to begin cultivation, had less rigorous
labor demands, could be grown profitably in small patches, and required no expensive manufacturing process—in short, tobacco
made possible an economic boom in Virginia without the necessity
of jettisoning traditional English laboring practices. The Chesapeake tobacco plantation economy was founded on white indentured labor.

This English aversion to things non-English included peoples
who were not English. Elizabethans, who disliked even the Irish,
hated and were suspicious of the Spanish, and quickly grew shockingly callous toward the Indians, certainly were prejudiced against
those most foreign of all, the Africans. It was almost as if the
English had a scale of acceptance ranging from white English Christian (read Protestant) civilization to black heathen savagery, with
each word as loaded with meaning as they sound to the modern
ear. The Africans' very blackness, associated as it was in Western

culture with evil, made only more visible and indelible his unflat-
tering identity. Yet such an automatic predisposition to denigrate
the African as existed among the English was more an abstract,
superstitious dislike of the unknown, a generalized and passive prejudice, than a systematic racism that shaped every black-white interpersonal relationship. The existence of the prejudice surely made
easier the acceptance of perpetual slavery for Africans, and toward
the end of the seventeenth century it became gradually transformed
into a peculiarly American racism, but it did not in the first decades
after 1619 push all Africans into the despised category of slaves-for-
life.

The half century or so of race relations after 1619 is very confusing. There is no doubt at all that many, quite probably most,
Africans were considered slaves, or at least servants whose period
of servitude was lifelong. Just as clearly, there were others who
served a set number of years—at least occasionally no longer than
similarly aged whites of the same sex—and then were freed. Not
every black was a slave, not every slave served for life, and the
treatment of black slaves/servants seems at times indis-
tinguishable from that accorded white servants. Because the legal presumption that blackness meant slavery did not yet exist,
the nature of one's bondage was subject to court decisions. The
judicial records of seventeenth-century Maryland and Virginia bear
testimony to freedom-seeking "slaves" who sought their liberty on
such grounds as having been baptized or having already served the
period of time previously contracted. On a number of occasions,
proof of their Christianity or documentation of their contractual
obligations having been met—in fact, often exceeded—resulted in
the court's declaring them free. There are still other examples of
blacks being adjudged free upon proof that one of their parents was
free. Precisely because such avenues to freedom existed in the first
decades, planters were sometimes troubled about the permanency
of their "slave" property. If baptism or paternity could lead to
liberty, then not only would some object to such otherwise
benevolent activities as missionaries might perform, but many
might also reasonably be worried about court costs and delays even
if the judgment were ultimately in the planter's favor.

Because laws usually protect the interests of those of wealth and
power, the status of slaves was hardened by a long series of

statutory enactments beginning about 1660. For example, because interracial sex was an act with tangible aftereffects that often led to problems, Virginia in 1662 legislated that all children born henceforth would have the legal status of their mother. Two years later Maryland declared "that all Negroes or other slaves already within the Province and all Negroes and other slaves to be hereafter imported into the Province shall serve Durante Vita"—for life. The children of slave women were to serve for life, according to the new Maryland law, and those white women who married slave men were themselves to serve as slaves for the lifetime of their husbands, and any offspring would likewise be slaves. In 1667 the Virginia assembly made clear by law "that the conferring of baptism doth not alter the condition of the person as to his bondage or freedom." While these and other such laws indicate that those who were currently slaves and their children, along with those slaves subsequently imported into the Chesapeake region, would find their bondage more ironclad than before, the laws also suggest something of the looser state of labor and race relations in the earlier period.

   The black population grew very slowly for the first half century after 1619; consequently it is easy to overemphasize the black presence during the formative years of the Chesapeake tobacco society. The scarcity of blacks complicates the task of explicating their history, for the documentary record is extremely sparse. Two of the most revealing sources are the 1624 and 1625 censuses of the Virginia colony, and they are most significant in the information they do not contain about the blacks. The 1624 census enumerates twenty-two living Negroes, the 1625 twenty-three. While the census entries for white persons usually contains the full name, complete names are not given for any of the twenty-two blacks in the 1624 listing; for almost half no name at all is recorded, and they are accounted simply as "one negor," or "A Negors woman," or in the case of one district, six blank lines followed by the descriptive word "negors." While the 1625 census provides more complete entries for five blacks, in only one entry is the listing complete. The age and date of arrival are given in only one instance, and this kind of data was of critical importance to white indentured servants whose period of servitude dated from the time of their entry. While not much can be drawn from such scant documentation as blank lines denominated "negor," one conclusion seems warranted. At least in the eyes of officials, blacks occupied a distinctly inferior position. The casual manner in which they are enumerated suggests that they were perceived as a category of people quite unlike any other group. Here perhaps is evidence of the English predisposition to assume blackness to be a natural mark of separateness and inferiority.

A spirited historical controversy has raged around the issues raised in the preceding two paragraphs. Because of the cultural connotations of the word *black* and because of rampant English ethnocentrism, was America born "racist" in the sense that Africans were automatically considered inferior and slaves because of their race or color? Or did slavery evolve primarily in response to labor and economic forces, and only afterwards, because Africans were the ones most conveniently enslaved, did blackness come to be synonymous with lifelong bondage? In other words, did slavery come first and racism emerge as a consequence, or did racism precede and make possible slavery? Did the two—racism and slavery—develop symbiotically, each reinforcing the other? It is clear, as the 1624 and 1625 censuses indicate, that a profound prejudice against blacks as an ethnic group existed from the beginning, but this did not instantly lead to the enslavement of all blacks, nor did it preclude a white-black fraternization that suggests a degree of lower-class biracial harmony seldom experienced in American history.

Perhaps the imprecision that marked social boundaries is nowhere better illustrated than in the position of the struggling free black population of the Chesapeake colonies. Their absolute number is unknown, but their relative numbers were probably substantial. There were several ways for Africans to become free. Some evidently entered the mainland as free persons, having lived previously in the West Indies or England and there learned English and been baptized. Others upon arrival were purchased with a set term to their labor; after working the requisite time, they were set free. Others of mixed parentage were declared free because of the laws establishing legal status according to that of the father (in Maryland) or the mother (in Virginia). Still others apparently purchased their own freedom, or had it given in reward for meritorious or special service. However the status of free black was obtained, it was a condition conferring rights and privileges far beyond those accorded either slaves or servants. Free blacks controlled their own labor and chose their place of residence. Free blacks like Anthony Johnson of Virginia and later Maryland could own property, and court judgments against them often carried fines indicating a presumption that they had an earning capacity sufficient to make sometimes quite substantial payments. Free blacks possessed land, livestock, white indentured servants, and slaves. Not until 1670 did Virginia, for example, legislate that "no negro . . . though baptised and enjoyned their owne ffreedome shall be capable of any such purchase of christians [read whites]," though they could still own blacks or Indians. Free blacks brought suit in court, were themselves sued, testified against whites, borrowed money, extended credit to others, paid taxes, served on juries, held minor public offices, and on occasion even voted. In fact, it is hard to see any severe discrimination against free blacks until the 1670 proscription of their having white servants. While English prejudices against blacks existed, both custom and law seemed to have moderated its impact during the first two generations of black-white coexistence in the Chesapeake region.

Of course one might expect the force of prejudice to abate somewhat when free blacks were involved, for however it is acquired, freedom has always carried with it at least a modicum of respect. What is more surprising in the light of precolonial English attitudes toward Africans and especially the repugnance felt toward blacks at a much later date is the degree of colorblindness that marked white servant/black servant or slave relations throughout most of the seventeenth century. The Chesapeake society that emerged in the mid-1650s was hardly a segregated one, especially at the lower ranks, and upon closer study one can see why rigid segregation was so slow to develop.

Before the 1660s the huge majority of the Chesapeake population was white, with the total black numbers in the low hundreds. These figures alone testify to the colonial preference for white laborers. Yet whatever their relative numbers, living conditions for white and black workers were remarkably similar. For the first fifty years the death rate for unseasoned newcomers remained simply devastating. In fact, many indentured servants died before they fulfilled their term, inadvertently being servants for life as surely as their black co-workers. Impartial death rates homogenized the status of the two races. The "typical" planter employed several white servants and possibly a black servant/slave or two. Because blacks had a greater initial cost, as long as death rates were high and the lifespans limited, the relative cost of a white servant's four or so years of labor was less than a similar or even somewhat longer period of service from a more expensive slave. Consequently, whites were not spared from difficult or dangerous tasks, nor were the worst jobs sloughed off to blacks. Whatever the racial mix of a particular planter's work force, the chores to be done were similar in kind.

If the planter had only two or three laborers, they probably boarded in the planter's house, sleeping in the attic or in a lean-to attached to the rear. Hands of both races worked side by side in the fields, and often their master labored with them. All workers, along with the planter's family if he were so lucky as to have a wife, ate the same monotonous food, which was probably prepared in common by the planter's wife, or a white servant girl, or less likely, a black woman released from field work for enough time to cook. If the planter had more servants/slaves than could be reasonably accommodated in his own house, then separate quarters were provided. Because purchasers of labor for either limited or extended time preferred males, men significantly outnumbered women among both the white and black laboring populations. Family life was very stunted as a result, for a pregnant white servant—whose offspring would be free—only represented a loss of time to the planters, and neither the legal status nor the long-range profitability of slave children was yet clear. Penalties were prescribed for pregnant servants, extending their servitude to make up for the time lost while carrying the child. In the absence of family patterns, workers were housed together, separated only perhaps by sex. Blacks and whites thus worked together, ate together, slept together; they likewise suffered the rigors of the sweltering sun and swarming mosquitoes in the summer, the damp cold of the winter, and the anger of impatient masters in season and out, and enjoyed the kinds of relaxation their rural bondage afforded: hunting, fishing, sleeping, carousing.

As the laws trying to prevent it make clear, black and white workers, slave and indentured, ran away together, had sex together, in fact lived, worked, played, and died together with apparently little racial antipathy. There were so few blacks they in no way threatened the whites, and their common experiences as laborers whose behavior was controlled—at least for the time they were together—by their masters outweighed any vague cultural prejudices. The blacks were widely dispersed among the whites and had to learn enough English to communicate; many had already been acculturated in the West Indies and, in the absence of large numbers of their fellows where their African heritage could more effectively be preserved, seemed more like co-workers than frightening savages. Most important, however, as long as black slaves were scattered by ones and twos across a white working-class population that numbered in the thousands, individual blacks were perceived more as fellow sufferers and friends than as despised, alien, degraded slaves. Many Africans became quite Europeanized in the mostly white society. This comparatively benign racial relationship was revolutionized, however, as the relative proportions of black to white began to shift in the last quarter of the seventeenth century.

The evidence is overwhelming that the English planters in Maryland and Virginia greatly preferred that the Chesapeake be a white man's country. By comparison, within a decade of its settlement, Barbados was in the midst of a sugar-slave boom, and its black population skyrocketed. In the Chesapeake colonies even as late as the mid-1670s, the number of white servants far outstripped black slaves. Then, starting almost imperceptibly in the 1670s, growing in tempo in the 1680s, and rising to a torrent in the 1690s, planters began the shift to African slaves that transformed the whole society. Twice as many African slaves were imported into the Chesapeake in the first decade of the 1700s as during the whole previous century. Why was the switch to African slavery delayed for a half-century, and why did it occur when it did?

In the first place, Englishmen naturally preferred to work with people of their own kind, people whose language and ways they understood and with whom they were comfortable. Living three thousand miles from dear old England, cast among a smattering of red men and subject to the whims of an unfamiliar climate, half-fearing a Spanish attack and unsure always of disease, worrying that the thousand leagues of choppy waves separating them from their motherland might also separate them from the civilization they desperately wanted to cling to, there was scant reason to let go of a familiar labor system and import hordes of the strangest people imaginable—blacks from the dark continent—into an already threatening environment *unless they felt they absolutely had to*. And for six decades they did not have to, for more or less voluntary immigrants—the indentured servants—met the ever-increasing labor needs of the Chesapeake.

Beginning about 1450 England experienced almost two centuries of sustained population growth, which, among other changes such as the enclosure acts that drove serfs off the manor lands and into the cities, led to a fall in wages and an apparent surplus of population. Such conditions, of course, had underlain some of the original justifications for colonization, and indeed these demographic conditions had produced an ample flow of willing migrants, most of whom were young males from the middle class. At the same time as these prime workers were coming to the Chesapeake (avoiding the West Indies for reasons of climate and the reputedly bad working conditions of the sugar-slave regions), the booming sugar islands were absorbing as many prime Africans as slavers could deliver. Few Africans were left over for the mainland, their prices relative to indentured servants were prohibitive (the price differential was exacerbated by the high death rates for blacks as well as whites in the first decades), and the small size of the available market in Virginia and Maryland made large-scale trade direct from Africa unprofitable to slavers as long as the sugar island demand stayed firm and the Chesapeake demand uncertain.

For reasons that are not entirely clear, but certainly including the English Civil War, the birth rate in England fell sharply in the 1640s, with the consequence that twenty years later the supply of ablebodied potential indentured servants dropped. In the mid-1660s the Great Plague resulted in changes in the population structure of England that led to a gradual rise in wages, and job opportunities there in general seem to have improved. Many, for example, were employed in the rebuilding of London after the Great Fire of 1666. Moreover, with the settlement of other colonies in America—particularly the Carolinas and later Pennsylvania—would-be migrants had alternative destinations. The sum of these social developments was a relative and then an absolute decline in the number of white indentured servants entering the Chesapeake starting at the very end of the 1660s. By the 1670s we detect more frequent complaints about the shortage of labor, and the relative price of servants increased in the 1680s, indicating that planter demand for white servants remained strong. In response to this severe labor shortage planters at first began to lower their qualifications for acceptable English servants—after the mid-1660s they were more willing to take younger males, women, Irishmen, the almost totally unskilled laboring poor, finally even convicts. In other words, the quality of the white servant working class fell in the final decades of the seventeenth century. So drastic did the labor shortage seem that planters reconsidered enslaving American Indians.

It was in the midst of this insufficiency of workers, in 1674, that the Royal African Company (the joint-stock corporation authorized to engage in the slave trade) first began direct shipments of slaves from Africa to the North American mainland. From that date on, ever-increasing numbers of slaves were sold in the Chesapeake, and, while most were probably purchased via the West Indies, a larger volume than previously estimated now appears to have been imported directly from Africa. After 1698, when the Royal African Company's monopoly was ended by a parliamentary act, and numerous enterprising merchants with smaller vessels—more appropriate to the kind of plantation-to-plantation slave peddling that existed in the Chesapeake—entered the trade, the slave imports to the Chesapeake reached flood-tide proportion. Yet the unfilled demand for white indentured servants remained high. Clearly the Chesapeake planters still preferred whites, but when for reasons beyond their control the English supply was insufficient to meet their needs, they turned to large-scale slave importations. As they came to realize that the lowered death rates now made the initially more expensive Africans more cost-efficient in the long run, and related to this, as there slowly dawned the recognition that slave offspring represented an additional permanent benefit, African slavery increasingly was accepted as the permanent solution to the labor supply of the tobacco colonies. Accommodating laws soon followed, and within a few years of 1700 the Chesapeake system of slave plantations was sustained by strong legal sanctions. Yet more had changed than the complexion of the laborers.

The character of race relations underwent as far-reaching a change as did the nature of the plantation work force. For two generations white and black plantation laborers had related to each other as equals to a greater extent perhaps than ever since in southern history. Living and working together, sharing drudgery and a common master, whites often failed to apply to the particular blacks with whom they toiled and cavorted the generally prejudiced attitudes embedded in their English culture. But with the demographic changes occurring in the Chesapeake society in the decades on either side of 1700, the vague, implicit, abstract racism of the English was transformed into a far more concrete, legally precise, and individually applicable societal racism that would in myriad ways poison the interpersonal relations of whites and blacks for the following two and a half centuries.

As the number of blacks rose abruptly at the turn of the century, they for the first time began to be perceived as a tangible threat to whites. Heretofore most blacks in the Chesapeake had arrived via the West Indies (some were even from England), and upon arrival already evidenced a degree of acculturation. Many spoke Spanish or English, or at least a pidgin language understandable to planters, had been "broken in" to the agricultural tasks expected, and in their small numbers seemed not irreconcilably different from whites. Now increasingly blacks were arriving directly from Africa, since the ending of the Royal African Company's monopoly allowed smaller vessels trading opportunities in the Chesapeake. American planters preferred to buy cheaper if less acculturated "unseasoned" slaves, having feared for a long time that those purchased from the West Indies would be rejects or troublemakers dumped without warning on them.

Not only was the Chesapeake labor force changing complexion, but also, and equally important, it was being Africanized. These frightened, dejected, half-naked raw imports, who at times courageously resisted the regimen expected of them and at others gave in with a sullen and sometimes suicidal passivity, seemed far more alien than their predecessors. With their total number rising and the size of slaveholdings increasing, Africans were able better to retain aspects of their own culture and began to evolve creative adaptions of it, an Afro-American culture, that permanently set them apart from white workers. Whites feared the black increase in numbers and were repelled by their new strangeness—fresh African imports came to be known as "outlandish" slaves as compared to more familiar "country-born" slaves. As blackness came to be practically synonymous with perpetual slavery (the proportion of free blacks to slaves fell precipitately), whites unconsciously, then consciously, sought to differentiate themselves from the black labor force.

A far more virulent racism emerged, and an apparent repugnance toward blacks arose that had not existed earlier. The laws of the 1660s and 1670s were intended more as a convenience to slave owners than as a denigration of blacks or an outlawing of interracial relationships. An owner's property was jeopardized as long as religious conversion could be interpreted as voiding bondage, or if mixed parentage could facilitate freedom suits. Hence obliging laws were provided to ensure property "rights" in slaves. Virginia, for example, in 1662 levied a special fine on interracial fornication—all fornication was sinful and therefore illegal, but sex between unequal classes was especially frowned upon—yet not until 1691 was interracial marriage prohibited by law. A flurry of statutes in the final decade of the seventeenth century flagrantly discriminated against blacks and sought to separate the races as far as possible. Also in the 1690s private manumission of slaves was made more difficult. After 1700 the laws against blacks hardened dramatically, and roughly after that date it is accurate to speak of the Chesapeake as a chattel slave society where blacks had few rights protected by law.

The increasing Africanization of the labor force, however, was not the only significant social change occurring in the 1680s and 1690s, nor was it the sole cause of the rampant white racism that emerged toward the end of the century. The nature of the white society was changing too. Before about 1660 those white servants who lived long enough to complete their term of service could find cheap, easily available land, plant several acres of tobacco, eventually import a few servants of their own, and in general share in the developing prosperity of the colony. For a variety of reasons—overproduction of tobacco with a resultant drop in price, the

restrictions of the Navigation Act of 1660, an increase in the cost
of land because of increased population, the growing success of far-
sighted and self-serving big planters in engrossing the best land in
the tidewater regions—opportunities for new white freedmen
decreased. Because of falling death rates, the numbers of such new
freedmen grew rapidly just as their chances for land ownership and
prosperity were decreasing. The result was growing population of
young, free males, landless, indigent, frustrated, increasingly
estranged from the planter and governing establishment. The situation seemed to be made worse by the necessity to accept ever-lower
standards in order to attract fresh indentured servants from Britain.

Bacon's Rebellion in 1676 showed the potential of violent social
unrest posed by a lower class of free, poor whites. While no one
in the planter aristocracy seems to have deduced logically that
lifetime black slavery was a "solution" to this problem, the drying
up of the supply of new indentured recruits and the increasing
availability of Africans offered an unforeseen way out of the dilemma. Slaves never became free and thereby would not be competitors for land or labor; accommodating laws made them more
susceptible to control; and the rising racial antipathy to blacks—
which the statutes reflected or perhaps intensified rather than
caused—generated an identification on the part of even the poorest
white freedman with the white establishment rather than with the
despised black. Black denigration elevated the lowest white to a
level above the most talented slave into a pseudo fraternity of white
equals. The transformation of the Chesapeake into a racist society,
possessing a virtual caste system, laid the foundation for the social
myth of white equality, defusing white social tensions and allowing
the growth of white democracy. Thus ironically American slavery
and American freedom were both born in the temperate clime of
the Chesapeake toward the end of the seventeenth century.

Despite their obvious importance to American history, events in
the Chesapeake do not exhaust the story of slavery's origins in this
nation. The developments in South Carolina reveal a different
route to bondage. While it is quite possible that the very first
Africans to set foot on the North American continent were those
accompanying the Spanish adventurer Lucas Vásquez de Ayllón
who planted a short-lived settlement near Cape Fear in 1526,
significant colonization of the Carolinas did not begin until 1660.

Newly restored to the English throne, King Charles II in that year gave to eight supporters a huge tract of land south of Virginia. A Barbadian loyalist and planter, John Colleton, led the group of royalists, who successfully requested of the thankful king an empire of American territory in reward for their steadfast support. The eight proprietors upon whom Charles II so bountifully bestowed the Carolinas were all familiar with slavery, and most of the early settlers—white and black—came from Barbados. This tiny speck of an island was already in the midst of its sugar boom, with a surging slave population and several hundred large planters quickly expanding their land holdings. Hundreds of less prosperous white planters, feeling opportunity slipping away from them in England's first plantation society, were eager to seek the greener pastures of Carolina. Consequently they moved to the newly opened mainland colony, bringing their families, their property (including bondsmen), and their commitment to a slave plantation economy. For the pioneers of Carolina, which was practically a colony of Barbados, no special decision to enslave Africans was required once they arrived on the mainland. The acceptance of slavery had been an earlier Barbadian development; the institution was simply transferred to Carolina.

From the very beginning then, Negroes came with white Barbadians to Carolina, and, though their legal status as slaves may not have been precisely established, they were treated much as chattel slaves later came to be treated. Barbadian custom dictated that blacks served for life, children followed the status of their mother, and they could be sold as property in payment of debt, while their legal status was left purposely ambiguous to avoid any possible conflicts with the officials in England. Less concerned with definitions of status than with controlling the behavior of the slaves, the Fundamental Constitutions of Carolina, drafted in 1669 and perhaps influenced by John Locke, provided that "Every freeman of Carolina, shall have absolute power and authority over his negro slaves, of what opinion or Religion soever." A South Carolina statute in 1690 expanded the police functions of masters, but it was disallowed by the proprietors in London. However, the local economy—cattle, lumber products, and increasingly rice— expanded so rapidly that by 1696, with approximately two thousand slaves in the provinces (a far higher proportion than in the

1696 - South Carolina
1st comprehensive Slave Code.

Chesapeake colonies), the South Carolina assembly passed its first truly comprehensive slave code, based on the Barbadian code of 1688. Except that they could be used for payment of debt, slaves in South Carolina were not legally chattel property until 1740. During the first generation after its founding, in the colony's pioneer period, white-black relations were less rigid than they later became. Slaves pursued a variety of occupations, often worked with whites—either indentured servants, hired laborers, or even their owners—in ways that suggested a degree of equality. But the quickly achieved prosperity of the colony, and the rapid increase in the number of slaves, soon brought a close to this first age of relative racial harmony. As the preface to the 1696 Act for the Better Ordering and Governing of Negroes and Slaves (often mistakenly dated 1712) vividly indicates, the evolution from befriended co-worker to feared black slave was as complete in Carolina by about 1700 as it was in the Chesapeake, and the process had taken less than half the time in Carolina.

> Whereas, the plantations and estates of this Province cannot be well and sufficiently managed and brought into use, without the labor and service of negroes and other slaves [Indians]; and forasmuch as the said negroes and other slaves brought into the people of this Province for that purpose, are of barbarous, wild, savage natures, and such as renders them wholly unqualified to be governed by the laws, customs, and practices of this Province; but that it is absolutely necessary, that such other constitutions, laws and orders, should in this Province be made and enacted, for the good regulating and ordering of them, as may restrain the disorders, rapines and inhumanity, to which they are naturally prone and inclined, and may also tend to the safety and security of the people of this Province and their estates; to which purpose. . . . [The assembly went on, in thirty-five sections, to outline measures to control the rapidly growing black segment of the population.]

The Chesapeake planters, having come directly from Britain and having no direct prior experience with slavery, turned to bondage only when white laborers were no longer plentiful; the Carolina planters, having accepted boom-time slavery in Barbados, instantly established bondage and bought slaves as soon as they could. The joint result, by 1700, was full-fledged slave plantation economies in both regions primed for unprecedented growth in the next century. The coming decades saw a dramatic increase in the number of African imports, the beginning of population growth among American-born blacks, and the resultant rise of an Afro-American people with a distinct culture. The rise of the black community was to be the most important development in black history in the eighteenth century.

2. The Crucial Eighteenth Century

Europeans harbored a series of conflicting ideas about the New World lying across the seas. America held forth the promise of both utopia and savagery; America was the hope of mankind and a monument to man's greed and folly, a mission field for Christian evangels and a burying ground for most of the early settlers. Death, failure, profound frustration, and the ache of loneliness were the constant companions of the first pioneers, and decades were to pass before hope, then success, and finally pride in accomplishment began to find a way into the emotions of seventeenth-century Americans. After midcentury, with falling death rates and rising tobacco production, enslaving blacks became an even more attractive option. By the final decade of the founding century, planters in the Chesapeake and in South Carolina had accepted slavery with few philosophical reservations.

Out of the hope, and the death, and the promise of New World settlements there had emerged by 1710 booming slave economies. Not only were imports from Africa growing in number, but indigenous population growth began among slaves in the southern mainland colonies, as it did nowhere else in the Americas. With the size of the slave population increasing, profound changes occurred in southern society. Whites, feeling more threatened by the presence of ever larger numbers of blacks, tightened social controls as racial attitudes hardened. Yet the slaves were more affected by subtle changes largely of their own making. Blacks learned to communicate with one another through a pidgin language, they began to create families and develop a sense of black community, and slowly a black culture—part African, part American—emerged by the mid-eighteenth century. These processes were to have great import for blacks, for the quality of their lives in general improved significantly even as legal proscriptions against them increased. On the one hand, the eighteenth century is the story of the creation in the colonial South of a harsh caste society based upon race, and on the other, it is the story of a separate black culture being forged by the slaves themselves. This Afro-American culture was to flower in the two generations before the Civil War, but the eighteenth century proved to be critical for the black experience in the South.

The African slave trade, whereby approximately eleven and a half million African people were shipped against their will as cargo to the Western Hemisphere, constitutes one of the most tragic episodes in history. The enormity of the trade and its human costs almost transcend comprehension, but its story, realistically faced, is an essential element of the heritage of this nation.

There had, of course, been slaves and a thriving slave trade in Africa long before northern Europeans were even conscious of the continent. African slavery was a diverse and complex system in which individuals ranged from plantation agricultural workers to candidates for religious sacrifice, but primarily it was a domestic institution. While slaves were essentially the property of their owners, they usually did have recognized rights, could own property, could marry (even into their owner's family), and had avenues of achievement and sometimes freedom open to them. Slaves were acquired in a variety of ways, with capture in war being the most common, but some lost their freedom because of debts, or crimes, or even—in the case of some of the Ibo—through the machinations of religious leaders who took victims ostensibly offered as sacrifice to the Chukuwu deity and spirited them away to waiting slave traders. For centuries variously acquired slaves had been shipped between kingdoms, and then from Africa via Arab middlemen in places like Timbuktu to markets in the Arabian peninsula. When Europeans intruded themselves into the ongoing merchandising of humans, African traders—as schooled in the wiles of barter and commerce as the Europeans—quickly saw the profits to be made in a wider market. The transatlantic African slave trade required Europeans willing to buy people simply as trade goods, and

Africans willing to sell people as merchandise. Both sorts there were aplenty, and with New World labor needs increasing as Old World diseases killed off the native Indian populations, the ultimate destinations of the victims and the total scale of the operations changed, as did the nature of the slave system itself. The dimensions of the tragedy are not lessened by the joint nature of the blame.

The Portuguese first perfected the mechanics of the European involvement in the trade, and the Dutch, who by the mid-seventeenth century dominated the commerce only to share it increasingly with the British in the eighteenth century, made few innovations in the nefarious traffic. Europeans quickly learned that the disease environment of Africa was so different from Europe and so deadly to white interlopers that actual invasion of Africa and slave raids were self-defeating. And where was the need, so long as African merchants, properly feted and their prices met, would furnish even the greediest slaver with ample supplies of human captives? By virtue of their greater immunity to tropical diseases and often their military prowess, the African tradesmen were in the dominant position, and it suited best the purposes of both parties for Europeans to lease offshore or beachfront trading posts—called castles or factories. The Europeans paid the local chieftain an annual rent, purchased water and provisions from him, and depended upon him to supply them with slaves. The African chief or king sold his war captives, those of his own people enslaved for whatever reason, or victims captured by his agents deep in the interior or bought "wholesale" at interior slave markets, for a whole spectrum of European goods ranging from gunpowder and cloth to iron bars and cowrie shells. The interior slaves were marched, chained together single file in coffles, sometimes hundreds of miles to the seashore market, or were ferried there in huge wooden canoes down the slow-moving rivers. Once arrived at the seashore they were imprisoned in hot, disease-ridden cages called barracoons until enough were gathered to fill the sea captain's ship. Here the captives, branded like cattle with a red-hot iron, prodded and poked and examined by the rough-handed slavers, became fully conscious of the horror of their predicament.

Until the moment newly captured slaves came into contact with European slave dealers, their situation, despite the brutality of their treatment, was quite comprehendible. Whether as a result of war or debt, the fresh slave would have been familiar enough with the institution of slavery to have some idea of his or her fate. But when queer-smelling, light-skinned Europeans began their rude examination of the captives' bodies, and in the distance, dancing menacingly on the waves, lay a ship the size of which staggered even those Africans familiar with the sea, the imprisoned Africans feared the worst. Many must have expected to be eaten by their strange captors, and fought back with crazed fear and anger and sometimes almost superhuman strength and courage. Others, exhausted by their overland march and weakened from hunger and mistreatment, acquiesced with such numbing passivity that they seemed almost to lose the spark of life. These responses represented the spectrum of behavior for newly enslaved Africans, with individual behavior usually falling somewhere in between, even though various situations could elicit either extreme from the same individual.

Assuming the white slaver had the goods or combination of goods to suit the African middleman and the price was agreeable to both, then a bargain in human souls was struck, and the persons bought were transported to the ship in either long African canoes or the ship's rowboats. After purchasing additional provisions from the chieftain, the slavers with their living cargo raised anchor for the voyage of six to nine weeks to the New World. At other locations in Africa, where there were no castles or factories and an uncertain supply of slaves, the European ships roamed along the coast, stopping now and then to take on a handful of Africans. Sometimes this kind of coastal buying trip lasted for months, after which the vessel with its human freight headed for plantation markets in the New World. Despite all the agony behind them, now began the worst part of the slaves' trek to the New World. For this horrendous Middle Passage between Africa and America the slaves were packed like sardines between the narrow decks into a space that averaged less than four feet in height. As the demand increased, callous shippers devised even more efficient ways of packing humans aboard, and at times the distance between the "decks" was less than two feet, with the slaves lying chained on broad shelves. Sometimes slaves were forced to lie on their sides, front to back, "spoonlike"; at other times, when the between-deck height allowed it, they were forced to sit up in rows, almost in each other's laps. For the slaves, shackled and chained with no freedom of movement, closely confined, almost suffocating in the furnacelike temperatures and dark, muggy, stale air of the hold, the Middle Passage was a forty-to sixty-day nightmare. The stench of vomit and excrement and festering sores became so rank that slave ships could be smelled for miles at sea. The moans of the seasick, frightened, bewildered, and undernourished blacks mingled with the groaning and creaking of the ship as it rolled seemingly without end on the sea.

At this far remove in time and comfort it is nearly impossible to imagine such horrors in their fullness, but some attempt must be made to measure the effect of the voyage on the emigrating Africans. The old charge that Africans accepted their fate without resistance because they had been slaves in their homeland is without substance. Most of those offered for sale were recent war captives, persons with the memory of freedom fresh in their minds, and many of them, when not physically and psychologically incapacitated by their ordeal, resisted the capture and shipment with a vengeance. The annals of the slave trade are filled with stories of slaves attacking sailors, fighting against muskets and cannons with their bare hands, even taking over the ships. Of course, given their hunger-diminished strength and their cramped muscles, much less the disparity in weapons, few shipboard rebellions were successful.

Other slave captives, having already experienced one hell and unwilling to undergo still another at some unknown destination, chose to escape a future possibly worse than death by taking their own lives. They jumped overboard (captains sometimes rigged nets along the side for this exigency) or refused to eat (captains employed funnels and special screw-type devices to pry open unwilling mouths). Still others with a kind of stoic refusal to accept their status as commodities simply gave up the desire to live and, foiling the best medical efforts of the shipboard doctors, quietly died. Slavers, calculating their profits from live bondsmen landed in America, sought to overcome at least temporarily some of the worst features of the cramped inner quarters by having the slaves come on deck every day for forced exercise, fresh air, and saltwater baths. Often one African was forced to beat a makeshift drum while the rest went through their melancholy shuffling. Vinegar was splashed in the holds to combat the stench, and medicinal remedies-of-a-sort were supplied to obviously ill slaves and daubed on open sores—less for reasons of humanity than out of concern for the possible loss of anticipated profits. On rare occasions a ship made the entire voyage without a casualty, while on other passages all the slaves perished, but the death rates averaged between 15 and 20 percent. The survival rate was higher than might be expected, and in fact is roughly comparable with that of white immigrants in the seventeenth century, but after all, slavers' profits were based on the number of live blacks landed in the New World. Perhaps it was a kind of poetic justice that the death rate for the whites aboard ship was about twice as high.

All in all, the uprooting and transporting of millions of Africans to America could hardly have been more brutal, more shocking, more devastating to a person's self-pride. Undoubtedly many carried the scars in their flesh and in their souls for life. No one was left unaffected, although some rebounded more quickly and more completely than others. Many were so weakened by the ordeal of the passage that they soon fell victim to disease in the New World; estimates of first-year death rates for new imports range up to one-third. For those women who survived, the ability to conceive and carry a healthy child to full term seems to have been delayed several years. After having endured the rigors of the voyage, nothing else could seem more threatening. As a consequence, many new slaves adapted themselves to their expected plantation work routines with an almost distracted willingness, though after a period of recuperation a human rebelliousness sometimes broke through the quiescence and manifested itself in running away or revengeful violence. There was no one response, no uniform behavior.

The African heritage was not erased by the Middle Passage, nor was it transported to America practically intact. One must simultaneously bear in mind the severity of the wrenching from Africa and the resiliency of the human spirit. The African cultural component varied from place to place, from time to time, from person to person. Transported Africans gradually became something new, Afro-Americans, but that complex and still incompletely understood process is better comprehended in the demographic context of import and survival rates, female fertility, and population density.

Estimates of the total slave imports into the Americas have ranged wildly from a few million to 50 million and even 100 million. The consensus today is that, for the entire period 1451-1870, about 10 to 12 million were brought to the New World, imports averaging less than 2,000 annually before 1600 and rising to a mean of approximately 60,000 per year during the eighteenth century, the height of the trade. Of these total numbers imported, no more than 5 percent, or 550,000 Africans (including those delivered by way of the West Indies), came to the North American mainland colonies. Brazil, in comparison, received more than 3 1/2 million, and individual West Indies islands like Jamaica and San Domingo imported more than the thirteen colonies that became the United States. The relatively small number of native Africans brought into the southern United States must be considered when analyzing the black culture that arose, as must such evidence that despite the disparity of imports, in 1825 the U.S. South contained approximately 36 percent of the slaves living in the Western Hemisphere compared to Brazil's 31 percent, and the British Caribbean islands' only about 15 percent. The relatively few Africans who landed in the South became the largest slave population in the Americas, a development that suggests much about the southern slave society and the resultant Afro-American culture. Why did southern slaves multiply so rapidly, and what did that mean for the emerging black community?

The number of blacks in the mainland British colonies increased very slowly in the 1600s. By 1700 perhaps 5,000 slaves had been imported into the Chesapeake region. Before 1690 most arrived via the West Indies, but afterwards the majority came directly from Africa, and after 1720 upwards of 90 percent did. The overwhelming majority of slaves brought to the mainland colonies over the entire period were directly from Africa. The number imported in the first decade of the eighteenth century averaged about 1,000 annually, and this figure rose during the second decade. During the 1730s about 2,000 per year arrived in the Chesapeake, dropping off slightly thereafter till the Revolution. The situation in South Carolina was similar, rising from annual import rates of several hundred before 1700 to more than 1,000 before the Stono Revolt of 1739 produced a conscious restriction of new African slaves. After about 1750 the rate rose again until, in the five years after

1770, more than 4,000 per annum were being sold in South Carolina. Charleston became the third largest United States entrepôt for slaves, receiving in the century following 1672 approximately 90,000 to 100,000 Africans, almost one-fifth of the total, for the British colonies in North America.

When the total imports are analyzed by decade, the rising rate of the slave trade is clear. The peak decades were 1740-60, when 100,000 over the twenty years were received. All together, almost 60 percent of the slaves imported into the territory that became the United States arrived between 1720 and 1780, the beginning of Afro-American cultural life in this nation. There were more blacks of African birth in the colonies during that period than ever before or afterwards. Yet the concrete African impress on either American culture as a whole or the emerging black community was less in British colonial America than anywhere else in the plantation Americas because simultaneous with the upsurge in African imports was an even larger increase in the number of American-born (or "country-born" or creole) slaves. In a situation unique in the New World, slaves in the mainland colonies of North America after several decades were able to reproduce quickly enough not only merely to maintain their numbers but also to sustain population growth. This seems to have occurred nowhere else—certainly not in the West Indies or Brazil, where a continuous heavy importation of African slaves nevertheless resulted in a slave population in 1825 substantially smaller than in the United States. The ability of slaves here to reproduce was of great moment, and discovering why it occurred and interpreting its significance constitute major breakthroughs in understanding the black experience in the South.

It now seems evident that a New World slave population composed overwhelmingly of African-born Negroes could not sustain itself through natural population growth. The Chesapeake colonies, for example, during the first half-century of slavery probably had a net natural decline in their black population that was concealed by the increasing import figures. That is, the total black population in, say, 1710, was significantly less than the total of all imports. The years from 1710 to 1730 were a transition period during which natural population growth began, but after about 1730 the country-born black population soared. Even with substantial numbers of imports, the overall Negro population was increasingly

American born and less African. In South Carolina natural increase probably began earlier, maybe by 1700, in part because a higher percentage of the first slaves had previously been "seasoned" in the West Indies and because the denser black population, confined largely at first to the sea island district and owned in larger groupings, facilitated the finding of suitable spouses among the blacks. Yet after 1720, with rice production increasing and African slave imports booming, the percentage of African born increased to two-thirds of the South Carolina slave population by 1740. One result was a cessation of the net natural increase. Not until after midcentury did natural growth emerge again for the total black population. These similar though significantly different developments in the Chesapeake region and South Carolina suggest answers to the puzzle of slave reproduction.

The nature of the slave trade had a devastating effect on initial population growth. Reflecting the labor needs of prospective buyers, slave ship cargoes usually contained far more men than women. The sex ratio (number of men per woman multiplied by 100; that is, if there were one and a half men per woman, the sex ratio would be 150) on commercial slave ships ranged to 200 or greater. Obviously the relatively few slave women would have to be prolific to sustain the population under normal conditions with such an imbalance of the sexes. Given the first-year death rates that were as high as one-quarter or sometimes even one-third (the primary culprit in the British mainland colonies being disease and the aftereffects of the Middle Passage, not overwork and undernourishment as was often the case in Latin America and the West Indies), clearly population growth was difficult. Moreover, the women who survived the first year were still so affected by the experience of the transatlantic voyage, particularly the malnutrition, that their ability to conceive was often delayed two or more years. Assuming the average slave woman was in her early twenties when imported—as seems to have been the case—then her childbearing period was reduced by about seven years, from approximately 25 to 40 instead of an otherwise natural 18 to 40. Because so many African women came from polygamous societies where breastfeeding lasted for about three years, with intercourse prohibited by custom before the child was weaned—and there is physiological evidence that lactation produces a natural contracep-

tive effect that significantly reduces the chance of conception—
the length of time between births would have been nearly four
years.

Imagine a slave ship containing 200 young males and 100 young
females, arriving in 1700. Assume 25 of the women died the year
following and the remaining 75 lived until they were past childbearing age. If each mother conceived a child within 3 years of arriving,
at age 25, and continued having children every 4 years, each
woman could bear a maximum of 4 children. If every child lived,
then the 75 mothers would produce 300 children (75 x 4 = 300),
hence reproducing exactly the number of persons who came on the
ship. Of course most African-born women in the early years did
not live long enough to bear 4 babies, and the infant death rate was
extremely high, with perhaps only half the infants surviving. Under
unrealistically ideal conditions then, a slave ship with a sex ratio
of 200 would not achieve population growth; in reality, the net offspring from such a ship would be about 150 surviving infants,
representing—when the parents died—a net population loss of 50
percent. In Latin America and in the Caribbean, where the labor
routines were far more harsh and the disease climate more severe,
fewer African women survived long enough to bear children, and
far fewer infants survived childhood. In the mainland colonies,
however, even though the few children born of African women
could not initially sustain the population, since they were equally
divided by sex and grew up adjusted to the New World disease environment, they as adults would be significantly more fruitful than
their parents. The key to potential black population growth, then,
was the presence of a plantation environment where the normal
work routines were reasonable enough, the food supply plentiful
enough, and disease sufficiently under control to allow the initial
African women to survive and produce children. This made possible the emergence of a generation of American-born slaves who
survived to maturity. The development of a sizeable pool of creole
slaves occurred only in the mainland colonies of North America,
where the women were not literally worked to death in a few years,
and it began in the early eighteenth century.

The severe demographic and biological deterrents to black
population growth in the early years were exacerbated by geographical and cultural factors. Before 1700 in both Carolina and

the Chesapeake, the majority of slaves lived in units of less than ten, where, given the sex ratios, it was often impossible for a male slave to find a mate within his age range. With the total number of slaves quite small and dispersed widely across an under-populated rural landscape where plantations were often miles apart, opportunities for finding sexual partners, much less forming families, were drastically limited.The dearth of roads, bridges, fer-ries, sometimes even pathways, further constrained the possibilities for population growth. (These same factors resulted in a net population loss for whites too in the early decades of Virginia.) Since some slaves evidently felt an inhibition about mating with someone from their own plantation (a vestige of the custom of ex-ogamous societies in Africa of marrying outside the tribe, family, clan, or other social unit), considering it tantamount to incest, the dispersed nature of plantation settlement and the meager black population further aggravated the difficulty of finding suitable spouses. The combined result of these varied factors—unbalanced sex ratio, high initial death rates, reduced childbearing period, lowered female fertility, inability to find a mate—was negative growth for the earliest African population in the mainland col-onies. Between about 1710 (for South Carolina) and 1730 (for the Chesapeake colonies) the situation began to change, but in order to understand the significance of this change one must analyze the cultural consequences of this initial period of naturally decreasing population.

Perhaps 75 to 90 percent of African slaves arrived at the main-land colonies in the summer, there to experience the humiliation of being sold. In South Carolina most new slaves were purchased in Charleston, probably within two weeks of their arrival, and usual-ly in groups of five to twenty. In the Chesapeake, where there was no dominant port city, the vessels peddled their human cargoes up and down the estuaries at the wharves of large planters who served as temporary agents. Many weeks might be consumed in depleting a ship's supply, with the tall young men going first, the women and children last. In the Chesapeake not only were the sales more dispersed, but they were also often in smaller units, mostly in twos, threes, and fours. Perhaps slaves played some role in their purchase by appearing either sullen or "likely" (willing, cooperative), no doubt the latter as the ship's captain hawked his wares up and down the broad rivers for what must have seemed an interminable time.

Before 1700 in both Carolina and the Chesapeake, newly bought slaves were then marched overland (or canoed through the sea island districts) to their ultimate destination. Since many were Ibos, or came from Angola or Senegambia, they may have been able to converse as they traveled to their new homes. Because of the high percentage of African born in the early slave population, some could find another slave who understood their language. Fragile friendships from the Middle Passage were possibly continued, bonds of shared experience that transcended nativity and language differences. But most slaves, placed amidst a babel of incomprehensible tongues, and with the necessity to understand the commands of their white masters, quickly learned a pidgin language composed of both African and English phrases, with even Spanish and Portuguese words linking the institution to its New World pioneers. From the very beginning, the scattered presence of some slaves who knew English facilitated the development of the pidgin as a lingua franca for communication between blacks and whites.

As the American-born black population grew, the pidgin language evolved into more complex forms, absorbed more English words, and became the first language of many slaves (hence was "creolized") particularly in areas of dense slave populations and few whites like the South Carolina and Georgia sea islands. In fact the creolized language persisted there into the twentieth century as the Gullah and Geechee dialects. In the South as a whole by the nineteenth century a distinctive and definitely black English had emerged. For those first Africans who disembarked in the New World, their inability to converse not only with whites but especially with other blacks must have only made more frustrating their already bleak situation. Their isolation magnified by their loss of verbal communication, estranged from the comforting presence of their former village with its familiar faces, customs, and places, pioneer African slaves must have often felt lost and hopeless. Breaking the language barrier was an inspiring accomplishment, for it allowed bonds of friendship and shared emotions to start wearing away the alienation, even disorientation, and begin creating the matrix of black solidarity out of which arose the slave community. This process of language evolution, from African tongues to pidgin speech, a New World creation, and beyond to black English, in general terms illustrates the larger process of acculturation whereby Africans became neither quite African anymore nor European, but rather Afro-Americans with a subtle blending of the various cultures.

The immense difficulty in transporting African ways to the mainland colonies and planting them intact in the emerging American societies can hardly be overemphasized. During the initial years the high death rate and short life span in the colonies hampered the continuation of any but the barest forms of African life. Because slavers and their intended customers preferred young males, few if any full-fledged religious specialists (almost always elderly men) were imported to the colonies. Even had some been delivered and allowed to practice their craft, the differences between tribal backgrounds would have rendered the complete duplication of any single African religious system impossible. With slaves numbering in the hundreds during the first few decades and stationed in small units widely spaced, it would have been practically impossible to gather together a group with common beliefs. Yet even had all these difficulties been somehow overcome, the differences between the flora and fauna of Africa and North America would have posed insurmountable obstacles to any religious specialist attempting to maintain his sophisticated symbolic system with a degree of purity. The rituals of the West African peoples were elaborately intricate, drawing on a wide range of symbols and beliefs. Particular ritual ceremonies required a long list of specific elements: a certain kind of bark, a special leaf, the wing feathers of a distinct bird, the sap of a particular tree, the stomach contents of a specific animal, and so on, each ingredient chosen because its color, or consistency, or the nature of its source represented definite virtues. These necessary constituents of a ceremony were simply unavailable in any one New World location. Moreover, a working population composed primarily of young, unmarried males, with no family (either wives, children, or elders) to be concerned about, was the least likely to preserve a cultural system.

The Africans in the New World were not alone; they were thinly scattered among and vastly outnumbered by white Europeans. For two generations blacks in the Chesapeake numbered in the hundreds, and in South Carolina, the only colony where blacks ever outnumbered whites, they did so only after 1708, a half-century following initial settlement. During these early decades, handfuls of Africans, living in units of one or two and very seldom more than ten, boarded and lodged with white indentured servants or in quarters attached to their master's house. They worked very closely with whites, farming, sawing timber into lumber, doing domestic chores. Blacks cast adrift from familiar African traditions and finding it largely impossible either to practice or revive African folkways experienced a significant culture shift away from things African to the ways of the Europeans. Pidginization was probably the first noticeable result, but a tendency for country-born slave women—in a land where men outnumbered women—to reject polygamy and the long lactation period associated with it, may have been another important illustration of acculturation. Whether this change came from following the example of white women, or from the insistence of the owners, or from the sexual pressure exerted by black males, we cannot say.

For whatever reason, American-born or creole (from the Portuguese *crioulo*, meaning a Negro born in his master's house) slave women adapted the European-like custom of weaning their children after about a year. This seemingly minor modification in childrearing meant that child-spacing for creole women was reduced from about four years to a little over two. Since creole women, though few in number at first, were present in America when they reached menarche (the first occurrence of menstruation, after which conception is possible), at age 17 or 18, and did not suffer the delay in conception experienced by imported slave women, their childbearing age extended from about 18 to 40. Creole women thus began having children at an early age, and had them almost twice as often, as African-born slave women. The result was almost a quadrupling of the raw birth rate, with the sex ratio of the offspring essentially even. For example, imagine 300 plantation slaves, with a sex ratio of 200 to match our earlier imaginary slave ship population. These 100 creole women would in their lifetime, making the same assumptions as in the earlier case, give birth to 1,100 children. This population "wave" of American-born children would, twenty years later as adults well adjusted to the disease environment, produce rapid population growth.

The adult children of the first generation of creole mothers hence

Why didn't this occur in West Indies or Brazil.

enabled the slave population to begin reproducing itself. Of course, this development had a snowball effect, since American-born children had good chances of survival, better chances of choosing mates from the enlarging Afro-American community, and still better chances of bearing numerous children. By 1710 in South Carolina and by 1730 in the Chesapeake the number of creole blacks soared, soon surpassing imports and producing an Americanized slave population. The net natural increase was demographically significant, for it explains why the United States slave population grew so spectacularly compared to those of the rest of the Western Hemisphere, but its significance for the emergence of an Afro-American community was no less important.

As the black population grew, both the density of black settlement and the average size of slaveholding units increased. Roads were cut through the forest-carpeted landscape, rivers bridged, and interplantation communication was made easier. Decreasing sex ratios and increased access to fellow slaves aided the development of black families. By the 1730s slaves on large plantations like Robert Carter's in Virginia often lived as nuclear families. On smaller plantations males were able to visit their spouses on neighboring farms, and a dispersed family system arose, the children living with their mother and both owners at least tacitly acknowledging the slave father's visiting rights. The health of the slaves improved, and those on large, successful plantations were rarely sold. Even when death or debts forced a sale, slaves were likely to be purchased by slaveholders who lived close by. These cumulative changes produced a more stable, less precarious life for typical slaves. Healthy, able to form relatively permanent families, and having a network of friends and relatives reaching across the fields and forests to tie neighborhood plantations into a slave proto-community, Afro-Americans succeeded in transforming their situation from one of isolation and death into one of growth and creativity. A slave population in which families existed, with children to be taught and parents to teach them, was obviously far more concerned with holding on to, creating, and passing on cultural values than an earlier society composed mostly of young males. The creation of an Afro-American culture followed the development of black families and a black community.

Those who look for African "survivals" in New World ceremonies or rituals that are recognizably African and who tabulate words of African origin that have entered the American language are apt to underestimate the creative force of the culture they are exploring. For the reasons discussed above, the highly visible symbols and artifacts of African life could not be replicated in the mainland colonies. Yet something more subtle, more lasting, was transmitted to American posterity. Slaves came from a wide geographical swath of Africa, spoke different tongues, carried with them a variety of customs and beliefs, and did not even conceive of themselves as Africans; instead they identified themselves by tribe or clan, considering other black peoples no more related to them than contemporary Englishmen felt related to Italians. There was no one African culture. When an African chieftain sold to waiting slavers blacks captured from an enemy, he was not selling his "brothers." It is one of the ironies of the history of slavery that out of their common bondage in the New World the multiplicity of Africans found unity in their color and came to recognize a common identification in their Africanness. As this ultimate acceptance of themselves as a people suggests, there was among the many African ethnic groups a cultural common denominator.

This inherent unity is to be found in broad philosophical concepts—such as the perception of time, ideas about causality, belief in a deity, attitudes toward social relationships, and rites of passage—that lie beneath the surface of readily observable folkways yet shape their expression in ways roughly analogous to how an almost unconscious grammar shapes one's speech. This subconscious, generalized heritage, especially basic notions about such things as family, one's relationship to the spiritual or supernatural universe, music, distinctive modes of what we today call body language (a certain gait, a style of gesturing with one's hands while in conversation, a fluid, loose way of undulating one's body in unison with rhythm), was brought to the New World. Like involuntary muscles that keep the heart beating without one consciously thinking about it, this generalized African heritage helped shape the slaves' response to their American situation. Most surface manifestations of the former African customs—adapted to the texture of a particular social and natural ecology—were stripped away when confronted with a new social and natural world so unlike their native one. Yet the way enslaved Africans adjusted to what life presented them in the New World—how they borrowed and subtly transmuted European language and religious beliefs and white and Indian medicinal lore and cooking traditions; how they accepted and remodeled to their own purpose plantation work routines and developed extended families complete with kinship networks and distinct naming patterns; how they adapted New World flora and fauna to modified versions of Old World rituals, smoothing out the differences between tribal ceremonies—all suggest the influence of an underlying African principle. The ultimate result, less African than some have wished and more African than appearances once seemed to indicate, was in fact a new person, the Afro-American.

Slaves of course were, even in the best situations, severely limited in how they could shape their lives. The lack of freedom was an overwhelming and constant presence; they had to work with what they had. While one must be careful not to romanticize the ability of slaves to develop stable families—the two-parents-present household was probably never the most common arrangement—or carve out areas of cultural autonomy, neither should one minimize what slaves achieved. We have already mentioned how some African males, by virtue of their exogamous traditions, refused to pick mates on their home plantation and instead chose spouses living on another plantation. In West African societies an individual did not exist in isolation; everyone belonged to a complexly structured kinship network. One's identity was found within the group of persons to whom one was related. Elaborate kinship networks stretched across households, linking many persons together into an organic unity.

As soon as survival rates, population density, and interplantation communication in the mainland colonies allowed it, similar kinship systems began to emerge. Obviously, large kinship groups did not migrate intact to America, but slaves from different African backgrounds shared a belief in the basic importance of kinship. At first in the New World, conceivably even on the slave ships, before biological kinship could exist, slaves may have created fictive kin relationships to give some semblance of familiarity and structure to their lives. Beginning with the second generation of creole slaves, individual blacks had New World parents and siblings; by the middle of the eighteenth century persons identified themselves in relation to quite extended kinship networks that were often actually genealogical: grandparents, parents, siblings, aunts and uncles, nephews, first and second and third cousins. When families were broken up, husbands and teen-age children would typically be sold to nearby planters; at a master's death slaves were often willed to elder sons and moved to new locations—usually only a few miles away in the eighteenth century. By this process kinship and friendship networks expanded spatially. A young child sold away to another plantation might find there an uncle, or an elder sibling, or a relative of a friend on his prior plantation. In the absence of biological relatives, fictive aunts and uncles could serve quasiparental functions.

Such associations eased somewhat the pain of separation from one's primary family. Slaves visited among plantations, sharing news and gossip with friends and relatives. Temporary runaways often visited loved ones then either returned voluntarily or were captured and returned to their home plantation. Runaways seeking to escape slavery (or, more commonly, by their absence protesting particular mistreatment) could find refuge among friends and relatives on nearby plantations. Such associations gave slaves a sense of belonging, helped structure their attempts at self-identity, and eased both the process of escape and involuntary separation. Nothing earthshaking had transpired, and whites seemed either oblivious to or unconcerned with what was occurring. Quietly, naturally, perhaps without conscious intent, slaves had developed a pattern of relationships that in part alleviated one of the most destructive aspects of the peculiar institution, the separation of families and loved ones.

How slaves named their children and chose surnames (and the black parents, not the owner, normally did the naming) suggest other ways deep-seated African concepts may have emerged in the New World, with the names themselves nearly always being European but the pattern of naming being African. In Africa one's name, and the occasion of naming, symbolically placed one in a kinship structure. Detailed studies of plantation listings of slave families and other plantation records reveal that many sons were named after their fathers, but black daughters were very rarely named after their mothers. (White sons were similarly named, but white daughters were often named after their mothers, so the slave practice was not merely a copy of the white.) Since in many cases a slave father lived on another plantation, naming his son after him was a symbolic way of linking the two together. Children of both sexes were named for grandparents, further evidence of the importance of families and kin relationships. In a society where slave marriages were not legally recognized and families could be separated at the whim of a master, genealogically significant names gave permanence to otherwise fragile family arrangements.

In Africa one's identity was also tied to location, specific places venerated because ancestors were associated with them. A vestige of this African concept, transformed by the harsh reality of being a slave always subject to sale and forced relocation, might very well be seen in slaves' choices of surnames. While most slave listings give only a first name, there are indications from the early eighteenth century through emancipation that slaves had double names. Often their surnames were not the surnames of the slave's current owner. Rather, slaves identified themselves with their original owner (or their parent's or grandparent's owner), so that, for example, Nat Turner, Joseph Travis's slave in 1831, called himself Nat Turner, not Nat Travis, because he had been born on Benjamin Turner's farm (and he had belonged to Putnam Moore before belonging to Travis). Even though a slave might be forced to move from a location linked to his ancestors, retaining the original name bound him to the ancestral homeplace. As suggested above, the children of slave parents with surnames different from their current owner carried their parent's name too. Clearly all slaves were not culturally adrift, without role models, identifying only with their owners. Genealogical identification helped slave families persevere despite the vicissitudes of living under a system of bondage.

One must never lose sight of the laws restricting slaves' freedoms, of the police control over their behavior exercised by whites, yet the plantation of 1730 or 1770 (or 1850 for that matter) was not a rationalized, strictly supervised "total" institution like a modern high security prison. On a large plantation, when the day's work was done and the master and overseer (if there was one) had retired to their respective dwellings, those in the quarters were left essentially undisturbed. Planters and overseers checked the quarters nominally and on an irregular basis most nights; they tried to control the daytime work routines of their slaves, and within limits monitored their coming and going. Some planters required that clothes be washed, cabins cleaned and occasionally white-washed, bedding aired, and other such minimal housekeeping duties performed. But what slaves did in their cabins after sundown—the tales they told, the songs they sang and dances they danced, the way they talked, how they named and disciplined their children, the patterns in the baskets they wove, their characteristic gestures and loose, disjointed way of walking—the master cared lit-tle for such matters. And yet, here in the arena of the slave quarters, so much of what constituted the Afro-American was created. In particular, the slaves' music and religion evolved to become significant parts of the black world view, and though the masters were aware of the music and largely regarded it as harmless, though they hoped to supervise the Negroes' religion, both music and religion were primary constituents of a distinct black culture. Song and worship became perhaps the major forms of black expression, with music less affected, religion more so, by the dominant white culture within which the Afro-American con-sciousness emerged. Black music and religion were participatory folk devices that united the plantation communities. But both topics are so important that they will be discussed in a later chapter.

So far, when speaking of Africanisms present in the New World, we have mentioned only things of the mind and spirit. Perhaps in the long run these were—are always—the most important. The planters were apparently oblivious to such things (like blacks creating real and fictive kinship networks) or considered them harmless (Africans dancing to the lively music of their banjos, tell-ing stories, carving wood). Hence, unregulated, some African styles and patterns of behavior survived the rigors of plantation life to become hallmarks of black culture. Yet also, in readily observ-able objective ways, Africans contributed special skills and knowledge to the society taking root in this hemisphere. In Africa certain individuals were knowledgeable about wood and metal working, and such persons found avenues for utilizing those skills in America. Every colony had black craftsmen locally renowned for their ways of shaping wood into handsome cabinets or elegant chairs. African herdsmen, transplanted thousands of miles, found their ability to handle cattle a valued skill in the early colonies, and Africans may have developed the pioneer cattle industry in South Carolina, using open grazing and cow pens. Perhaps the reason cattle handlers, the quintessential American hero, are called cowboys rather than cowmen is related to the race of the prototype cowherders. Slaves experienced with canoes and river navigation became adept at ferrying their masters through the labyrinthine waterways of the sea islands and piloted ships into various southern ports. Quite probably slaves from the "rice coast" of Africa showed their masters in South Carolina the secrets of successful rice cultivation, for certainly the techniques of planting the seed in America exactly resembled the process in the old country, and planters sought out slaves skilled in African rice production.

Most Africans had lived in villages and subsisted on crops planted and harvested by time-tested agricultural techniques. Accustomed to agricultural tasks, they found adjustment to the labor requirements of plantations in the New World not impossible— unlike the far more primitive North American Indians, who as simple hunters and gatherers could not make the transition to advanced agricultural life. Rather than being savages into whom skills for the most menial tasks had to be drilled over and over, Africans "made good slaves" because their own style and level of civilization had prepared them for the kinds of routinized labor New World crops required and masters desired. Contemporary observers often commented that slave women, unlike white women (even indentured ones), often worked in the field, but in Africa women had been the primary agricultural workers.

Because they found the kinds of tasks assigned not too foreign, slaves quickly devised ways of to some degree influencing their work routines. Blacks slowed the tempo of their labor, working at a deliberate pace to husband their strength. Work songs in American fields as previously in Africa united the laborers in rhythmic fashion, and choppers moved across a field with their tools swinging to the measured cadence of a chant. Just as the Africans' agricultural heritage acquainted them with the tasks required in America, their preindustrial work discipline slowed the routine to more acceptable levels. Africans were not, as one early historian wrote, simply what the white man made them. To an extent only recently realized, Africans had a hand in shaping what and who they became in America.

It has already been suggested that as the eighteenth century advanced, the average size of plantations (in terms of slaveholdings) increased, with major implications for the formation of black families and an incipient black culture. The increased size of slaveholdings also brought significant changes in the work routines for many slaves. In the pioneer period slaves had been employed in a variety of tasks from clearing land and cultivating crops to fishing, driving wagons, serving as carpenters, coopers, sawyers, and the like. At first most agricultural tasks were quite simple, but as plantations grew larger, and more successful, they also became more complex, with a greater division of labor. Certain blacks became slave drivers (foremen) or even overseers (farm superintendents);others acquired specialized roles such as plowmen, millers, livestock tenders, gardeners, carriage drivers, and a wide variety of domestic positions (cooks, valets, maids, governesses). Such gradations in the plantation work force offered limited avenues of advancement, a refreshing respite (even if only temporary) from monotonous tasks year after year, and opportunities for increased self-respect in one's upward mobility or complex task well done. Obviously incentive was limited, upward mobility quickly curtailed, and so on. But slaves, like other people in tight circumstances, earned and appreciated small pleasures; like other people aware of their worth they felt a sense of accomplishment over a bountiful crop, a succulent meal that pleased their master, any achievement requiring real skill. Such individuals were not, to use a modern phrase, being "co-opted by the system." Relatively few choices were open to them, and they made the best of their world. Who can read of the skilled slaves on George Mason's eighteenth-century plantation, Gunston Hall—as described by his son—and not be impressed with how much slaves contributed to the life and society of colonial Virginia during its Golden Age?

It was very much the practice with gentlemen of landed and slave estates in the interior of Virginia, so to organize them as to have considerable resources within themselves; to employ and pay but few tradesmen and to buy little of the coarse stuffs and materials used by them. . . . Thus my father had among his slaves carpenters, coopers, sawyers, blacksmiths, tanners, curriers, shoemakers, spinners, weavers and knitters, and even a distiller. His woods furnished timber and plank for the carpenters and coopers, and charcoal for the blacksmith, his cattle killed for his own consumption and for sale supplied skins for tanners, curriers, and shoemakers, and his sheep gave wool and his fields produced cotton and flax for the weavers and spinners, and his orchards fruit for the distiller. His carpenters and sawyers built and kept in repair all the dwelling-houses, barns, stables, ploughs, harrows, gates, &c., on the plantations and the outhouses at the home house. His coopers made the hogsheads the tobacco was prized in and the tight casks to hold the cider and other liquors. The tanners and curriers with the proper vats &c., tanned and dressed the skins as well for upper as for lower leather to the full amount of the consumption of the estate, and shoemakers made them into shoes for the negroes. A professed shoemaker was hired for three or four months in the year to come and make up the shoes for the white part of the family. The blacksmith did all the iron work required by the establishment, as making and repairing ploughs, harrows, teeth chains, bolts, &c., &c. The spinners, weavers and knitters made all the coarse cloths and stockings used by the negroes, and some of finer texture worn by the white family, nearly all worn by the children of it. The distiller made every fall a good deal of apple, peach and persimmon brandy. . . . All these operations were carried on at the home house, and their results distributed as occasion required to the different plantations. Moreover, all the beeves and hogs for consumption or sale were driven up and slaughtered there at the proper seasons, and whatever was to be preserved was salted and packed away for after distribution (Edmund S. Morgan, *Virginians at Home: Family Life in the Eighteenth Century* [Williamsburg, Va.: Colonial Williamsburg, 1952], pp. 53-54).

Like William Byrd II before him, George Mason might have claimed to "live in a kind of independence on every one but Providence." But clearly such large, well-organized, self-sufficient plantations were always the exception, never the rule, even in mid-eighteenth-century Virginia. Tens of thousands of blacks lived on struggling farms with only one or two slaves, often a woman used primarily for domestic chores. Other thousands labored on middling farms with between five and fifteen slaves composed of men, women, and children, representing families and fragments of families. Most slaveholders owned only a handful of slaves, but most slaves lived on larger plantations. One wealthy planter might own more slaves than several dozen smaller slave owners together. Describing the "typical" slave is far more difficult than describing the range of slave situations. The black experience on any one farm or plantation depended upon an extensive list of factors. Population density, sex ratios, percentage of African born in the population, and the like were circumstances that established the broad outlines of black life. But the size and kind of plantation, the vagaries of a growing season, the price export crops were bringing in the world market, and the personalities of individual slaves and their masters or overseers all helped to shape an individual slave's world. For some, given their temperament and that of their master, perhaps the best situation was on a very small farm, working in the fields with the owner, living under the same roof, sharing the same food, the same joys, frustrations, and accomplishments. No doubt for many the close supervision one received in this environment, with an identity sometimes necessarily molded in response to one's owner, was psychologically suffocating. For one so stifled, being sold to a large plantation where black life in the slave quarters approached a degree of cultural autonomy could be liberating.

Only the most general conclusions should be drawn. The southern plantation system never became so standardized that the Negroes' history could be aggregated from examples drawn from across the region. Both slaves and slave owners were individuals whose diversity accentuated the soil, climatic, crop, and other varieties within the region. On the whole, colonial slaves must have received at least minimally sufficient diets and reasonable work loads to have survived, reproduced, and formed a black community of over a half million by 1775. Yet even the causes of this population growth are a mixture of white and black actions.

There was no standard slave diet, but the food whites distributed to their slaves, while monotonous, was adequate to sustain them. Just as important, it became customary for whites to allow slaves to cultivate small, private garden plots to supplement their diets. Enterprising slaves also hunted, fished, and gathered berries, pokeweed, and other wild nutrients. By permitting slaves to supplement the food allotment—or by being indifferent to their ingenuity in doing so—planters wittingly or unwittingly, directly or indirectly, allowed access to a diet adequate to provide reasonably good health, stamina, and the ability to conceive and rear children. The eighteenth-century South was the only large-scale slave society in the Americas to enjoy a net black population increase, a development arising out of such basic aspects of treatment as sufficient food and reasonable workloads.

This was done in Jamaica

The labor required of slaves of course varied widely, but in aggregate terms slaves were not worked to death in the British mainland colonies. Because of the planter's self-interest and occasional benevolence and the absence of the man-killing labor needs of the sugar islands, together with the blacks' ability through their wiles and collective efforts to manipulate the work pace, slaves as a population group survived reasonably well. They worked hard, though no harder than they had to, because they were pressured and forced to be industrious. But they also had both direct and indirect positive incentives to do so. Slaves quickly perceived that, other things being equal, they were better fed and housed, and less apt to be separated from their families, on more prosperous plantations. And of course a plantation's economic well-being was ultimately in their hands.

Whites controlled important segments of a slave's life. However, in ways we are just beginning to understand, slaves carved out areas of self-control, seized and multiplied their limited opportunities, and resisted becoming simply human property. White sufferance, black strength, or a mixture of both? In every imaginable category of human need, slaves in the South had a more difficult, less pleasant life than whites. But for the humanity, self-interest, and laxity of their owners, their lot would have been far worse; but for the humanity, self-interest, and creative skills of the slaves themselves, their lot would have been still worse. In the final analysis the horror of slavery is not to be measured in dietary insufficiencies or work routines or even survival rates, but in the absence of freedom, especially in a land where, relative to most of the world, economic and political liberty flourished as never before. The black response to the American Revolution, in which perhaps as many as 50,000 blacks fled to the British, reveals both the slaves' longing for liberty and the caution with which they held in check that desire until propitious occasions offered reasonable expectations of success.

The previous chapter indicated the deterioration of relations between whites and blacks in the final decade of the seventeenth century. With the slave population growing by leaps and bounds, with more African imports and recognizable African culture traits, whites in the various southern colonies conjured up images of black domination and white destruction. Soon southern planters sought by a series of legislative enactments to control slave behavior. Beginning about 1700 harsh, rigorous codes were passed in each southern colony. In successive decades these laws were elaborated, made more inclusive, and utilized to maintain total white hegemony. In retrospect it is easy to see repressive laws pyramiding as the black population grew, but it is probably a mistake to overemphasize the effect these increasingly racist codes had on blacks. Similarly, whites in the middle decades of the eighteenth century seem to have treated slaves more brutally, to have conceived of them more often as things or beasts of burden, than at any other time in American history. Gone were the early days of the seventeenth century when blacks were so few as to appear unthreatening, when they were simply other workers, more or less the equivalent of indentured servants. Now their numbers and their Africanness set them apart, and before the moderating influence of Enlightenment ideas and paternalistic ideals became widespread, and the implications of the end of the slave trade (1808) were well established, North American slavery went through its harshest phase.

Yet at the same time as the legal restrictions on black freedom were being drawn ever tighter and white attitudes became more racist, developments in the countryside worked to make slave living conditions more tolerable. With black population growth came increased slave density and larger units of slaveholding, along with better communication among plantations. Blacks established families, shared concerns, created a culture and a community. What was happening in the quarters affected slave life in the long run as much as white prejudice or laws passed in Annapolis, Williamsburg, and Charleston. With families and a common language, the terrible isolation early slaves must have felt largely disappeared. In special regions where highly unbalanced sex ratios (and net population decline) continued, black resistance may even have been more extensive than whites dared to think. The slave-Indian insurrection of 1709 in Surry County, Virginia, and the great Stono Revolt in South Carolina in 1739 showed that, among populations composed primarily of young, unattached males, unrest could be almost endemic. After all, very little was to be lost. Yet such unstable regions became increasing atypical after the mid-eighteenth century.

In one of the most ironic twists of southern history, the astonishing growth of black population that so worried whites and led to repressive legislation simultaneously enabled slaves to ameliorate the quality of their lives so significantly that insurrection became a far less attractive option. (More private acts such as running away and, far less common, arson and poisoning, continued.) Not only was one's condition more endurable, but, with wives and children to think about, black males were far less willing to risk open rebellion. Now there was too much to be lost. Although the human desire for autonomy and freedom still burned in the breasts of peaceful slaves, sensible strategy cautioned against community-threatening actions. When in the final quarter of the century the American Revolution held forth in different guises an opportunity to achieve freedom, thousands of slaves took bold action to gain their liberty. While the white colonists were seeking independence from the British, some black colonists sought independence from the whites. The contagion of liberty knew no racial boundaries, but relatively few slaves actually gained their freedom from the Revolution. By wresting national control from Britain and placing it in the hands of local representatives, the Revolution's ultimate effect was to ensure the continuation of the institution of slavery that had evolved in the previous three generations.

3. The Maturation of the Plantation System, 1776-1860

Slavery in the North American mainland colonies was approximately a century old when the American Revolution sundered the British colonies from the crown. The black response to the "epochal rupture" was largely conditioned by the previous history of black-white relations and the aspirations nurtured by the Afro-American community. Although blacks participated in the Revolution, many in support of the American cause, most who found themselves living in the new United States had little freedom in which to rejoice. Several thousand slaves in the South were emancipated at the high point of egalitarian fervor, and those in the northern states witnessed the beginning of the end of slavery above Mason and Dixon's line. But the huge majority of blacks lived in the South, where—after the Haitian revolt in 1791—their numbers raised the specter of black domination if freed and the fear of slave insurrection if control over them were relaxed. Good men might dream of abolition and move to prohibit slavery's spread to virgin territories, but racial fears and political timidity prevented even Jefferson from boldly striking out against slavery where it already existed in the early and mid-1780s. Paradoxically the Revolutionary era, by legitimating the political control of resident slaveholding whites, confirmed the plantation society that had developed in the eighteenth century and laid the foundation for the mature slave society that evolved in the nineteenth century. Home rule's ultimate significance was to ensure that nonresident legislators would not be able to end slavery by legislative fiat, as Parliament did for British West Indian slavery in 1833.

In many ways the Constitutional Convention of 1787 was a conservative movement to slow and control the democratic tendencies that had taken root since 1776, and on no other issue were the Founding Fathers more conservative than in defense of private property, which included the right to own property in humans. Thus the new nation in its charter guaranteed the prolongation of African bondage and allowed slave imports until 1808. The Constitution was ratified in 1788, a new government was in place the following year, and the United States began its meteoric rise among nations.

For most Afro-Americans freedom was still a vague dream. Slaves outnumbered free blacks twelve to one (twenty to one in the South) in 1790, and though the small free black population grew faster than the slave population for several decades, the next seventy years were to be the heyday of American slavery. The first census in 1790 listed 657,527 slaves in the South, and that number almost doubled by 1810 to 1,163,854. The numbers still rose: 2,005,475 in 1830, 3,204,051 in 1850, almost 4 million on the eve of the Civil War. Human bondage spread west and south as new states were formed and the areas planted in cotton and sugar expanded. Jefferson's empire of liberty grew to encompass a giant slave empire, and the development of a mature plantation society in the South in the antebellum period saw the fruition of white practices and a black community pioneered in the previous century.

Before the Revolution free Negroes had served in the various colonial militias, quite commonly in the North and, though rarely, also in the South. Blacks had been caught up in the revolutionary ferment from the beginning of the imperial controversy; the mulatto Crispus Attucks was the first casualty at the so-called Boston Massacre in 1770. Within a year of the beginning of armed hostilities with Great Britain, however, the Continental army forbade the use of black troops. The southern militias already had adopted that policy, for the arming of slaves presented supposed dangers for plantation societies. When the royal governor of Virginia, Lord Dunmore, pioneered the use of black troops, his actions struck fear in the hearts of the planters and ignited hope in the hearts of their bondsmen.

In April 1775, the month of Lexington and Concord, a group of slaves had come to the governor volunteering their services in exchange for freedom, but Dunmore had hesitated. Dunmore began to reconsider his options as the crown's position in Virginia worsened. By June the royal governor had left Williamsburg and taken refuge aboard a ship off Yorktown. Faced with rebellious subjects and bereft of British reinforcements, Dunmore in November issued the proclamation that cast him as a liberator to the slaves and an infamous villain to the whites. Calling the rebel colonists traitors, Lord Dunmore then stated, "And I do hereby further declare all indented servants, Negroes, or others, (appertaining to Rebels,) free, that are able and willing to bear arms, they joining His Majesty's Troops. . . ." A nightmarish chill swept down the backs of the whites, and they quickly took emergency police action to prevent a slave stampede to the British banner. Patrols were doubled, slaves removed from sensitive areas, rumors spread that the nefarious British would simply ship the unsuspecting slaves to the West Indies; attractive offers were issued to tempt bondsmen to remain with their owners. Despite the precautions of the whites, hundreds of slaves fled to the British forces, and soon 300 uniformed blacks constituted what was officially called Lord Dunmore's Ethiopian Regiment. But before Dunmore's army had a chance to prove itself, it was routed by patriot troops in December. For the next few months Dunmore's forces, white and black, operated aboard a flotilla meandering about Chesapeake Bay. Black foragers were sent ashore for supplies, and slaves came in droves whenever the freedom flotilla came near, but a smallpox epidemic decimated the shipborne slaves before any further military engagements occurred. In August 1776 Dunmore fled to Bermuda; perhaps 300 blacks went north to further military service and eventual freedom. Less than a thousand slaves in all escaped to join Dunmore's Ethiopian Regiment with its banners announcing "Liberty to Slaves," but Lord Dunmore's proclamation reverberated throughout the colonies for the duration of the war.

By 1777 the need for manpower forced both sides to reconsider the use of black troops. Colonials in the northern states were quite willing to employ free blacks, and with the growing realization that slavery itself stood in contradistinction to the ideals of the Declaration of Independence, numerous whites freed their slaves in return for their service in the army. Free blacks often on their own initiative chose to fight, perhaps because they shared the patriot ideology, or sought adventure, or—more probably—desired to gain the land bounties being given recruits. To the south both Maryland and Virginia accepted the employment of free blacks in the army, with numerous masters manumitting their bondsmen for that purpose. Yet South Carolina and Georgia resisted to the very end the use of black soldiers. It is impossible to know how many blacks served the patriot cause in a military capacity; the best estimate is about 5,000, mostly in the North.

Some black soldiers actually bore arms and fought side by side with their white compatriots. Far more served ancillary functions. The typical black soldier of the army of the Continental Congress was in the infantry, and was primarily engaged in supporting the white troops. Blacks did duty as cooks, wagoneers, and servants. They built roads, made camps, constructed fortifications, and dug trenches. They worked in tanneries, ropewalks, munitions factories. Serving as foragers they scoured the countryside provisioning the regular army. Other blacks found still more specialized ways to aid the rebel forces. Some Negroes functioned as spies, giving colonial officers invaluable information about British troop locations and numbers. Still other blacks utilized their intimate knowledge of the terrain to guide troops through swamps; many who were skilled in navigation piloted American and French ships to their harbors. Scores served in the Continental navy.

As the theater of war shifted to the South after 1778, black involvement became much more important. In addition to those many hundreds of blacks who performed military duties in the expectation of freedom, thousands of slaves were pressed into temporary service by the white military and public authorities. Few of these slaves received freedom as a reward for their labors. These blacks were called to emergency duties to build fortifications, to forage supplies for hungry troops, to repair roads, and otherwise relieve the soldiers of noncombat labor. Not only were slaves "borrowed" from their owners, but they were also leased for longer terms and even bought for public use by military and state agencies. As the war dragged on and the need for manpower reached a crisis level, patriot leaders like Nathanael Greene actively considered large-scale utilization of black (freed slave) troops, but South Carolina and Georgia officials overruled such ideas out of the fear of arming slaves. Those blacks who served in the patriot cause seem to have done so willingly. They had comparatively little choice in the matter, they had some hope of freedom as a result, and the opportunity to prove they were the military equals of the whites was no doubt attractive.

Yet in the South by far the majority of slaves involved in the Revolutionary War were attracted to the British forces. Lord Dunmore's abortive campaign had been of little immediate military import, but for tens of thousands of southern bondsmen, the proclamation of 1775 symbolized the possibility of freedom by joining the British. London officials did not look favorably on black regular soldiers, but toward the end of the war, with the major campaign in the densely black-populated southern tidewater and the transportation of men and provisions from England proving to be nearly impossible, hard-pressed local officers began to employ blacks in practically every capacity. Lord Dunmore, in South Carolina in January 1782, made plans to raise 10,000 black troops, but his hopes were dashed by London; by then, the British cause was too far gone to risk such a bold departure. Throughout the war the British, as did the Americans, primarily used blacks in a military support capacity. Both sides also occasionally used slaves as property to be bartered for supplies and services.

The British less often than the Americans resorted to impressment of slaves. Rather, they simply received the hordes of expectant bondsmen fleeing their masters and flocking to His Majesty's forces. At times the British feared they would be inundated by blacks seizing the chance to be free. The British did not hesitate, however, to raid rebel plantations and seize the slaves, less to free them than to cripple the opposing side. Thousands of blacks were used as laborers or foragers—these hardworking volunteers (and involuntary captives) performed functions identical to those performed by blacks serving the patriot cause. They kept artillery units rolling, armies marching, soldiers and displaced slaves fed. Only the scale of the black contribution to the British differed. The rebels called upon the efforts of several thousand blacks, the British had the benefit of tens of thousands. The slaves had much stronger expectations of freedom from the British—and the British needed their cooperation more desperately. Blacks gave indispensable assistance by spying on patriot forces, leading British troops through strange territory, and piloting British naval vessels through treacherous coastal waters. Such actions were even more valuable to the British than to the patriot army.

The Americans tried to dissuade slaves from flocking to the British by threatening punishment and offering rewards for loyalty, but primarily they continued to use the ploy of spreading rumors that the British planned to resell their helpless minions to the West Indies. Such rumors failed to stop blacks from joining Lord Dunmore's Ethiopian Regiment in 1775-76, and they failed in the last years of the war to slow the far larger slave efforts in behalf of British victory and black freedom. In some regions, like Maryland's Eastern Shore, white and black Methodists, whose religious beliefs inclined them toward Toryism and whose mutual disdain of patriot planters produced a kind of populist Loyalism, worked together to aid the British forces. In many areas of the South, the Revolution was more nearly a civil than a revolutionary war, and those who have focused on white divisions alone have underestimated the black role.

Vicious fighting continued in the South (and among naval squadrons in the Caribbean) for two years following Lord Cornwallis's surrender at Yorktown, which determined the outcome of the war. Even before the treaty was signed in 1783, the British began the process of evacuating their troops and supporters. Here arose a problem. Americans expected all property seized by the British to be returned, and that included those slaves who had joined the British forces in return for the promised freedom. The British faced a moral dilemma: liberation of slaves had never been a war aim; instead, it had been a means to an end. Yet to dismiss the promises of freedom and callously return the blacks to their vengeful former owners seemed dishonorable. Their honor at stake, the British refused to give in to the demands of American negotiators and officials. The issue was to rankle British-American relations for a half-century, but the British evacuated possibly as many as 50,000 ex-slaves with their departing troops and scattered Loyalists. (It is impossible to say now how many unwilling slaves were seized by the British and how many escaped to the British.)

Many of the blacks went to Canada, others to England, still more were ultimately colonized in Sierra Leone. An unknown number of blacks eventually did end up being sold as slaves in the West Indies or pressed into military service there. It seems evident that some, now possessed of their freedom, chose to remain in America to be near their loved ones and located near their former owners, though certainly some went to the young nation's cities and began new lives as free black craftsmen, artisans, and laborers. How many slaves took advantage of the chaos associated with the war to escape and emerge as free blacks in southern towns and northern cities is anyone's guess.

For white Americans 1776 is the birth of political freedom from Great Britain. Less appreciated is how the ideals so eloquently expressed in Jefferson's Declaration found their way into the hearts and minds of many slaveholders and helped open their eyes to the evil of slavery. In the northern states, where there were far fewer slaves, no large-scale plantation slave economy, and previous sentiment for emancipation, the ideology of liberty pushed hesitant conservatives over the brink. Slowly, beginning with Pennsylvania in 1780 and culminating with New Jersey in 1804, every northern state provided for gradual emancipation of its slaves. (Massachusetts by court decision declared slavery illegal in 1783, becoming the first state actually to end slavery, although the slave trade had been ended almost a decade earlier in some New England colonies.) Hundreds of southern slave owners, smitten with the revolutionary ideology—and on many occasions their hearts warmed by waves of evangelical egalitarianism just beginning to take root in the South—provided for the manumission of their slaves. As a result, thousands of former slaves received their freedom from patriot Americans in the generation following 1776. The number of free blacks in the United States increased several fold between then and 1790. The first federal census of that year showed 59,446 free blacks in the nation, 32,357 in the South. Ten years later that number had almost doubled again, with 108,395 in the U.S. and 61,241 in the South. Together with their black brothers who had departed with the British, these Revolutionary freedmen represented the first great gains in liberty achieved by Afro-Americans. Eighty years later, in another great war, hundreds of thousands of slaves would flee to liberating forces and eventually all would win their freedom. But between the Revolution and the Civil War the plantation system came to maturity.

The postwar South faced many problems. Physical property had been destroyed, particularly in South Carolina and Georgia. New trade agreements, including certain markets for agricultural products, had to be negotiated. Tens of thousands of slaves had fled or been taken by retreating British ships. In the confusion and turmoil of the 1780s, tobacco, rice, and indigo production fell far below prewar levels. A decade and a half passed before such staple crops regained their old standing, and their production stagnated thereafter, in part because of soil exhaustion and the region's inadequate transportation network. Farmers in the Chesapeake region increasingly turned to wheat as a money crop, a grain whose smaller labor needs combined with liberalized ideas to produce a willingness to end the African slave trade. In the rice and indigo growing areas of the South, however, the desire to replace wartime slave losses and rebuild destroyed levees and rice irrigation canals soon produced a clamor to keep the African trade open. Out of such compelling needs came the constitutional compromise delaying the federal prohibition of slave imports until 1808.

During the mild agricultural depression of the 1780s and early 1790s, there actually seemed to be a region-wide surplus of Africans, an excess aggravated by marketing problems and the shift from tobacco to wheat in the Upper South. The agricultural future of the South looked clouded as the value of slaves dropped and crop production failed to spurt ahead after the war. But various changes—technological, agricultural, and territorial—were unfolding that in combination were to change the whole structure of the southern economy and drastically shape the black experience for the next century and a half. The latter two changes occurred in this nation, but the technological developments were largely British.

For countless centuries most of the Western world's clothing had come from wool and flax, with only the rich able to afford fine cotton goods imported from India and bearing names, like muslin, calico, and madras, that hinted of their exotic origins. Cotton spinning and weaving had begun in England before 1650 but a century later was still a minor industry. Yet precisely because it was a new trade, tradition-bound guilds and other vested interests were less able to control its direction and sabotage labor-saving innovations. Beginning with John Kay's flying shuttle in 1733 came a parade of technological breakthroughs, culminating with James Hargreaves's spinning jenny in 1763, Richard Arkwright's water frame in 1769, and Samuel Crompton's mule, which combined the previous two ideas, in 1779. The result was an industrial revolution in the production of cotton cloth, and with cotton factories spreading to supply the ever-cheaper cotton goods to a constantly expanding market (Europe had simultaneously begun a sustained population explosion—increasing more than a third between 1750 and 1800—accentuating the need for cloth), the British demand for raw cotton far outstripped the world supply.

Minute amounts of cotton had been grown in the American mainland colonies since the settlement of Jamestown, and large plantations usually cultivated a small patch entirely for domestic consumption. Several species of cotton were known in the South before the Revolution, the hardy green-seed variety, whose short lint adhered tenaciously to its fuzzy seed, and the smooth black-seed variety, with its more luxurious lint that was easier to separate from the seed and its greater susceptibility to a fungus known as the rot. Before the Revolutionary War plantations up and down the seaboard used simple roller gins that, in a fashion analogous to old-fashioned wringer washing machines, squeezed the lint through to fall in bags and left the seeds discarded on the inlet side of the parallel rollers. Neither the strength of the demand nor the efficiency of the gins recommended cotton as a viable money crop. Some time in the mid-1780s a more rot-resistant, smooth-seed cotton was introduced from the West Indies, and this long-staple species spread throughout the sea islands. With the lint separated either by hand or by roller gins, "sea island cotton" became profitable as the British demand raised the price. Between 1784 and 1791 British imports of cotton increased 216 percent, and they were to double again by 1800. Clearly hand and roller ginned cotton could not meet such a demand even if sea island cotton cultivation could have been expanded into the upland. As shrewd planters observed the rising cotton prices and contemplated the wider geographical range of the green-seed cotton, whose only serious drawback was the difficulty of separating its short staple from the seeds, many would-be inventors began to ponder the problem of freeing the lint from the grasp of the seed.

Several people achieved the breakthrough almost simultaneously, a situation that ultimately prevented the inventor of legend, Connecticut-born Eli Whitney, from capitalizing on his contraption. In 1793, while visiting the Georgia plantation of the late Nathanael Greene, Whitney made a simple refinement of the old roller gin. He added wire teeth to one roller and rotated it in such a fashion as to grab and tear the lint from the seed of cotton fed into a slatted box; another roller, with small brushes, whisked the separated lint from the teeth of the first. Thus, Whitney had made an inexpensive, workable, and easily duplicated improvement on the roller gin. The result was that upland-grown greenseed cotton could now compete for the expanding British market. Quick improvements—especially circular saws replacing the wire teeth—by Whitney and others multiplied the efficiency of the gin, with the ultimate result that cotton soon became the most promising money crop in piedmont South Carolina and eastern Georgia.

In the seven years between 1793 and 1800 millions of acres of fertile land became available for enterprising—some would say greedy—southern farmers. Between 1783 and 1796 a series of treaties with the Indians opened central and western Georgia to the advance of agriculturists, and land speculation further beckoned cotton growers. Fraud and avarice were the hallmarks of the land grants in the Yazoo River country, but the final result was the westward march of the cotton frontier. Anglo settlers had already established residence in the Natchez area of what is now Mississippi, and though the region was nominally in the hands of the Spanish, the transmission of American agricultural technology was rapid. As in the southern part of the United States, the cultivation of cotton had preceded Whitney's gin, but in Natchez too the inefficiency of the roller gin lessened marketing prospects. However, in 1795 Daniel Clark, hearing a traveler's description of Whitney's invention, put a local mechanic, a blacksmith, and a skilled slave named Barclay to work on replicating it. Within a short time Mississippi had entered the modern cotton age, and when, in 1798, the Mississippi Territory (including present-day Alabama) became a part of the United States, the advance of the fluffy staple all the way to the Father of Waters was assured.

Cotton, however, was not the only new crop amenable to slave labor in the Deep South. At the same time as the development of the gin, the growth of the British demand, and the settlement of new territories were ushering in the age of cotton, advances in the cultivation and manufacturing of sugar in Louisiana were occurring that would turn the southeastern section of that territory into a region of wealthy sugar plantations employing thousands of slaves. For decades before the 1790s sugarcane had been grown in French Louisiana for domestic use and for rum. In the early 1790s sugar-cane production increased, but not until 1795 when Etienne de Boré imported a skilled sugar maker from San Domingo, built a modern sugar mill on the site of the present-day campus of Tulane University, and began large-scale cultivation of sugarcane did the crop bear promise of great profits. De Boré persisted in his efforts until success came several years later. Soon hundreds of sugar-wise refugees from revolt-torn San Domingo brought their expertise with the crop and its manufacture to Louisiana. By 1801-2 as many as seventy-five sugar plantations were producing between four and eight million pounds of sugar each year, much of which supplied the American appetite for sweets. The territory acquired by the United States in 1803 was entering a prolonged sugar-slave boom. The size, the wealth, and the work routines of the Louisiana sugar plantations served to differentiate Louisiana from the rest of the South, but the important point is that, before 1800, technological breakthroughs at both ends of the South— accomplished by Eli Whitney in Georgia and Etienne de Boré in Louisiana—made possible the remarkably rapid rise of a slave-staple crop society in the Deep South.

Slaves were employed in the cultivation of various crops in the South, wheat and tobacco in Maryland and Virginia, tobacco in North Carolina and Kentucky, rice in the sea islands of South Carolina and Georgia, hemp in Kentucky, sugar in Louisiana, and foodstuffs like corn, sweet potatoes, and peas practically every-where. But it was cotton that provided the Old South its identity, cotton that gave the region its major money crop, cotton that dominated the minds of southern entrepreneurs and statesmen, cotton that employed the labor of perhaps three-fourths of all south-

ern slaves. For that reason the spread of cotton cultivation is a significant aspect of the slave experience in the Old South.

In the same way that Virginia was the key theater for the
development of colonial slavery, Mississippi was the quintessential
cotton state, leading the South in bales produced in 1860 and being
second only to South Carolina in the percentage of the total
population that was slave. In developing a new hybrid breed of cotton, called Petit Gulf, Mississippi farmers made a contribution to
cotton culture that rivals Whitney's gin. Petit Gulf's superior traits
(it grew well in a variety of soil conditions, its bolls were easy to
pick, it was immune to rot, and the lint was not knocked off as easily by late fall rains, thus lengthening the picking season and improving the yield) led to its being adopted across the South, widening significantly the geographical spread of cotton and increasing
annual production. Mississippi also became the South's leading
breeder and supplier of high-quality cotton seeds.

One very important feature of the Old South (a chronological,
not geographical, term by which most people mean the five- or six-
decade antebellum period, excluding the eighteen or nineteen
decades of southern history before 1788), was how *new* it was. Emphasizing Mississippi will help keep the nearness of the frontier in
mind. Mississippi became a territory in 1798, and far greater
numbers began to migrate there than ever before, but the presence
of Indians and the War of 1812 prevented a wholesale migration of
southerners, black and white. By 1815 both these deterrents had
been essentially overcome—though the removal of the Indians continued until the woeful Trail of Tears in 1836—and the period of
great migration to Mississippi began in 1816. In that year the
population was approximately 60,000, and by the end of 1817,
when Mississippi became the twentieth state, the population was
over 75,000. The subsequent growth of the white population, of the
number of slaves, and of the production of cotton—all quite spec-
tacular and closely interrelated—footnote vividly the newness of
the Old South's leading cotton state.

Before 1815 the cotton economy had spread slowly, primarily in
upstate South Carolina and east central Georgia. With the Indian
problem "solved," the trouble with the British resolved, the British
demand still growing, and available land suited for cotton nearly
exhausted in the seaboard states south of Virginia, slaves and cot-

ton cultivation grew and pushed westward in the decade after 1816. Cotton production in the United States almost tripled between 1816 (259,143 bales) and 1826 (731,452 bales), and hundreds of thousands of southerners, black and white, began the massive human migration across the face of the South, east to west, from the Peedee River eventually to the Brazos, creating the Old South of romance and reality. Thus were the plantation pretensions and aristocratic ambitions of white Virginians and South Carolinians spread to the raw frontier states of Alabama, Mississippi, Louisiana, and Texas. Numbers never tell the complete story, but the figures on pages 66-67 speak volumes about the quick rise of the cotton kingdom.

The dimensions of this migration to the western portion of the South—what was once called the Southwest and now the Old Southwest—suggest several important aspects of the cotton kingdom. First, it accentuates the geographical mobility of antebellum southerners, white and black, and suggests the measure of social mobility that existed for white southerners. In this new land, with rich black soil, available slaves, and a strong cotton market, many small white farmers through hard work, good management, and the smile of luck bought more acres, acquired slaves, improved their homes, and successfully made the transition from pioneer to planter. Such self-made men were often supremely confident of their own ability though terribly insecure in their new-found status, a combination conducive to exaggerated defenses of honor, outbreaks of arrogance, and political intransigence. A certain rawness, a frontierlike readiness to brawl, and an eagerness to put on the trappings of "culture" and "civilization"—that is, imitate the seaboard South—were other characteristics of the developing sections west of Georgia. Land, good land, lay waiting to be acquired and cultivated, and quick money from cotton and slaves beckoned thousands of would-be farmers and planters from the seaboard states. A certain gold-rush mentality prevailed as the cotton frontier surged across the region, and the chance of abolitionist sentiment prevailing amidst the ensuing cotton rush was infinitesimal. Conscientious souls in the Chesapeake, shifting to wheat on their tobacco-worn soil, might contemplate emancipation and free labor, but in the flush times of Alabama and Mississippi, slavery seemed the key to a prosperous future. The Old Southwest became the heart of Dixie.

In the older states of the South—Maryland to South Carolina—most of the good land was already settled, and erosion, soil exhaustion, and the loss of international markets hindered the future of rice, tobacco, and indigo production. With the white and black populations growing, there was quite naturally pressure to move westward. When cotton, and to a lesser extent sugar, offered strong economic incentives, and successive Indian treaties opened up vast acreages, the southern population surged westward. Clearly many slaveless whites seized the opportunity to obtain land, and while many of these continued as yeoman farmers, raising corn, cattle, hogs, and perhaps some cotton as a money crop, others prospered and competed for slaves. Still other whites, often a planter's younger son accompanied by his family, with their belongings in a covered wagon and their slaves and livestock walking behind, journeyed overland in small caravans much like those associated in the popular mind with wagon trains to Oregon and California. The slave migrants often came in family units, traveling with their master from worn-out regions of Virginia or South Carolina to Alabama or Mississippi. Still other slaves were sold to the Southwest by slave traders, who purchased their cargoes in Maryland, Virginia, or South Carolina and sent them, usually by foot, to the boom regions. No one questions that the Southwest was settled in this fashion. The continuing controversy is over how many slaves came, and whether they came in family (or plantation) units or were mostly individual victims of the internal slave market.

Perhaps as many as a quarter million slaves were involved in the interstate slave migration in the peak decade of the 1850s. For the entire period 1790 to 1860, some estimates place the total beyond one million. The declining slave populations of Maryland and Virginia, and the slowly growing one of South Carolina, suggest that they were essentially seller states, and the booming cotton and slave states of Georgia, Alabama, Mississippi, Louisiana, and, after 1850, Arkansas and Texas, were the buyer or importing states. The volume per state varied over time, but as the charts on page 67 indicate, the peak periods for each state came in succession as the cotton kingdom extended westward.

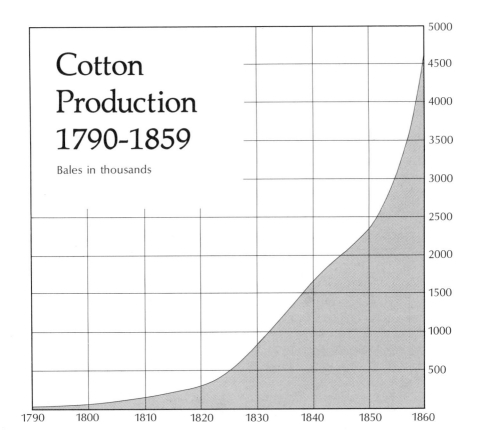

Cotton
Production
1790-1859

Bales in thousands

| 1790 | 1800 | 1810 | 1820 | 1830 | 1840 | 1850 | 1860 |

5000
4500
4000
3500
3000
2500
2000
1500
1000
500

The Cotton South

Population 1790-1860

(in thousands)

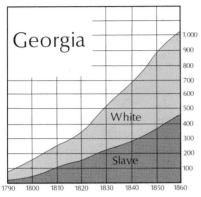

Georgia

White

Slave

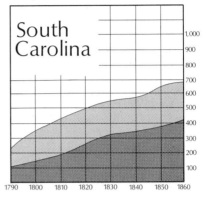

South Carolina

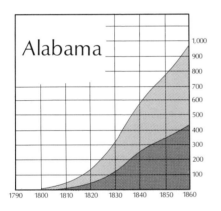

Alabama

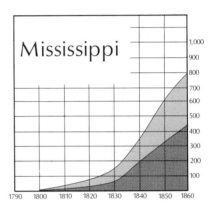

Mississippi

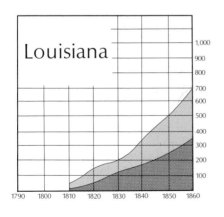

Louisiana

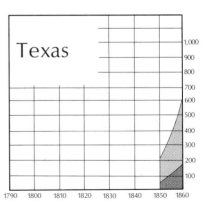

Texas

Despite all the research done on the internal slave trade, only rough estimates of its volume and form can be made. Approximately 75 percent of the million slaves involved in the interstate slave migration came with their owners in company with members of their families. The remaining 25 percent suffered the trauma of individual sale from their original place of residence, though many were bought and sold in large enough lots to preserve a fragment of old relationships in their new homes. Suffering such separation from relatives and friends back in their home states, slaves again utilized their expansive notions of kinship—real and fictive—to preserve a semblance of order and coherence in their lives. Insurmountable obstacles prevented separated slave families from visiting or corresponding, but the cords of memory bound many together. As in the eighteenth century, fictive aunts and uncles also provided a sense of family and a source of advice for young slaves removed from their biological parents. But in one of those tragic paradoxes that often occur in history, the very sense of family and kinship that to some extent lessened the pain of separation, especially after the initial shock, often deepened the sorrow, loneliness, and frustration caused by the involuntary uprooting from all that was familiar and beloved.

Virginia and Maryland planters sent thousands of surplus slaves southwestward, and the profit from that internal slave trade promoted the idea that they purposely bred slaves. From abolitionist days on there have been charges that slaveholders bred slaves like cattle and annually sent their human crop in coffles to the new cotton regions much as, later, Texas cattle drivers drove their longhorns to Abilene, Kansas. Such charges are very difficult to document. Certainly slave owners desired their slave women to be fruitful, and they often promoted marriage and stable family life by constructing family-unit slave cabins, gave bonuses to mothers who bore healthy babies, increased rations to pregnant and nursing women, and in other ways symbolically and materially gave their blessing to prolific black mothers. Surely there was a large measure of self-interest in such behavior, for owners knew the price young hands brought in the marketplace and were aware of the demand for slaves in the developing southwest. In particular young planters on the make shrewdly calculated the gains to be made by an expanding slave force.

Yet this was an era when large families were considered one of life's natural blessings, when publicists like the inimitable Parson Weems advocated whites marrying early and having many children, when effective methods of contraception were unknown. Reduced work schedules and improved rations for mothers were also the result of plain humanitarian impulses. The growth of the black population in the slave selling states, the de facto recognition of slave marriages and families, the relatively light work routines, particularly in the Chesapeake, and nutritionally adequate diets were all factors contributing to high slave fertility rates. The comparatively humane physical treatment of slaves in the seller states (vis-à-vis the Caribbean), partly because the overwhelming majority of U.S. slave owners were resident on their plantations, resulted in more slaves than the changing economies of Maryland and Virginia could employ.

There is no reliable evidence that slave owners as a general practice interfered with the sex lives of slaves so as to maximize reproduction. There is no evidence of gross sexual imbalance as one would expect had slave stud farms existed. Moreover, careful demographic analysis of the age and sex composition of slave populations in seller and buyer states does not substantiate the idea of slave breeding. The percentage of women of childbearing age and small children in Maryland and Virginia was not disproportionate and neither was the percentage of males and prime field hands in the major buying states. In fact, in Texas in 1860 (the leading buyer state in the major decade of slave selling), there were more slave women between the ages of 15 and 49 than there were men; there was a higher percentage of children under age nine than in the selling states; and the slave fertility rate (infants per thousand childbearing-age females) was higher than in Maryland and South Carolina and very similar to that in Virginia. Evidently, while slave owners wanted their slaves to multiply and provided advantageous conditions for them to do so, little interference with natural sexual behavior existed.

Slave population growth was in large measure the result of the marriage of individual black men and women who had large families and successfully reared a high percentage of their children to maturity. Slave owners did not discourage or prevent slave marriages, did not prohibit slave families, did not employ work routines so severe as to drastically shorten life spans and lower fertility rates, did not starve their slaves into such a state of malnutrition as to interfere with reproduction. Perhaps attention should focus on what slave owners in the South did not do and on how slaves in large measure controlled their own lives. Shifting labor needs and the desires of slave marriage partners, not calculating slave breeders, chiefly determined black population increase and indirectly its gradual relocation southwestward.

When one reflects on the expansion of cotton acreage in the decades following 1793, the huge increase in the number of bales produced annually, and the population onrush to the newer states of the Southwest, perhaps the question of the profitability of slavery would seem to answer itself. Yet few issues in American history have generated so much scholarship and controversy. One must recognize initially that there are many variables and much imprecise data that preclude any simple answer. Clearly a large, well-run plantation on fertile delta land in Mississippi was more profitable and efficient (when efficiency is measured in terms of dollar profit per worker) than a farm on worn-out soil in Virginia or shallow, rocky soil in Appalachia. But soil fertility, not slave labor or even size of farm, was the crucial factor. Because for many years cotton brought a good price thanks to a persistently strong worldwide demand, and cotton—unlike wheat—was not perishable and could easily be stored or shipped long distances, a productive cotton farm in Alabama might well produce more profit per worker or per acre than a wheat farm cultivated by free laborers in Wisconsin. But the high price of cotton, its imperishability, and the long overland distance from Wisconsin to the major wheat markets in the East—not something intrinsic to slave labor or plantation routines—were the crucial factors. Cotton, barring crop failure, was usually profitable precisely because, throughout the entire antebellum era, Britain's need for it did not abate, and consequently the price of cotton was not severely dampened for long periods by overproduction.

Cotton requires a long growing season and thrives best with moderate springtime rains and dry autumns. Excessive rain in the summer can rot the stalks, and pelting rain in late autumn can make the lint fall from the bolls onto the ground and be soiled. Because most of the South lay below the 37th parallel of latitude, the length of its growing season was well suited for cotton. The monthly distribution of rain also favored its culture. With new fertile lands, proper climate, and sustained demand, cotton indeed became king in the Old South.

Still other natural factors aided the rise of cotton, attributes not caused by slavery or the plantation system, though they were to have a significant impact on the lives of slaves and the profitability of plantations. Cotton harvest required more intense labor than any other season of the year. A fixed number of slaves (or free laborers) could plant, cultivate, and grow more cotton than they could pick. Since it made no economic sense to plant more cotton than one could harvest, and extra hands at harvesttime were practically impossible to hire, the picking limit of one's workforce determined the number of acres planted. Therefore a typical cotton farm or plantation planted substantially less cotton than *could* have been cultivated. This undercultivation meant the workers would have been under-utilized if cotton were the only crop. And too much leisure, whites believed, would promote dissoluteness and rebellion among the slaves. Clearly this "excess" labor potential, when expended on crops that did not compete with cotton for labor at the crucial planting and harvesting times, could produce a bonus harvest at very little additional cost to planters. And corn was just such a crop.

Corn could be planted either earlier or later than cotton, could be grown in less fertile soil, and could be harvested before or after the cotton was picked. Because on plantations corn was secondary to the money crop, and because in general southern soils and climate were not as favorable to corn as were those of the Midwest, corn yield per acre was fairly low. But it could be cultivated at practically no additional cost and was an extremely important crop in the antebellum South. In 1860, at the very peak of cotton production, more acres were devoted to the cultivation of corn than to cotton. The South's per capita production of corn was higher than the national average, with some states like Kentucky rivaling the corn-belt states in the Midwest. Mississippi and Alabama in 1860 had a per capita production of corn significantly above the national average.

According to the best estimates for human and animal consumption, the Old South produced many millions of bushels of corn in excess of its needs. Mississippi, the quintessential cotton state, in 1860 had a substantial corn surplus. The huge southern corn crop was especially important for feeding the livestock of the region. Probably about half the total corn yield served as animal feed, and the number of hogs and cattle raised in the South was enormous. In 1860 the South had two-thirds of the nation's hogs; the value of hogs and other livestock butchered in the South exceeded that in the North, and the value of southern livestock in 1860 was more than double that year's record cotton crop.

The details of the corn-livestock industry in the Old South are irrelevant here; even such colorful and relatively unknown southern character types as the herdsmen and hog drovers who raised and marketed tens of thousands of animals, and small farmers whose basic crop was corn both for home consumption and for sale either to plantations or to livestock herders, claim no space in this account. But their importance to the southern cotton economy was crucial. The South in the last decades of the antebellum period was essentially self-sufficient in foodstuffs. It had not always been so. In the early decades of the nineteenth century the South had not grown enough food. Two periods of lower cotton prices, at the end of the 1820s and for several years after 1837, had led to an emphasis on agricultural reform, especially crop diversification. Agricultural fairs, farmers' periodicals, country agricultural societies, all advocated more local production of foodstuffs. Certainly by the final two decades of the antebellum era significant amounts of food crops were cultivated, though always in deference to cotton's labor needs. Sweet potatoes, wheat, rice, and peas were major food crops, with cow peas, intended for human and livestock consumption, planted between the corn rows at the time of last plowing ("lay-by time").

Because the labor needs and growing season of cotton allowed substantial food production, and the picking limit on cotton made food production not only possible but a sensible way to maximize the slaves' labor, the South did not suffer a significant monetary drain to the North or Midwest for food. The campaign for crop diversification was quite successful. Large plantations devoted a larger percentage of their land to cotton production than did small ones, and yeoman farmers typically emphasized corn production with only a few acres planted in cotton for a money crop, yet in the aggregate the South fed itself. (Louisiana's sugar plantations along the Mississippi River were usually not self-sufficient in food, but their extremely fertile soil and long growing season, so well adapted to sugar cultivation, which brought high profits, and the cheapness of river transportation for Midwestern foodstuffs, made emphasis on the money crops simply rational.)

The high price of cotton and the compatibility of cotton production with corn cultivation made King Cotton and the plantation system profitable throughout the antebellum period. The situation changed drastically after 1865—but that is getting ahead of our story. Certainly the plantation system slowed the growth of towns in the South and may have hindered to some degree the development of southern manufacturing, although inadequate transportation facilities seem to have been the major cause of the lag in industrialization. However, that liability was not really felt until after 1861. After all, the South was booming in the late 1850s, and no one could foresee either the Civil War and Reconstruction or the changing rate in the growth of the cotton demand. Certainly many planters and smaller farmers were living, on their own terms, quite comfortably, and they found little reason to question or repudiate their social economy. Cotton farming was a profitable business even if it wasn't a profitable regional economy.

Like tobacco and unlike rice and sugar, cotton was a crop well suited to the small farmer. No expensive equipment was needed for its cultivation, no extensive and costly construction of irrigation canals or protective levees was required in order to bring a field into production. Cotton did not rot or spoil after being picked. It could be easily stored until enough was gathered to justify a trip to a gin; after ginning and pressing into a bale its value per volume was high; and its imperishability made transportation easy. For these reasons cotton could be grown profitably on any scale, from the subsistence farm where only a few acres were planted just for some cash, to the largest plantation with its hundreds of slaves and thousands of acres.

Cotton could be grown profitably by small farmers, and plantations seem to have offered little gain through economies of scale. The yield per worker was apparently no higher on large plantations; in fact, moderate-sized or small plantations (really, large farms), closely supervised by the master himself, were probably

more efficient than larger plantations, especially absentee ones
situated in several locations and managed by overseers. Because
large plantations had their own gins and could on occasion buy
their goods in bulk lots, they enjoyed some savings. Sometimes
they could afford to withhold their crop until the price increased,
or gain a slightly higher price because of their volume, but such
margins were slight. The most significant economic advantage of
slavery was that it allowed farm size to increase significantly.
Because of the shortage of free farm workers in the North and
South, free farms were typically restricted in size to the labor output of the farmer and his immediate family. But a slave owner
could increase his acreage as he increased his labor force, hence
there were no size limitations other than the planter's ability to purchase slaves. Consequently the average farm in the cotton South
was more than double that in the Old Northwest (present-day
Midwest) in size. Since bigger plantations could devote a larger
percentage of their land under cultivation to cotton and still supply
their food needs, and since the price of cotton was inflated by European demand, large plantations earned a higher profit per acre. Yet
there was no significant economy of scale, no peculiar slave-
plantation efficiency. Small farmers could compete quite profitably
in the Old South.

This democracy of cotton cultivation helped unify the antebellum white South, for small, slaveless landowners with their
insignificant cotton acreage had something tangibly in common
with their more prosperous neighbors. The larger planters had a gin
and cotton press to satisfy their own needs, and they also ginned
and pressed the cotton of their less affluent neighbors and relatives
for a percentage of the yield. Further, no doubt on many occasions
the large planters bought surplus corn, hogs, and beeves from the
yeoman farmers. These transactions—ginning and the buying of
foodstuffs—created not only an economic nexus between the
classes but also a common society. Small farmer and grand planter
together had a stake in the cotton economy. The whites developed
a complex society that blended paternalistic and democratic
tendencies, and capitalistic men-on-the-make, genteel planter
aristocrats, and self-sufficient yeoman farmers intermingled usually
with little social friction at courthouse, church, and cotton market.

This absence of most class conflict in the Old South often

obscures one very basic fact. Slaves were distributed unequally among slaveholders and unequally across the face of the land. Throughout the antebellum period (here defined—because of the availability of census data—as 1790 to 1860) slaves averaged 33.4 percent of the total southern population. This proportion stayed remarkably constant, being 33.5 percent in 1790 and 32.3 percent in 1860. As the Deep South developed following the rise of the cotton kingdom, the black presence grew enormously in absolute numbers and slightly as a proportion of the total population, from 41.1 percent in 1790 to 44.8 percent in 1860. In that year 2,423,467 of the South's 3,953,760 slaves, or 61.3 percent, lived in the eight Deep South states: Alabama, Arkansas, Florida, Georgia, Louisiana, Mississippi, South Carolina, and Texas. In both South Carolina and Mississippi slaves comprised over half the population (57 and 55 percent respectively). Throughout the era the black percentage of the total population fell in the border states, dropping to 22.3 in 1860. Perhaps the slave presence in the Deep South can be better comprehended if it is remembered that in that region there were 82 blacks for every 100 whites, while in the Upper South there were fewer than 30 blacks per 100 whites. Clearly the most densely black region was the Deep South, and in the cotton belt that swept through these states from South Carolina to Texas (those counties producing more than 1,000 bales of cotton each in 1860), slaves constituted 48 percent of the population. Still, while they were concentrated in a black belt, they were also scattered across the entire region.

Most southern whites did not own slaves, and most of those who did possessed only a few. Slaveholding was concentrated in the hands of a significant minority of the population, and plantation-sized slaveholding was confined to a tiny minority. In 1860 approximately 1,918,175 southern whites (or 24 percent) were members of slaveholding families, and 6,120,825 (76 percent) were not. Of the 385,000 heads of households who owned slaves, almost 49 percent possessed fewer than five. If the ownership of a total of twenty slaves is taken as the minimum for running a plantation as opposed to a farm, then only 12 percent of all slaveholders qualified as planters in 1860. Substantially less than 1 percent, or about 2,300 families, owned 100 or more slaves and constituted the planter aristocracy—out of a white population of 8 million. During the last antebellum decades slave ownership became more concentrated. The percentage of all southern families who owned slaves fell from 36 in 1830 to 31 in 1850 and to 25 in 1860, and the size of slaveholdings was increasing. Those who owned fewer than 5 decreased from 50.2 percent in 1850 to 48.5 percent in 1860, and those owning more than 20 increased from 10 to 12 percent.

The implications of these figures have been widely debated. Emphasizing the growing concentration of slaves in the hands of a few and that minority's overwhelmingly disproportionate share of all southern wealth, some historians have argued that planters were gradually squeezing nonslaveholders out. Other historians, emphasizing the huge numerical majority of nonslaveholders and those who owned fewer than five slaves, have pointed to the landholdings of such yeoman farmers and spoken of a democratic South politically dominated by the plain folk. Recently the planter-dominance school has reemerged, with attention placed on the disproportionate political power of the planters. Still another school of interpretation has focused on that one-quarter of southern families that possessed slaves and has shown that slave ownership was remarkably widespread given the investment represented. No consensus, no new synthesis, of these disparate viewpoints has arisen.

At issue is the nature of the southern society: was it a slaveocracy controlled by the planter minority for its own benefit, or was it essentially a plain folk democracy where the yeoman majority, for complex cultural, racial, and economic reasons, accepted political rule by the planter minority? Both viewpoints can be justified. Moderate to large-scale slaveholders controlled a vastly disproportionate share not only of the wealth but also of political offices. Yet the inequality of wealth in the South was less extreme than in northern urban areas, and the yeoman farmers prospered and in no way seemed (or apparently felt) threatened by the slaveholders. Perhaps the region can best be understood as consisting of two separate but interrelated societies, each partially dependent on the other and partially independent. Like intersecting circles, most of the life of either society was untouched by the other, yet at their intersection there were many relationships binding the two societies together in support of the basic southern institution, slavery.

In many areas of the South—western Maryland; western

Virginia; mountainous regions of Kentucky, Tennessee, and North Carolina; Missouri; northern portions of Alabama and Mississippi; central Texas—there was practically no slavery. Here the yeoman farmers owned their land, grazed cattle and hogs, grew most of their foodstuffs, and lived, self-sufficient, with little to do with the outside world. In other regions, particularly in the Deep South, almost half the white families were slaveholders, and in the fertile black belt the percentage was much higher. Here commercial agriculture was the key to the economy, and even those small farmers who grew little cotton supplied corn or livestock to those larger planters who did. In a real sense there were two societies, two economies in the Old South, the one slaveholding and market-oriented, the other nonslaveholding and largely self-sufficient.

Class conflict was largely absent by the 1840s because the regions where each society was most conspicuous were geographically separate; the legitimate political interests of one seldom interfered with the other (the self-sufficient yeoman who produced no commercial crop had little need of government services, and the planters already had control of the government); Jacksonian era reforms had already democratized southern political life, equalizing representation and judicial administration; and family ties usually stretched across class lines, lessening potential alienation. Thousands of small farmers with only patches of tobacco or cotton could identify with the local planters because both were growing the same crop, which may well have bound them together more than the different source of labor separated them. For those small farmers who marketed their surplus corn and hogs to planters and depended on them to gin and even market their few bales of cotton, a real economic nexus existed between the classes.

The plain folk and planter aristocrats came together at church services, election rallies, and the crossroads store, and slave-owning political aspirants knew where the votes lay. Deference was still a factor in politics. Yeomen looked up to their "betters," admired and took local pride in the occasional mansion, and may have longed for self-advancement to the slave-owning class. There were no strong sources of ill will against the ruling establishment, little resentment that might have produced significant opposition to rule by slaveholders. Whatever antagonism existed toward control by the planters was submerged by the practically universal belief that slavery was the only method of controlling millions of blacks. Race ultimately united the white South. Racial fears, not planter hegemony, were at the root of the southern determination to maintain slavery in the face of northern opposition.

This resolve, manifested in laws, institutions, and behavior, determined the place of blacks in the Old South. In the Deep South from South Carolina west to Texas, where the majority of slaveholders (and slaves) resided, the recognition that slavery was slowly becoming less pronounced in the border states and the fear that, as these states were "bleached," they might shift allegiance to the North merely strengthened the political determination to defend the peculiar institution against all threats, real and perceived. It was no accident or mere coincidence that the first states to secede were from the Deep South. Here was the heart and soul of Dixie.

Another perennial controversy in slavery scholarship has been the question of how productive slave labor was. Contemporary sources range from remarks that one free farm laborer in the North outworked four slaves, to slave owners congratulating themselves on their slaves' industriousness. Historians have been equally diverse, even contradictory, in their judgments. So many variables are involved—the merits of a particular season, labor demands of different crops, soil fertility, disease, age and sex ratios of individual plantation work forces, managerial skill of the planter, incentives both intended and implicit—that definitive, quantifiable, answers will never be attained. The use of present-day industrial or factory analogies is not appropriate, for the vagaries of weather, disease, and pests, along with a work pace defined by mule-or-ox-drawn plows, the absence of modern conveniences, and the unclear boundary between work and recreation common to most agricultural societies, require that slave labor in the antebellum South be described in its chronological and geographical context.

Agricultural work routines of more than a century ago are difficult to describe to modern urban readers. The punctuality, the regularity, the monotony associated with industrial labor was largely absent. Work animals had to be fed after dawn, then harnessed and walked to the fields; they had to be rested and watered at mid-day; in the evening they were unharnessed and fed before dark. When plowing, the slow-stepping mule, completely impervious to considerations of efficiency, set the work pace. Hand chores such as chopping cotton could be done only in good daylight. Rain, and wet ground, normally brought cultivation to a soggy halt. In emergencies where inclement weather threatened an entire crop, for example, slaves were required to work in adverse conditions, but so were free farmers North and South. Such rescue labor was less an aspect of slave treatment than a commentary on how the vagaries of weather plagued agriculturalists in the nineteenth century. Typically, in good weather gangs of hoers moved together up and down the rows, talking and singing as they worked long hours in often hot, muggy weather. By today's nine-to-five standards the workdays were long, but the physical labor was not especially demanding except for the plowmen and sugarcane harvesters. On most plantations cotton-picking time was the period of greatest demand, when every available hand worked all the daylight hours, dragging heavy cotton sacks or baskets and stooping and bending to pick every ripe boll.

Slaves were forced to work by fear of punishment or hope of reward, and usually by some combination of both, with the threat of chastisement always hovering in the background. Through a form of low-scale resistance to bondage, slaves worked at less than a feverish pace and over time a certain rate of performance came to be considered the norm by planters. Whites generally accepted rather sluggish labor, in part because the heat and humidity sapped their vitality as much as it did that of the slaves, and in part because whites had internalized a conception of the black as naturally lazy and irresponsible, and hence expected little better. Even so, agricultural labor was tiring and, like the proverbial woman's work, never really done; there were always fields to clear, fences to mend, firewood to chop, meals to cook, livestock to feed, hogs to butcher. A lifetime of labor, with no real hope of freedom, very limited reward for individual accomplishment, and little control over one's workplace or duties, must have threatened to deaden the souls of many slaves.

One of the achievements of the slave community was its discovery, in the midst of a smothering work environment, of narrow pathways to self-advancement and brief moments of self-esteem. A small number of skillful, industrious slaves became plantation overseers with authority over the black work force. On occasions even the master deferred to the agricultural expertise or managerial acumen of such black leaders. Far more bondsmen, perhaps chosen because they had strength and leadership in addition to skill, served as slave drivers, a position roughly analogous to a foreman, who was the link between overseer and slave hands. While some drivers may have mistreated the slaves under their control to curry favor with the owner, and others may have routinely misled the owner in order to protect or gain the favor of their fellow blacks, most seem to have mediated the interests of owner and owned in an attempt to minimize punishment and overwork and maximize crop output. Persuasion and put-on were meted out to both sides, and it was a skilled driver who could avoid antagonizing one or the other.

Other slaves became plantation specialists—perhaps a plowman, cook, gardener, carriage driver, nursemaid, or houseservant—or occupied a variety of artisan positions ranging from blacksmiths to weavers to carpenters. There was some social mobility for slaves on plantations, and though severely limited it did provide enterprising bondsmen an arena for self-advancement within the plantation system. Still other spheres of achievement existed within the slave community itself, spheres not dependent on the white man's concurrence and possibly more important for that reason to the blacks—but more of that later. In small, personal ways at least some slaves gained a sense of fulfillment and even pleasure from the performance of their agricultural duties. Surveying a well-built barn, gazing across cotton fields white with open bolls, striding briskly through newly plowed fields in the spring when the warm color and rich aroma of the turned soil suggested new life and fresh beginnings, eyeing arrow-straight furrows—few slaves were so spiritually deadened by their bondage as not to experience a spark of exhilaration at such visible evidence of their achievement under adversity.

One should never forget that slavery was a system based upon force. Slaves did not have the liberty to be idle, or to choose their jobs, or to determine the allocation of labor even within their own family—slave wives and children worked at the master's call. For the recalcitrant worker there was always a spectrum of punishments ranging from the removal of small privileges to brutal whippings. On occasion slaves were threatened with being sold to the Deep South, a threat that has helped nurture the belief that conditions were worse on expansive cotton plantations in the black belt. The frequency of punishments like whipping has been hotly contested by historians, and the variables involved from planter to planter make any kind of numerical analysis futile. Clearly, in the minds of everyone involved, white and black, the lash stood as an ever-present reminder of where authority lay. The public whipping of one bondsman, with all his fellows looking on and seeing his grimaces as the blows fell, hearing the brutal crack of the whip, and vicariously suffering with him in his agony, had an effect on the local slave community that cannot be appreciated by the simple tabulation of the frequency of such punishment. Surely slave parents reared their children to fear the lash and taught them behavior that would avoid it, and the visible scars on many black backs bore silent testimony to the pervasive reality of force.

At the same time, slaves were not sullen beasts of burden who performed just enough work to stay on the safe side of punishment. Slaves were members of a production unit, ranging from the small farm to the large plantation, and they were members of a family both biological and fictive. Especially when their supervisors were blacks, or when their white overseer or master was reasonable, slaves sometimes took pride in their work and performed at a level of competence and efficiency that often pleased their masters. Making the best of a bad situation, some bondsmen found a portion of their self-respect in the skill with which they conducted the affairs of a plantation. It was not lost on slaves that in their hands largely lay the prosperity of their master, and hence it was to their direct benefit to ensure agricultural success. Good crops brought monetary profits only to the master, but they also usually meant at least somewhat better clothing and shelter, and better food, to the hands. Certainly unsuccessful farming hurt the slaves, for when rations had to be cut, doctors' bills eliminated, and other shortcuts taken, blacks were the ones who suffered first and longest. If the plantation were perennially unsuccessful, slaves were sold and families separated.

Slaves could see their own self-interest at stake and consequently worked with what sometimes seems surprising industry precisely because they benefited indirectly from prosperity. Contemporary observers often noted how energetically slaves toiled during the feverish harvest times on sugarcane plantations, probably the most physically demanding labor in the Old South. Caught up in the camaraderie of the occasion, when everyone of working age exerted himself to the fullest in a carnival of cutting, hauling, and boiling the cane, slaves often astounded their masters with intense bursts of labor that lasted for several weeks. A season was made or lost at harvesttime, and not only the following year's food and supplies, but also a well-earned holiday depended on performance at that crucial period. Slaves seldom developed the work ethic of their masters because they had such limited avenues of profit and self-advancement, but they often worked with remarkable skill and determination because their well-being was so intimately tied to the prosperity of their plantation, and the threat of the whip always existed even on the most scientifically managed plantation.

From time immemorial employers have complained about employees in all kinds of work situations from domestic to industrial to agricultural; consequently, masters' complaints about slave inefficiency, stupidity, and laziness must be tempered. Inefficient agricultural practices were as much the result of planter conservatism as slave behavior, as was the southern proclivity for using sturdy, simple, heavy agricultural implements. Because the labor bottleneck for cotton cultivation was at the picking end of the season, there was little pressure to increase the efficiency of preharvest cultivation. Critics have blamed slavery or the plantation system for cotton planters' slow move to mechanization, overlooking the fact that existing cultivation techniques could already produce more cotton than could be easily picked. Agricultural invention has been invoked to solve particular problems in the production chain—mechanical reapers for wheat, gins for cotton, and, much later, caterpillar tractors for unstable soil in the San Joaquin Valley of California. With the picking restraints on cotton production in the antebellum South, there was relatively little pressure for mechanical innovation to increase acreage. The difficulty of harvesting cotton, not the ineptitude of blacks or the backwardness of planters, kept cotton cultivation essentially unchanged until the twentieth century. Not until chemical defoliants (to make the leaves fall off the cotton stalk) were developed did mechanical cotton pickers become practical.

The work routines of slaves depended on a large variety of factors: the season, the crop, the size of their master's slaveholdings, the personality of their owner. On the smaller farms slaves worked side by side with their master, and here personal relationships were often formed that transcended color. Planters with five to twenty field hands usually supervised all labor, perhaps utilizing a trusted slave as a driver to set the field hands to their daily jobs. Only the largest plantations had professional overseers who operated the plantation for the owner. On most cotton plantations slaves worked by the gang system, being sent out to the field by the driver and put to planting, chopping, picking, or whatever task was at hand. Such a labor practice lessened the chance for individual initiative, but it probably aided the well-being of the slave community. Strong workers could help out those who were slower or weaker, and gang work added to the sense of group solidarity. The workers together could slow down the work pace more effectively, and with less danger of personal blame, than could individual workers. Slaves and their masters acquired through give and take a mutual understanding of how much work was to be done in a normal day, and slaves on each plantation considered excess work a severe infringement of their "rights." Planters realized intuitively that they were supervising other humans, who could retaliate in numerous ways against treatment judged too harsh even in the context of slavery. Slaves revolted less against slavery itself than they protested transgression of what they considered the limits of service reasonably owed their owner.

Bondsmen knew how to appeal beyond an offending overseer to the master, and the masters' frequent willingness to back their slaves in such matters bears testimony to the slaves' power to shape within limits the work routines on a plantation. Mules inexplicably let out of the barn lot, tools left in the rain, cotton plants accidentally plowed under, chores that required double the normal time to complete for mysterious reasons, sickness that struck down a large portion of the field hands—maladies too vague to doctor but too "real" to ignore—such were the weapons "defenseless" slaves could bring to bear against rigid taskmasters. (Workers everywhere have learned to use such forms of sabotage against those in authority.) Punishing the whole gang of slaves was both too time-consuming and potentially counterproductive, and hence the slave community found strength in its unity. The institution of slavery was a constant process of accommodation and mutual adjustment, with masters always having the upper hand but with slaves controlling a larger fraction of their lives than the system would logically seem to allow.

The institution of slavery became so widespread across the South in the decades after 1800, whites became so accustomed to being surrounded by blacks, and blacks became so adept at adjusting to the system, that white southerners no longer felt constantly threatened by what they now called their domestic institution. With slavery accepted as a natural part of southern life, whites underwent a slow, subtle shift in their attitudes toward blacks. The harshest features of the mid-eighteenth century were moderated, slaves in general were better fed and treated, and the paternalism that had its roots in eighteenth-century manor houses came to characterize the ideal of slave management. Professional slave traders were ostracized, and planters prided themselves upon their reputations for mild treatment of their "people." By the 1840s southern society seemed, at least to whites, stable, democratic, and benevolent—the best of all possible worlds for free and bond alike. But as always, there was a significant gap between ideal and reality.

4. Life and Death in the Old South

Legend and Hollywood have successfully fixed in the popular mind a luxuriant southern landscape of moss-festooned live oaks and blooming magnolias interrupted now and again by white-columned mansions. Cotton fields laden with ripe bolls stretch to the horizon, and off behind the big house, in neat rows, are attractive slave cabins. In truth, most southern regions with rich soil were adorned by a few such plantations, just enough to legitimate in the eyes of whites the correctness of their institutions, but this scene never was typical. Such mansions were goals for struggling small planters and generated respect and deference for their wealthy owners—necessities in this paternalistic, patriarchial society—but an investigation of the life of slaves must move beyond pleasant images and self-serving models. Even on large plantations slave quarters were usually crowded and uncomfortable, the diet of nearly everyone was monotonous and at times inadequate, and the ravages of disease and death lay just beneath the veneer of prosperity and gentility. Slave morbidity, however, was not simply the result of ill treatment by planters. Biology and the unanticipated medical and ecological consequence of living close together in an age before modern health care shaped the physical quality of life for slaves as much as did more obvious human factors. What planters did not know about food and sickness affected their slaves almost as much as conscious white policies did. Life and death were a seamless web, interconnecting biology, history, and culture in the Old South.

Shelter, clothing, food, and health care were as important to the slaves' quality of life as the type and circumstances of their work.

As with other aspects of the black experience, the range of conditions was enormous. Examples of good and bad shelter, food, and health care can be found, but the more appropriate task is to seek to describe the normal or typical—the average—experience of slaves. Housing was inadequate for most slaves, as it was for many white yeoman farmers. Houses were cold and drafty in winter, hot and fly-infested in summer, and leaky when violent thunderstorms strafed the structures with wind-blown rain. When a farmer owned only one or two slaves, they often slept in a cramped lean-to or shed attached to the farmer's cabin or upstairs in an attic. Larger planters had log cabins away from the main house, and slave families usually had their own cabins, which, on some of the largest plantations, were erected in parallel lines to form a "street." On occasion two families shared one cabin. Some slave quarters were frame houses, or even brick, but most were primitive cabins with dirt or rough wood floors. Such quarters afforded no privacy and little comfort. Living conditions were hardly better for countless whites, but when frustration with poverty and a hope for greener pastures turned their fancy toward the west, free farmers hitched up the wagon and moved in quest of independence and happiness. Similarly discontented slaves had no such choice; they were not at liberty to seek better opportunities elsewhere. Far more than dirt floors or squalid cabins, that immobility was the real measure of their bondage.

Masters were sparing in their allotment of clothing. The typical bondsman received two suits of clothes a year, one for winter and one for summer, with one pair of shoes. Often men were given a hat and women a handkerchief to cover their heads. Children ran around naked in warm weather until they were six or seven or wore a one-piece shift; later they were given oversized and worn-out hand-me-downs. Everyone went barefoot as long as the weather would allow. In the warmer months no one probably complained much about the clothing, but in the winter cold spells slaves often suffered severely. Luckily farm tasks could be curtailed in the coldest weather, but slaves with thin coats, no socks or gloves, and makeshift sweaters and other wraps felt the bitterest stings of old man winter. Surely everyone suffered in the cold, particularly poor whites, but slaves were in the weakest position to provide themselves with suitable clothing. Because of their low tolerance for cold and heightened susceptibility to diseases like pneumonia and frostbite, they bore the brunt of winter hardships. When bondsmen did accumulate spending money (from overtime work or selling the produce of their gardens, for example), they very often augmented their clothing allotment with purchases from rural storekeepers, who always stocked what was labeled "negro clothing."

As storekeepers' inventories suggest, the clothing provided slaves differed in quality as well as quantity. The cloth was coarse and dull colored, and the garments were cut with an eye to loose-fitting comfort, not style. Shoes for both sexes were stiff brogans, themselves an invitation to go barefoot as long as possible. Some cloth for slave clothing came from New England or England, though most was manufactured domestically. On plantations and farms the slave women spent many a cold, rainy winter day at the loom or spinning wheel. Homespun was colored with locally available dyes, often made from hickory bark or vegetables.

On many plantations slaves—especially the house servants—were given the worn-out, out-of-fashion, and outgrown clothing of the whites, and such items, even when worn to pieces and cut up and reassembled, added a touch of color and sheen to their otherwise drab clothing. Many slaves displayed ingenuity at finding ways of sprucing up their meager wardrobes with snatches of material from the planters and pieces of finery bought or bartered from storekeepers. Bondsmen became artful scavengers, seizing everything thrown away or discarded and finding uses—practical and decorative—for a vast kaleidoscope of items on their persons and in their homes. In clothing as in food, and, indeed, in their whole culture, slaves never simply accepted what the white man gave or left them; in ways insignificant individually but profound in accumulation, they took what was given, shaped and reshaped it, supplemented it with what skill and nature provided, and produced something unique. The result was often quite literally a crazy quilt of colors and forms and influences, but it was, most importantly, something of the slaves' own creation. Travelers in the South and planters' careful descriptions of runaways again and again exhibited an implicit astonishment at the variety of slave clothing and the aplomb with which the idiosyncratic adornment was worn. If clothes make the man, those worn by slaves bear testimony to the unquenchability of the human spirit.

Food was if anything even more basic to the slaves' well-being than clothing and shelter, and the quality and quantity of food available varied at least as widely. Ignoring atypical extremes of food distribution and speaking in the most general terms, the diet of most slaves was sufficient quantitatively to sustain reasonably good health and vigor for the time and region. The food often lacked variety and, at certain periods of the year, balance; clearly many bondsmen had to augment the rations allocated by the master; planter ignorance of nutrition often contributed to less than optimum food choice; certain genetic traits may have heightened the slaves' need for specific nutrients. Nevertheless, despite all the qualifications, the fact remains that slaves, except in truly exceptional cases, were neither starved nor kept in a passive state of malnourishment as part of a policy of mistreatment. On many farms where the several slaves lived in an attic or a lean-to attached to the owner's house, whites and blacks ate essentially the same food even though they typically ate separately. The choice of foods was, however, limited and surely became monotonous.

Both necessity and choice determined that corn and pork would be the foundation of the southern diet for blacks and whites, although rice was the staple in portions of South Carolina and Georgia. Corn grew fairly well in the South, accommodated itself easily to cotton cultivation, was plentiful and easy to preserve, and could be cooked in a great variety of ways. It also was widely used as a food for pigs, which easily adapted to the southern climate. Hogs could run wild in the forests of the South, surviving on acorns, other nuts, and roots until they were penned up and fattened on corn. Southerners of both races preferred pork to beef. As discussed earlier, the South produced prodigious amounts of corn and pork, and it was quite natural that southern tastes adopted the two as the staple foods of the region. Had they not existed in abundance in the South, the slave diet would have been inestimably worse.

Existing plantation records indicate that there was for all practical purposes a standard minimum slave ration provided by masters. With some variation depending upon the work season and the age and sex of the slaves, this standard was a peck of cornmeal and three to four pounds of bacon (i.e., pork) per slave per week. This represented the food measured out and distributed by the plantation owner; it seldom if ever amounted to the total diet of the slaves.

On an almost regular basis molasses was distributed, and when possible coffee, sweet potatoes, peas and beans, squash, various greens, poultry and eggs, and beef were provided. The corn-pork basic element was normally given out every week, and other foods were available on a more seasonal basis. When, as was usual, these were grown on the plantation, they were plentiful enough not to be subject to detailed record-keeping, were sufficiently available not to be kept under lock and key, and were provided according to need. Some large, rationalized plantations gave a certain acreage over to truck crops cultivated and harvested by the slave hands, under close planter supervision. This produce would then eventually be prepared in a common kitchen by cooking specialists and fed armylike to the black work force. Occasional large planters who ran this type operation believed there was less theft and waste, better prepared food, and more rest time for their bondsmen as a result. A variant of this system was for the planter to allow the slaves to grow vegetables in their own individual garden plots and even raise chickens and pigs, and then to buy produce from them both for their common kitchen and for his own family's food. With their hard-earned money slaves would then buy extra clothes, presents for spouses and children, whiskey, and perhaps save up in hopes of eventually buying their freedom. However, the huge majority of farmers and planters ran much less organized plantations, leaving a larger proportion of both food production and preparation to the initiative and energy of individual slave families.

Most slaves, whether they lived on small farms or plantations of broad acres, were allowed to cultivate garden plots. They tended their own crops either at the twilight end of the day or on Saturday afternoon or Sundays—practically every owner gave his hands time off for at least part of the weekend. Often the planter would buy fresh vegetables and eggs from his slaves in order to provide them additional incentive, to make available to them some money so they could afford simple luxuries, and because by so doing he avoided the problem of theft commonly associated with a large plantation garden worked by slaves but for the table of the owner. Many slaves on Saturday would carry their surplus produce to crossroads stores or trading communities and sell or barter their items for money or other goods. Slave marketing of their own agricultural produce in southern towns never reached the level it did in some Caribbean islands, but neither was it negligible. Occasionally urban areas would pass ordinances against slaves coming in from the countryside to peddle truck crops and poultry products because the authorities feared such trade stimulated thievery, and they understood and feared that the practice provided slaves with a potentially dangerous pinch of freedom. But ultimately every town was too dependent on such sources of food to prohibit completely this quite literal black market. It was not uncommon for slaves to own pigs, cows, even horses, wagons, boats, and household utensils beyond those provided by the master. Slaves who were sold or moved to different regions were typically reimbursed for their property that the planter deemed inexpedient to move.

The bulk of vegetables grown by slaves in their own garden plots was consumed by the individual families who grew them. Much more common than the communal gardening and preparation of food was the practice of letting each slave family (or cabin group, which sometimes included the extended family along with an occasional single adult) grow and prepare its own food. Although some planters required this because they believed it lessened the spread of disease, most slave owners permitted it because slaves seemed greatly to prefer to manage this important portion of their lives. For bondsmen whose work hours and movement were regimented, the ability to control their garden plot, exercise their gardening skills, and choose their supplementary food crops was an important way of holding on to a portion of their self-identity. Especially significant was the slaves' commitment to cultivating garden vegetables and cooking them as a family activity.

By legal definition the black family was nonexistent, and forces as broad-ranging as the fear of slave sales and the emasculating authority of the owner threatened to destroy it, so slaves utilized every substantive and symbolic way to strenghten their families. Perhaps more important than any other activity cementing the family unit was the production and consumption of food. No other task has been as central to the survival of the family in human history, and here was a realizable and tangible way for fathers to be providers and for creative wives and mothers to show their affection. The family meal, shared by all around the domestic hearth, served to bind together those whose relationship was fragile for reasons beyond their control. Preparing a meal at the end of a long day must have been an onerous task for the tired slave women, but their preference for control over their home life speaks eloquently of their determination to preserve their own humanity. Often a stew begun at the lunch break cooked all afternoon in a heavy iron "spider" set amidst glowing coals on the hearth, where the slow-burning fire never went out.

Discussions of slave food supply have been controversial because it is difficult to quantify the supplemental portion of the black diet. The produce grown in slave garden plots seldom left a trace of evidence in plantation account books, but it made a world of difference to the diet of the bondsmen. Similarly, southern rivers and streams were teeming with fish, particularly the nutritious and tasty catfish, and southern forests offered bountiful game. Forests also provided nuts, herbs, grapes, berries, persimmons, sassafras roots for tea, pokeweed for salad. Rural slaves in their "leisure" time hunted, trapped, fished, and gathered, and the result of these activities added nutritional value and much-wanted variety to their meals. If slaves had had more free time, such delights offered by the fields and streams would no doubt have played an even greater role in their diet. Slaves also took quite liberally from their master's larder, especially on larger plantations. Taking food from another slave was considered stealing by the bondsmen, but helping themselves to their master's supply was not. When they were hungry, or craved some diversity in their diet, it wasn't even necessary to justify redistributing a portion of the plantation's goods. Many a mother risked punishment to provide a treat for her babies; many a male, through such sly augmenting of his family's or girlfriend's diet, felt his manhood enhanced. In a conspiracy of silence slaves helped one another steal from the master.

One rather obvious omission from the slaves' diet was fresh milk, for masters very seldom supplied it as part of the dispensed rations, and slaves—who sometimes had their own hogs and poultry—very rarely had milk cows. Cattle were considered by owners primarily a source of beef (there were surprisingly few "milch" [milk] cows in the antebellum South), and when slaves were given milk, it was mostly sour or buttermilk. For years this was considered by historians to be mistreatment, but biochemically it was appropriate because blacks were deficient in the enzyme lactase, which must be present for the body to break down lactose (milk sugar, a major food component of milk) into digestible form. Many people around the world have as a genetic trait this lactase deficiency (or lactose intolerance), which prohibits them from drinking more than very small amounts of milk without suffering diarrhea (infants could drink their mother's milk with no ill effect). Since present-day West Africans show practically 100 percent lactase deficiency, and contemporary American blacks a deficiency of about 70 percent (because of interbreeding with Caucasians, of whom only about 2 to 20 percent are lactase-deficient), antebellum American slaves must also have been overwhelmingly lactose-intolerant.

Ironically, clabber (sour milk), buttermilk, and several varieties of cream cheese could be digested by lactase-deficient slaves, giving a biological basis to blacks' noted preference for buttermilk. Whether owners realized that milk did not agree with slaves, or did not often distribute it because availability was severely limited by the adverse effect of hot southern temperatures on cows' milk production, or were foiled in providing milk by the absence of refrigeration, or whether, more likely, it was a combination of these factors, the result is clear. Slaves in the Old South drank very little fresh milk for reasons having less to do with mistreatment than with genetics and climate.

The perishability of milk suggests a problem that plagued efforts to maintain balanced diets for everyone in the Old South. Ice houses insulated with soil and sawdust in the Upper South, and spring houses there and in the Deep South, provided only an imperfect means of storing dairy products. The warm climate complicated efforts to preserve meats; pork could be salted and smoked, but such methods were better suited to regions where winters were hard. Generally beef had to be eaten within days, which meant that only large plantations could afford to butcher a yearling although sometimes several farmers would butcher a calf together. Fresh vegetables were simply unavailable throughout much of the winter, but potatoes, turnips, yams, apples, and other fruits could be preserved with sufficient preparation. Dried peas and beans could be kept, but mice and weevils were a severe challenge even to the most careful farm managers. The diet of bondsmen doubtlessly suffered in mid-winter when fruits and vegetables were scarce, and malnutrition posed more of a threat to slave health in January, February, and March than in any other season. Nutritional diseases like pellagra (characterized by skin eruptions, digestive and nervous disturbances, and eventual mental deterioration) probably afflicted some slaves in those months. Had the period of least sufficient food not also been the period of least physical labor, there might have been more widespread suffering from dietary deficiencies.

Much nonsense has been written about southern food and southern cooking. Contemporary travelers noted again and again the monotonous sameness of the cuisine, with corn and pork, always too greasy, served in the absence of vegetables (and southerners particularly disliked salads) and washed down with dreary substitutes for coffee. Black cooks were often as bad as white, giving lie to the romanticized belief that every slave woman was a secret gourmet. The largest plantations in the right season could mount mouthwatering feasts with menus as varied as the servings were generous. But most white farmers ate plainly, with an occasional serving of venison or catfish or wild turkey or squirrel to break the routine. The diet of slaves was less varied than that of their owners, and had not their own gardening, hunting, fishing, and gathering added to their rations, their food supply would have been even more limited. Blacks and poor whites who cooked their vegetables and meats together and then poured the extremely nutritious "pot likker" on cornbread, probably received more vitamins than those who ate in higher style.

However monotonous, however unappetizing to the cultured taste of contemporary travelers or present-day readers, the diet most southerners of both races received most of the time was sufficiently nutritious to enable them to maintain active, productive lives. The life expectancy of slaves was slightly less than that of whites, but the black birth rate and the rapid growth of the slave population (especially compared to the negative slave population growth rate in the Caribbean and South America, and even compared to the white population growth rate in the antebellum South) are evidence that starvation and malnutrition were less a worry to slaves in the Old South than their inability to control more than a small portion of their own lives. Again it should be emphasized that slave ingenuity at augmenting the ration dispensed by the master often made the difference between a bare-bones diet and one of some variety, flavor, and nutritional adequacy.

Controversy has raged over the precise English and African

origins of southern cooking, but the American Indians may have contributed more than either Old World cultures. Certainly the English wheat-mutton diet and the various African diets shifted to one based largely upon foods native to America and long utilized by the Indians. A great many of the foods associated with southern cooking—corn, peas, beans, squash, pumpkins, sweet potatoes (all of which can be preserved for long periods)—were adapted from the American Indians. Moreover, Indian ways of preparing food became the southern way: corn transformed into hominy and hominy ground into grits, cornmeal cooked as hoecake, johnny-cake, cornbread, and hush puppies; beans and corn mixed together to form succotash; green ears of corn roasted or boiled whole as corn on the cob; meat cured and smoked on a spit over coals or hickory logs and termed barbecue. Even the practice of growing peas intermixed with the corn (the peas sowed when the corn was laid by), and the planting technique of mounding the dirt around the corn or squash into "hills," were borrowed from Indian agriculturists. Since both Africans and Englishmen were unfamiliar with the flora and fauna of America, they had much to learn from the Indians, who were very visible in all the southern states through the 1830s. In ways historians are only beginning to understand, the first Americans left a permanent imprint on the American soil and not just in place names.

The preponderance of corn in the southern diet raises one important question about the health of slaves and other southerners. Nutritionists have known for decades that twentieth-century Africans and Europeans who depend on a corn-centered diet often suffer from pellagra, a disease caused at least in part by a deficiency of niacin. Corn contains niacin, an acid of the vitamin B complex essential to health, but it occurs in a form the body cannot use. To make matters worse, an amino acid (leucine) found in corn inhibits the metabolism of whatever niacin the total diet contains, and it also inhibits the body's ability to metabolize tryptophan, another amino acid often found in proteins, which normally allows the body to produce its own niacin. If the total diet provides sufficient protein from sources other than corn, then sufficient tryptophan can be produced. Pork—usually fat pork—was the other basic component of the slave diet, but unfortunately it would not supply enough tryptophan to meet the deficiency. Milk is an excellent source of protein and tryptophan, but of course most slaves were lactose intolerant and hence could not consume sufficient quantities of milk. Therefore, the slave would seem to qualify as a prime candidate for pellagra. However, it is possible that the peas, sweet potatoes, beans, and molasses so often found in conjunction with the corn-pork staples could have been a source of enough protein (and hence niacin and tryptophan), though none is particularly rich in either the vitamin or amino acid.

There is evidence that, when corn is treated by a lime or lye process to make it into hominy, the chemical transformation breaks down the molecules binding the niacin, freeing it to allow human digestion. If a substantial portion of the Old South's corn was consumed as hominy or grits, the additional niacin thus available may have lessened the danger of pellagra. Nevertheless, there remains the possibility that nutritional inadequacies in the comestibles available to slaves, however adequate the food may have seemed in quantity, may have caused physical ailments about which we can only speculate. Such illnesses quite likely may have afflicted whites as well, though less severely. Many nutritional diseases have few unique symptoms, and pellagra, for example, may very well have existed in the Old South, but been undiagnosed or misdiagnosed because of its multiplicity of symptoms. Still other diseases caused by poor diets might have produced symptoms that misled owners. Small children who have a nutritional shortage of proteins and calories (as slave children weaned from their mothers no doubt often did) can suffer from kwashiorkor, a disease (familiar today in war-torn countries) whose most obvious symptom is a distended belly. Slave children with mild cases of kwashiorkor may have been thought by their masters to be healthily plump. The controversial question of slave health, and health care, is enormously complex and just beginning to be understood.

The questions of the adequacy of the slaves' diet and their general healthiness are complicated further by certain genetic differences between Africans and Caucasians. The lactase deficiency of blacks is but one of several genetic characteristics that involve nutrition. The slaves' black skin reduced their capacity to synthesize vitamin D3 from sunshine, and though in tropical sunlight this was no liability, in higher latitudes (and during cold, overcast winters), slaves would require a better dietary source of D3 than whites.

Black also suffer with a much higher frequency than whites several varieties of hemoglobin abnormality that in centain circumstances (as with the sickle cell trait in regions where malaria is endemic— more on this later) have positive medical benefits, but also can cause medical problems. It may be that in the American climate Africans required a minimum diet somewhat richer in protein and various minerals than whites required; if so, all the computations about the adequacy of the slave diet calculated on the basis of present-day Department of Agriculture Minimum Daily Requirement figures (in which no adjustment is made for different racial types) should be reconsidered.

Researchers in the medical sciences have long known that there are differential racial and geographical susceptibilities to many diseases. This kind of information bears directly on the question of slave health both because of their African racial identity and because Africans were involuntarily transplanted to an alien climate and disease environment. Much is still unknown about these relationships, but surely they must play a role in any analysis of the health of bondsmen in the Old South. Many medical authorities in the Old South, along with planters, believed slaves had an inborn resistance to malaria, and they often interpreted this perceived immunity as an indication that slaves were suited by nature to work in the swampy rice-growing regions. Today we know that blacks did indeed have less susceptibility to malaria, particularly its more virulent forms, because of several genetic factors.

Significant numbers of blacks, for example, because they lack a particular red blood cell ingredient (called the Duffy antigen),are highly immune to one of the three major types of malaria. Many Africans, coming from a land where malaria was endemic, possessed the sickling trait—misshaped blood cells—which inhibits the growth of the more virulent forms of malaria. Those blacks who inherited the sickling trait from one parent were thus largely spared the ravages of "the fevers," as malaria was often called. That small minority of blacks who inherited from both parents the sickle-shaped blood cells—though they were still resistant to malaria— suffered from sickle cell anemia, and many died before adolescence. Even those who possessed the sickle cell trait, not the disease, probably had a mild form of anemia that increased their need (as compared to whites') for iron and folic acid. Still another abnormal hemoglobin condition that many slaves shared was a deficiency of an enzyme called G-6-PD, which also increased their resistance to malaria.

Again, these genetic immunities (relative, not complete) had evolved in an Africa where malaria was a constant threat, and they did prevent slaves in the Old South from getting malaria as often, or suffering as severely when they did, as did the surrounding whites. But because malaria was not endemic in the South, the medical complications arising from the hemoglobin abnormalities may have made the blacks' genetic traits a net disadvantage. All the hemoglobin traits cause a series of medical problems that have long been associated with slaves, though the causes of the diseases are only now being recognized. High rates of miscarriage, aching joints (often diagnosed as rheumatism), pneumococcal infections, and leg ulcers are all related to red blood cell defects, and all have frequently been pointed to as common slave maladies. Very probably one of the major causes of the high mortality rate for slave children was sickle cell anemia. Obviously the issue of slave health involves factors as diverse as genetic differences and planter treatment, and sometimes the two were intertwined in ways neither blacks nor whites understood.

Blacks are more susceptible to respiratory diseases than are whites, but the precise reasons for this are not apparent at all. Certainly the prevalence in blacks of red blood cell defects is a factor, but perhaps more important was the difference in historical experience with the diseases. In the colder climate of Europe, Europeans had for centuries lived and died with such pulmonary infections as pneumonia and tuberculosis (then called consumption), and as a result had over time developed immunities. For Africans, coming from tropical climates, both were new diseases. As we know from much epidemiological research, relatively mild, "domesticated" diseases can wreak havoc in virgin populations. Pulmonary infection is also increased by exposure to damp, cold weather, and blacks in several ways are less tolerant of cold than whites. Moreover, one of the major ways the tubercular bacterium is spread is by human sputum in close quarters. Hence slaves living crowded together in damp, drafty slave cabins were easy prey for pulmonary infection, far more susceptible than whites would be under similar circumstances. So even though slave living quarters may have seemed quite comparable to the cabins of many white farmers, the special genetic and geographical background of slaves may have meant that their living conditions did have unintended bad consequences for their health. Such was less the result of planned slave treatment than an accident of history and biology.

Yellow fever, another dreaded disease that periodically struck the South with drastic epidemics, was on the other hand not as virulent among blacks as among whites. There are no known genetic reasons for this differential susceptibility, though perhaps the disease's long history in Africa had resulted in the development within Africans of some kind of partial immunity. Certainly whites suffered more from yellow fever than did blacks, though there were some black deaths. The disease is spread by the bite of an infected *Aedes aegypti* mosquito, whereby the virus enters the patient's bloodstream. The best antebellum defense against yellow fever was flight from an infected area (and hence the carrier mosquitoes), but blacks were not free to flee. Were it not for their historical experience with it and hence partial immunity to it, slaves would have been prime victims of yellow fever epidemics.

Because slaves often lived crowded together, they, like large white families dwelling in small cabins, were susceptible to the various "minor" infectious diseases that afflict mankind. Mumps, measles, the common cold, rheumatic fever, diphtheria, whooping cough, and chicken pox caused great discomfort, sickness, even death, but it is difficult to relate these common diseases to any particular aspect of slave treatment, shelter, or diet. The drafty and ill-heated housing of slaves may have worsened some of the maladies, but the difference between black and average white shelters was usually only one of degree.

To a surprising extent planters from a mixture of motives tried to provide minimally adequate health care for their bondsmen. Certainly economic loss resulted from slaves too ill to labor, and the death of a slave was a severe financial blow to most slave owners. Humanitarian concern for the obvious suffering of persons under their dominion also clearly motivated many owners to seek relief for the sick. And since so many of the common illnesses were by sad experience known to be contagious to the whites as well as blacks, medical care was recommended by both the owner's crassest economic motives and the tenderest feelings of love for his family. The result was real concern for the health of bondsmen. This concern was in practice rendered at least partially useless by the medical ignorance of the day and the scarcity of doctors across the rural South. As in many rural communities even today, home remedies were the normal response to illness. For nearly every symptom there was some kind of traditional herb or patent medicine, and alternative medical theories competed with superstition and folklore (perhaps with many folk remedies borrowed from the Indians) for authoritative treatment. Only when amateur medicine seemed not to work (or when the symptoms clearly called for expert assistance) would parents or planters summon a doctor to treat either whites or blacks. Nevertheless, southern archives are filled with account books attesting to doctors being called to the slave quarters. Occasionally planters had doctors under contract, and larger plantations often had primitive infirmaries. In the cities where there were hospitals, whites often so avoided institutional medical care that doctors, wanting hospital patients, sometimes offered free care to sick slaves, and then practiced medical experimentation on their hapless patients. Given the state of medical science at that period—when some treatments, like purging and bleeding, only harmed the patient—no one would claim that slaves received good health care by today's standards. But because whites and blacks lived so close together in the Old South, self-interest alone, not to mention humanitarian and economic concerns, normally resulted in honest attempts to treat what were considered genuine cases of slave sickness. At times slaves rejected white medicine, preferring their own medicine drawn from African and perhaps Indian sources; likewise many whites disregarded the doctor's advice and turned instead to folk healing techniques. Impoverished free blacks alone in the anonymity of southern cities and destitute poor whites in isolated upcountry settlements probably suffered most from the ravages of disease in the Old South.

Since antebellum times much has been written about the supposed proclivity of slave mothers to smother their sleeping infants. The census mortality schedules do show that a hugely disproportionate number of slave babies under one year of age died of "smothering," sometimes reported as death by being "laid over" by the mother. Some have attributed these deaths to parental infanticide—the action of mothers who would rather their children die than live as slaves; but there is little evidence of this. Others have conjectured that overtired mothers in their exhausted stupor accidentally rolled atop their infants and, unconscious of doing so, woke to find the child dead from suffocation. However, evidence today suggests that it is practically impossible for babies to smother in that way. It seems clear that most slave children who died by "smothering" were victims of that baffling disease now called Sudden Infant Death Syndrome (SIDS), or crib death. The age and seasonal distribution of "smothering" deaths recorded for slaves in the mortality schedules is very similar to that observed today for victims of SIDS. Most "smothered" babies and most SIDS victims die between the ages of one and six months, and between November and February.

Today children of low-income families have a higher susceptibility to SIDS, but the exact cause of the malady is unknown. Perhaps nutritional imbalances are responsible, and several experts have suggested that calcium and magnesium deficiencies that probably existed in black infants' diet may have been the root cause of the disease. Because "smothering" was associated with the death of slave children and often attributed to the ignorance of the black mothers, it carried the connotation of being a black disease. Consequently, white children under one year of age who died mysteriously during the night were seldom said to have been smothered but instead to have died of unknown causes. But this cannot explain the shockingly higher black rate of death "by smothering" (the ratio of black to white was as high as 53 to 1). Today SIDS victims reveal no racial predisposition, but rather one of low socioeconomic position. A detailed study of the mortality schedules of the 1850 and 1860 censuses shows that the incidence of "smothering" deaths was many times higher in those regions of the South where there was large-scale production of cotton and tobacco. The far lower death rates in nonplantation areas (where small slave owners predominated) and the rice-growing regions (where the task system of labor was traditional) suggest that overworking of pregnant slave women was the major cause of SIDS. A pregnant woman who had to work in the fields also needed a more nutritious diet than other slaves, for she had to "eat for two persons." Since most victims of SIDS would have been conceived in the midst of the previous winter, when slave diets were most inadequate, dietary inadequacies and overworking of pregnant mothers were probably the twin causes of the high rate of SIDS among slave infants. Planters, who generally valued the birth and subsequent rearing of healthy slave children as a valuable adjunct to their agricultural crops, were obviously unaware of the probable etiology of SIDS.

Much illness was associated with pregnancy, childbirth, and infancy. Planters usually recognized both the humanity and the practicality of giving special treatment to expectant mothers, but there were examples of overwork and whipping that harmed the mother and child. New mothers were normally allowed several weeks of recuperation before they were sent back to the fields. Some slave women suffered from severe menstrual maladies, and occasionally after childbirth had a prolapsed uterus (where the supporting pelvic tissue was weakened and the uterus protruded down through the vagina and outside the body). It was not uncommon for slave women after childbirth to have puerperal fever, sometimes called "childbed fever," a potentially fatal infection of the placental site caused by contamination following delivery. Doctors and midwives often unknowingly spread this infection from mother to mother. None of these childbirth and gynecological problems was unique to slave women, though their possibility of being overworked or worked when indisposed might well have made their distress more common and severe. Similarly, the childhood diseases of black infants were the common illnesses of children, though minor infections probably spread more easily because slave children on large plantations were often kept in a crude nursery and sometimes may even have been fed from a common wooden trough. A nursing mother would either come to her baby several times a day, or have an older child bring the infant to her; she would then rest at the edge of the field while the baby nursed. Such conditions, with the mother hot and dirty, were not ideal hygiene, and the makeshift nurseries were also unclean. In fact, from today's perspective of modern laundry facilities, diaper service, and expert pediatric care, it often seems amazing that any children, black or white, survived. That they did is witness to their parents' love and skill and the resiliency of the human organism.

Some diseases, with complete impartiality, seemed to strike white and black, rich and poor, while others seemed more prevalent amidst the kind of living conditions in which slaves were likely to find themselves. Smallpox, for example, one of the three (along with cholera and yellow fever) most fatal epidemics that periodically struck the South, was no respecter of persons. Whites as well as blacks caught and spread the disease, and slaves and whites who had contracted it were quickly quarantined. In the eighteenth century planters often had their slaves and family members innoculated to prevent the spread of smallpox. Innoculation was an African and Asian practice brought to America whereby a tiny amount of smallpox material from the scab of a patient was introduced into a healthy person in an attempt to produce a slight case of the dreaded disease and thereafter immunity. After 1800 vaccination was increasingly used. After a smallpox scare planters (and in towns, public officials) would quickly institute a vaccination campaign because everyone had much to gain by immunity.

Another "disease" that afflicted white and black alike, but one that has more often been associated with poor whites, was dirt eating, variously called clay eating, cachexia africana, and, more medically correct, geophagy. Just why some persons in the South—and in fact all over the world—have shown an inclination to eat dirt has puzzled nonpartakers for years. Although it may very well be a culturally reinforced habit passed from one generation to the next, there is increasing evidence that the craving arises from a shortage in the diet of such minerals as calcium, magnesium, potassium, and iron, all of which have been found to be present in the clay thus consumed. While dirt eating seldom caused death, it did produce such symptoms as indigestion, severe diarrhea, a yellowish complexion, and a listless, always tired feeling. It has long been accepted that poor whites appeared lazy as a result of disease and dietary deficiencies; the same, accentuated by geophagy, may have sapped the vitality of many slaves, not disabling them but giving them a languid disposition often interpreted as laziness. Diet, culture, and perception are all parts of the complex problem of slave health and society.

Terrible cholera epidemics struck the South four times in the final three decades of the antebellum period, and though blacks had no special genetic susceptibility to the disease, they apparently contracted it more often, had more severe cases of it, and had a far higher mortality rate than whites. Since cholera was much worse in cities, where most free blacks lived, it was disproportionately deadly for the free black population. The major southern cities were all either seaports or riverports, and the poorest people— mostly free blacks and urban slaves responsible for their own quarters—were required by economic necessity to live in the lowest, dampest areas near the docks. Cholera is caused by bacteria and is primarily contracted through contaminated water: by drinking it, or by eating fish caught in it or other foods washed or irrigated with it. Because the causes of cholera were not then known, no effective countermeasures were developed, but because of its etiology it hit blacks, slave and free, with especial vengeance. Occasional efforts to clean up black neighborhoods and control the sale of nonfresh food did not prevent cholera but no doubt had other beneficial effects.

Many other diseases were at least in part caused by living conditions in the South, and though these afflictions usually visited white and black alike, the slaves' special circumstances may have made them especially susceptible. Bondsmen seldom had the freedom, leisure, or incentive to attend to their personal hygiene or to keep their quarters clean. Most slaves—and yeomen—did not have privies and relieved themselves under the cover of nearby bushes. With dogs, chickens, and children underfoot, human and animal feces and urine contaminated the yard, were washed into the sources of drinking water, and contaminated food and clothing by hand contact. Flies swarmed from decayed food and table scraps to excrement to the table. Food prepared under less than hygenic conditions and with no refrigeration made spoiling a constant problem. Dysentery, typhus, food poisoning, diarrhea, hepatitis, typhoid fever, salmonella, and intestinal worms often resulted from crowded living in such squalid conditions. This state of affairs was less a consequence of slave treatment per se than the natural result of humans living together in a warm, humid climate before the advent of modern hygiene, sanitary reform, and food preservation. No blame need be assigned; human suffering from disease was in the nineteenth century and earlier a common tragedy. What needs to be pondered is the possibility that the large numbers of blacks living together in overcrowded, unsanitary slave quarters may have produced real health problems that outweighed the social and cultural benefits of living together in such plantation "villages," where in many respects a separate black ethos could develop in those hidden hours between dusk and dawn when the black community was beyond the white man's purview.

Attention focused too narrowly on slave health may distort our picture of reality; everyone in the antebellum South was visited sometime in his life with sickness, and bondsmen may have suffered no more than many whites. Despite all the problems, people of both races persevered, increased in numbers, and even thrived. Life was difficult in an age with few mechanical conveniences. Human energy, not electric or gas, performed most of the work, and everything from bathing to preparing dinner was more trouble then than now. Memoirs from other regions and later times, such as those of Laura Ingalls Wilder from the upper Midwest in the 1880s, William Owens from East Texas in the early twentieth century, and Nate Shaw from Alabama in the first half of this century, remove much of the veneer of nostalgia from the past. The pang of hunger, the weariness of overwork, the chill of cold wind occasionally touched nearly every human soul. Because of their status, slaves usually had fewer advantages in every way than their free white contemporaries. And they realized their deprivation. Their condition probably seemed to them and their owners somewhat less severe than it looks to us in retrospect, and compared to slave conditions in the Caribbean and South America, bondsmen in the Old South were—in terms of physical well-being—much better off. Survival rates for slaves imported into the South contrast very favorably with those for imports to Latin America, and survival says much about the bottom line of physical treatment.

But the critical question about slavery is the absence of freedom, not the presence of relative physical comforts. No recitation of survival rates, daily caloric intake, and quality and quantity of living space can negate the psychological effect of bondage. The possibility of being whipped or being separated forever from a loved one and the reality of having little control over most aspects of one's life must have been ever-present burdens oppressing most slaves. One need not argue that slaves were worked down into listless drones or beaten and malnourished into states of semiconsciousness to indict the institution. Any labor or social system that defined persons as property and deprived them of basic autonomy over their lives was irredeemably evil. The system that planters called their peculiar institution can in no way be justified; we need only try to understand how it worked, for it condemns itself.

The system worked well enough to last for two centuries, and millions of blacks persevered under it in an almost unimaginable variety of circumstances. The diversity of situations in which antebellum blacks lived and labored shows how all-pervasive the black presence was in the Old South. Our next task is to understand how slaves were distributed across the face of the land and the diverse ways in which they contributed to the life and economy of the region.

5. Black Diversity in a Slave Society

The South as a region and its politics, economy, and culture have often been misunderstood and falsely depicted as an undifferentiated whole, uniform from the Mason-Dixon line to the Rio Grande. Geographically the states of the South were widely diverse, and their populations were surprisingly varied. No one political party dominated the Old South; even in the years after 1830 the Whigs and Democrats fought each other to a practical standstill. A number of regional folk cultures developed and persisted, from Eastern Shore Quakers in Maryland to German-speaking settlements in Texas, with Louisiana Cajuns, Appalachian hill folk, and thousands of native Indians in between. The economies of Baltimore, New Orleans, and Richmond had as many differences as similarities, and the backcountry areas in Mississippi and Alabama were almost a world apart from the salons of Charleston and New Orleans. Cotton dominated the Lower South, and those areas growing tobacco, wheat, rice, hemp, and sugar as commercial crops had their unique work routines, capital needs, marketing systems. In some counties there would not be a single plantation. Climate and soil types ranged enormously. The spectrum of black activities, occupations, and conditions mirrored this diversity. Despite the myths and movies, not all blacks in the Old South were slaves, and not all slaves were either uppity house-servants or alternately passive-rebellious field hands on large plantations. Somehow northern policies and perceptions, combined with southern self-images, created a South out of the many different souths.

A black people emerged from slavery more unified than their prewar condition (or indeed their diverse African backgrounds) might have suggested. One task is to emphasize the vast diversity within the society, and yet at the same time not forget that the whole was more than the sum of its parts. The white desire and wherewithal to maintain the institution of slavery clearly set the parameters for black life. Yet its texture was often determined more by local conditions and particular circumstances than by legal codes and racial abstractions. The day-to-day existence of a slave was largely shaped by such factors as the density of the black population and especially the size of slaveholdings, for, while the typical white slave owner possessed fewer than five slaves, the typical rural slave lived on a large plantation. This apparent paradox—of great cultural importance—is best explained by examining the statistics of slave ownership. Imagine a universe of ten slaveholders, eight owning two slaves apiece, one owning twenty-four, and the tenth possessing sixty. Obviously most slaveholders (80 percent) would own fewer than five slaves, but most slaves (84 out of a 100) would reside in units of more than twenty. Such an imaginary model suggests what the numbers reveal. In 1850, when 73.4 percent of the slaveholders held fewer than ten slaves, exactly 73.4 percent of the slaves lived in units numbering more than ten. Over half, 51.6 percent, resided on plantations of more than twenty bondsmen. These figures were more pronounced in the Deep South, and still more so in 1860, when fully 62 percent of the slaves in the Deep South lived in plantation units, and one-third on really substantial plantations of more than fifty slaves. Remembering that 2.4 million of the South's 3.9 million slaves lived in the Deep South, it is clear that most slaves lived on plantations in close proximity to numerous other slaves.

This proved to be a cultural fact of great significance. The ability to be with other blacks, to find companionship and marriage partners, made life much more bearable. Black religious and musical expression, black family life and folklore, all were the richer as a result of there being enough blacks congregated on plantations to approximate separate slave villages away from the constantly inquiring eyes of whites. Had most blacks been scattered in ones and twos across the rural South, slave families and cultural expression would have been far weaker. Later we will discuss in detail the social and cultural ramifications of the spatial arrangement of blacks in the Old South.

The implications for the work routines of blacks were equally profound. On small farms with fewer than five slaves, little specialization of labor occurred. A black woman gave domestic service, and in times of high labor need like harvest would shift her work to the fields. The black man would do whatever had to be done—plowing, planting, hoeing, picking, building fences, chopping wood, odd chores. Slave children over seven or so might do light work and usually became partial hands at ten or twelve. Slaveholders with fewer than five slaves normally had both sexes and a range of ages represented and worked in the fields with their bondsmen, and they and their small work force were jacks-of-all-trades.

On plantations with more than twenty slaves, where most slaves lived, there began to emerge a degree of labor specialization. This was more evident on the still larger plantations, and in 1860 in the Deep South, fully one-third of all slaves lived on plantations with more than 50 slaves. Division of labor appeared on agricultural units of this size, and here a range of slave vocations enabled bondsmen to develop their skills, earn prestige within the black community, sometimes even earn money for themselves, and exercise their leadership ability. Occasionally slaves acquired quasi-managerial positions on plantations, but most could at least aspire to positions of skill or artisanship. Real freedom, real control of their lives was, of course, beyond their grasp, but the possibility of achieving prized positions as carpenters, plowmen, cook in the big house, livestock handlers, or drivers added a degree of mobility to the institution of slavery. The limited variety of slave occupations on plantations provided some slaves with avenues of advancement that affected their whole behavior; some potentially rebellious slaves may have been co-opted by their owner's holding out to them positions of leadership.

Perhaps the most basic division of labor was the separation of hands into house-servants and field slaves. Actually the terms *servants* and *slaves* were used almost interchangeably, along with such phrases as *hands* and *my people*, but *servant* carried with it a slight connotation of respect—it was the polite term. Much nonsense has been written about house-servants. Black women were widely used for domestic labor, and, especially in towns and cities, those one or two slaves owned by most slaveholders were women domestics. Even on farms, often the single slave owned, or one of the two or three, was retained to help the mistress of the house. Such domestics who did the arduous cleaning, washing, ironing, and helped with the cooking had no particular class or status. Plantations with twenty or so slaves would normally have a black cook, who more or less was a full-time house-servant, one or two more women who regularly helped with washing and ironing, and probably a man who served as a part-time butler, coachman, perhaps yardman. Except on the largest plantations, these part-time domestics could expect to be shifted to the fields when the need arose, and certainly at cotton-picking time they joined in the harvest rush. The house-servants of moonlight-and-magnolia legend, who made up a special caste of bondsmen, existed only on that tiny minority of large plantations.

The several thousand grand plantations sometimes employed a surprisingly large retinue of house-servants, each assigned a category of tasks: cooks, laundresses, nursemaids, butlers, valets. Such servants lived in close and constant proximity to whites, were often always on call, were better fed and clothed than the field workers, and at times knew their owners in the most intimate ways. Always on hand, favored valets and maids heard all the conversations, knew all the friends, and witnessed the secrets and weaknesses of their masters. They were sometimes devoted to their owners, and the whites generally reciprocated their feelings, though occasionally familiarity did breed contempt for the master. One of the surest guarantees of good treatment that trusted servants and "mammies" (and their families) had was the affection and respect in which they were held. Trusted house-servants on occasion served almost as managers of the plantations, at times carrying the keys and even paying bills and handling business with outsiders. Masters and mistresses at times grew so dependent on the skilled services of certain house-servants that the slaves could within reason manipulate their owners. Life in the big house was a never-ending process of give and take, and masters sometimes found themselves psychologically almost as enslaved to the system as were the blacks. On many large plantations the mammy of legend and lore practically reared the white children, but, however important to the children involved, in the context of the whole white population of the South mammies were too few to have had a significant impact on shaping white racial, cultural, or sexual attitudes.

On the handful of genuinely preeminent plantations the approximation of a special caste of house-servants arose, but generally there were too many ties of kinship and affection between the servants in the big house and the slaves of the quarters for an attitude of separation to develop. The spouses of the house-servants were sometimes privileged too, though likely as not they were field hands. On all but the grandest plantations moments of agricultural crisis brought practically every slave to the field, and few house-servants were so immune to harsh treatment as not ultimately to identify with their less fortunate fellows in the quarters. Some, unhappy with the constant supervision in the big house and perhaps desiring the camaraderie of work in the fields, actually seem to have desired the more physically demanding outdoor work. Rarely did house-servants develop such pretensions to rank as to snub their black brothers in the field. Cooks and mammies were probably the most likely to do so, and at times they may have jeopardized their position and welcome in the quarters. But in most cases all slaves knew they were first slaves, secondly house-servants, and cast their identity with the black majority. For every beloved house-servant who sided with the master when Union troops came near during the Civil War, there were one or more who led the black exodus to freedom. Their greater knowledge of their master's foibles, and their increased familiarity with liberty, only resulted in a greater hunger for freedom.

The vast majority of all slaves were classed as field hands, though this term does scant justice to the variety of jobs they performed. Both men and women worked in the fields, along with children over the age of ten or twelve. On a typical plantation a planter could expect about 60 percent of his total slave population to be available for agricultural work at any one time. The other 40 percent represented small children, aged or infirm slaves, and specialized slaves such as cooks, weavers, blacksmiths, and herdsmen. When calculating workers employed in a certain task, owners and overseers used as a measure the concept of a "hand," meaning a male of prime age; women, children, and older workers were counted as fractions of a hand, as for example a child under fourteen might be considered half a hand. Laborers in the field were further subdivided into the plow gang and the hoe gang. Usually young men were the plowmen, but on occasion a young woman— by choice, apparently—also was a member of the plow gang. The majority of field workers wielded the hoe, and spent their spring and summer workdays chopping the grass away from the cotton plants and, once in the spring, thinning the cotton. Such routine labor required some skill, for a hoe swung an inch too far would clip the cotton stalk. The experienced hand could with a clean stroke gently cultivate the soil and cut down the ever-present grass that, if left alone, would take over a field. The plow gang, with light cultivator plows, kept the middle of the rows clean of grass, and the thin layer of fresh dirt thrown by the plow's wings covered up and killed or at least temporarily retarded the growth of grass along the edge of the rows. The grass atop the rows and between the cotton plants was, of course, the concern of the choppers. Keeping the cotton "out of grass" was a constant battle never really won, and a prolonged wet period could spell near disaster, calling out all available hands for a fast defensive skirmish against the grass. Good light and relatively dry fields were required for hoeing, and so labor even in the rush times was confined to the daylight hours of drier weather. Likewise, plowing required as much skill as strength, for otherwise the plow would dig alternately deep then shallow and wobble across the field, leaving a crooked furrow. Adept plowmen could plow even, straight furrows, with the fresh-turned dirt and arrowlike rows a testament to their skill.

The number and variety of jobs to be done on a plantation were almost endless, and on smaller plantations and farms individual slaves performed many different chores at different times. Crop labor needs varied, and workers were shifted to clearing land, cutting firewood, shearing sheep, husking corn, repairing barns and fences, and so on as circumstances required and time permitted. On rainy days certain women, rather than work in the fields, sat at a loom or spinning wheel and helped provide the clothing. There was ditching to be done, manure to shovel, food to be preserved and prepared, and the measure of a good overseer or manager was determined as much by his ability to keep his slaves usefully employed as by the crop yield. The general neatness and appearance of a plantation depended upon slave labor performed at less than peak load times.

On the largest plantations certain highly skilled slaves, who properly should be called slave artisans, worked steadily at their crafts. Slave blacksmiths not only kept the horses shod and tools sharpened and in repair, but made hinges, nails, and other metal items. Carpenters and cabinetmakers maintained the plantation's physical plant and along with the blacksmith sometimes were hired out or took in outside work for extra income for the planter and themselves. Slaves served as gardeners, stablemen, dairymen; they operated cotton gins and cotton presses; they supervised the grinding and boiling of sugar on sugar plantations; they ran mills for the grinding of wheat and corn and the husking of rice; they wove cloth and made clothing. On cattle ranches in Texas in the 1850s there were slave cowboys, mounted on horses and branding and rounding up cattle. Every imaginable kind of agriculture-related job was performed by slaves, from the simplest routine to the most highly skilled task. On large plantations slaves also served in managerial positions, sharing in decision making, discipline, everything but profits.

There was no job more difficult in the antebellum South than that performed by black drivers and overseers. As in so many other important aspects of the study of slavery, exactitude in calculating the number and influence of slave drivers and overseers is impossible. Several terms were used for such black work supervisors, census and plantation account books did not always recognize their titles, and many who performed this function did so in an unofficial, or impromptu, manner. On large plantations drivers probably served regularly and more or less permanently, but on the majority of agricultural units employing slave labor, the position was less formal and more temporary. There, the most senior or most dependable slave, while working side by side with his fellows, may have set the work pace and have been looked upon by both his owner and his co-workers as the slave leader. The owner might discuss the tasks with him, and he would be held responsible for the quality and quantity of work performed when the owner was not present. On small farms the owner often worked beside his slaves, but even so, one bondsman usually stood out. Anytime several people are working together, one of them, because of strength, or personality, or intelligence, or stamina, or some combination of all, will emerge as the virtual leader. Recognized alike by slave and master, the drivers were primarily workers like the other slaves and probably identified more with the slaves than with the owner. No doubt most took pride in their special relationship with the master and were careful to stay in his good graces, but because of the informality of their position they had to stay in the good graces of their fellow slaves too in order to retain the ability to command their respect and cooperation. A constant balancing act was required, with such leaders drawn in two directions. Because on small slave-owning units informal slave drivers were less likely to be required to discipline or actually whip slaves, they were more apt to be looked upon by their fellows as intermediaries and even protectors than cruel extensions of the master's power.

The majority of slaves, however, lived on plantations, and most plantations utilized some variety of black supervision. In 1850 there were 37,662 plantations of more than twenty slaves, in 1860, 46,274, and on most of these there must have been at least some variant of the slave driver. On those units of twenty to thirty, when the owner, or perhaps an elder son or other relative, actually oversaw the operation, the driver's position might have been much like that on the small farm. When the white owner-manager was away, or sick, the slave leader would often be pressed into temporary service as the real driver, and often he managed the plantation; in other words, he became in fact the overseer. While occasionally a driver might sieze this opportunity to push the slaves harder than usual in an attempt to curry favor with the owner and thus cement his new-found role, most drivers realized the impermanence of their status and were careful not to jeopardize their relationships in the slave quarters. On some occasions owners learned that the slave drivers were more skillful at plantation management than they, their white relatives, or overseers, and gave the driver permanent supervision of the slaves and crops. Many planters testified to the efficiency and harmony of slave-managed plantations, and they often deferred to the driver-overseer's judgment in agricultural matters.

On the large plantations the slave driver played a very significant role in the daily operation of what has been called the

agricultural factory, though the efficiency and routinization con-
notated by the industrial analogy seldom if ever obtained in the
rural South. As the total slave force neared fifty and went beyond,
most owners needed managerial assistance, and of course all
absentee owners employed managers of one sort or another. Again,
older sons, or brothers or other relatives, often served, and there
was a class of white overseers, usually berated and criticized, who
specialized in plantation supervision. In the organizational scheme
of plantations the black driver was beneath the overseer, who
established the basic guidelines. The driver (or drivers on giant
plantations) saw to it that the overseer's orders were carried out.
It was his responsibility to enforce the labor demands: he assem-
bled the slaves in the morning (the plantation bell usually awoke
them), counted them, set them to their tasks, watched to keep the
bondsmen laboring at a steady pace and to ensure that work was
performed reasonably well, made sure the draft animals were
periodically rested, fed, and watered, kept the tools in good order,
sent the slaves back to the quarters at dusk (often the plantation
bell signalled the end of the workday). In short, slave drivers were
the vital nexus between owner-overseer and the slave work force.
The day-to-day operation of the plantation rested more on their
shoulders than on anyone else's. From at least the mid-eighteenth
century on, perhaps a majority of slaves took their daily orders
from, and worked under the direct control of black taskmasters.

In important ways the slave drivers insulated the owners (and to
a lesser extent the overseers) from the worst aspects of slavery. The
hateful tasks of rousing the slaves, supervising their labor, often
meting out discipline were in the drivers' hands. The owner, by
staying in the background, could appear benevolent in contrast.
Since the driver was immediately responsible for their drudgery
and punishment, malcontented slaves naturally tended to direct
much of their resentment toward him. His favored position was
maintained by his effectiveness at maximizing the labor output and
minimizing slave complaints. He had control over both by wielding
the whip or extending work hours until a set task was completed,
and since he was the medium through which the overseer or owner
received the responses of the slaves, the driver could cover up
minor resentments. To protect their positions most drivers on large

plantations, where there was a visible elite slave corps, identified with the owner. Yet such drivers had to walk a tightrope, for if they treated those beneath them too harshly, the slaves, ever aware of what they considered their rights as bondsmen and of what was considered reasonable work expectations, would appeal to the master for relief.

Most masters were receptive to such appeals even when complaints were about a white overseer, for they knew that ultimately the surest guarantee of a profitable harvest was a reasonably contented work force. Overseers were dismissed as often for mishandling the slaves as for producing poor crops, and slaves quickly learned how to manipulate overseers by going beyond them to the owner. And owners had their paternalistic roles legitimated and revived by such maneuverings—they were perceived as benevolent protectors of their "people," and the slaves transferred their anger and resentment to the fired overseer. A driver too in a real sense served at the pleasure of those under his immediate control, and, while he could be a hard taskmaster and might even sexually exploit the female slaves, seldom was his position with the planter so secure that he could afford to brutalize the slaves.

Slaves in their memoirs and recollections directed much animosity toward their black drivers, and this record of resentment cannot be explained away. There were scattered examples of drivers who faked their whippings of the slaves, who looked the other way when hungry bondsmen stole food or illegally butchered another planter's beeves, but such glaring instances of a driver's identifying with his people rather than with the owner are rare. Drivers understood that their favored position—and often special treatment for their immediate family—was precarious. If they leaned too far toward using their role to benefit the slave community in general, they risked jeopardizing their own well-being and that of their loved ones. Of course, if they completely adopted the planter's interests and drove the slaves mercilessly, they risked losing their capacity to command the deference and obedience of the slaves. It was an impossible position, pulled as they were toward two different world views. Some did succumb to brutality and took pleasure in their ability to magnify their own power by debasing their fellows; others constantly hazarded their status by benefiting the bondsmen under their supervision. Most must have occasionally done both, hewing mainly to a middle line of maximizing slave labor and slave benefits.

No doubt skilled drivers could deflect much of the rancor of their fellows by blaming their actions on the demands of the overseer or planter and suggesting it was better that they rather than the whites administer the punishment. Drivers and overseers each played off the other, and the harmony of a plantation depended upon how effectively this was done. Since the drivers and the planters were more permanent, it was often the overseer, despised by both and easily fired, who became the scapegoat. It is quite possible that the absence of recriminations by freedmen against either their former drivers or their former owners can be explained by most of the black enmity having been projected onto the overseers. Former slaves could sincerely profess a degree of attachment to their former owners, but not because their plight had been easy. The former owners—detached as they had been via overseers and drivers from much of the harshness and routine irritations of slave management—could easily romanticize the days of yore when they had been masters and mistresses of great plantations. The romance and reality of life in the Old South were so intermingled that demythologizing the period remains an unfinished task.

The jobs on a farm or plantation, either in the fields or in the house, were enormously varied. The present-day student can well imagine the diversity of agricultural occupations and recognize that slaves gained an impressive range of skills. Slaves had less work-oriented occupations too, at least part of the time, and two in particular, those of musician and preacher, brought a bondsman respect and prestige within the slave community. While the antebellum South was overwhelmingly rural and agricultural, where there were industries and cities slaves toiled there too. One of the least recognized chapters in the black experience in the South is the black contribution to southern industrial, urban, and commercial life. While it would be an exaggeration to say that slaves built the South, to underestimate their role would be just as mistaken. If one were to compile a list of antebellum occupations, slaves would be represented in every category. From clerks to carpenters, from brick makers to coopers, from cobblers to ship caulkers, from train engineers to bridge builders, from typesetters to barbers, slaves were visible in the skilled trades that kept the southern economy functioning.

The South's economy was dependent upon transportation. Basically a producer of bulk raw products for manufacture elsewhere, the region required an inexpensive method of transporting bulk cargoes to port cities. The South was blessed with a system of rivers large enough to permit boat and raft traffic, and much of the river system was navigable without recourse to expensive locks and canals. The cotton empire spread westward at the same time as the steamboat was opening up the western waters to commerce. Not just the Mississippi but also dozens of smaller rivers could accommodate shipping for several hundred miles inland. Even places that seem unlikely today, like Jefferson, in northeast Texas, were linked by bayous, lakes, and rivers to the sea. Hundreds of flat-bottom steamboats plied these waters, carrying cotton, food, manufactured goods, lumber—all the stores the society demanded. Toward the end of the antebellum era railroads began to replace waterborne commerce, and post roads linked towns and cities with the hinterland. Slaves made significant contributions to each transportation system.

From the time the first primitive roads were built, slaves were employed to fell the trees, level the right-of-ways, and drive the wagons. Slave draymen and wagoners carted foodstuffs, lumber, and cotton from the countryside to the towns. At times critics charged that various southern cities were too dependent on such slave labor—fearing that slaves were gaining too much power and were profiting too much from theft of the goods transported—but in every instance the labor performed was too valuable to be curtailed. When railroads began to be constructed in the South, again slave labor was crucial. Companies purchased slaves and hired them; black workers built the roadbeds, cut the ties, laid the rails, built the bridges. There were even slaves who designed the bridges. Once the tracks were laid, slaves helped operate the trains: several served as engineers, but hundreds more worked on maintenance crews, chopped the wood for the wood-burning steam engines, and loaded and unloaded the freight.

On the steamboats and rafts that traversed the southern rivers, slaves played an even more prominent role. At every step slave labor was important. At shipbuilding yards slaves performed all manner of skilled work in constructing boats. Along the rivers they cut and stacked mountains of wood for the boilers, and then loaded it aboard when steamboats pulled to shore for refueling. At the ports of embarkation and debarkation, slave stevedores loaded and unloaded the ships. En route slaves fired the boilers, cooked and served the food, cleaned and maintained passenger quarters, and entertained the paying customers. But as glamorous and romantic as the gothic steamboats were, much commerce floated slowly down the rivers on lowly barges and rafts, where river current and men's muscles were the locomotive forces. American folklore has memorialized such white rivermen as Mike Fink, but thousands of slaves manned these craft too. Some of them, like Simon Gray, achieved remarkable independence. Gray, hired out for years to a prominent lumber company in Natchez, commanded huge lumber rafts downriver to New Orleans. With crews of whites and blacks under him, Gray displayed quite remarkable skills not only in river navigation but also in the wiles of trade. He was allowed by his white employer to make deals, buy logs, sell the lumber, contract future sales, collect and pay bills. Gray's employer permitted him remarkable freedom because his energy and skill earned the company money, and Gray, knowing he was an asset to the company, successfully pressed for more privileges. His independence was exceptional, but the river seemed to bring out the exceptional in many men.

Most southern industry was extractive, and thus was located away from the region's few cities. Because of the sparseness of population and the availability to whites of inexpensive land, there was a constant shortage of white laborers. Consequently southern industrialists—who more often than not were also planters who engaged in quasi-industrial pursuits like lumbering in the slack season, received their capital from planters, and were thus acquainted and comfortable with slave workers—typically turned to slaves for labor. In every industry some entrepreneurs owned slaves, but, in order to reduce initial capital demands, most of them hired slaves from surrounding planters. This dependence had an important effect on the treatment of industrial slaves.

The largest southern industry was lumbering, which employed 16,000 workers in 1860, most of them slaves. From Virginia to

Texas slaves worked in the forests, cutting hardwood and pine, hauling it by ox- or mule-drawn wagons to sawmills, and there cutting it into usable lumber. In the Dismal Swamp of Virginia and North Carolina teams of provisioned slaves disappeared for weeks at a time and cut and hauled thousands of cypress and oak logs. In the great swamps of Louisiana, skilled slave foresters girdled giant cypress trees, and, after they had died and dried out, the slave axmen, standing in boats, would fell the trees, trim their limbs, and tie the logs into monstrous lumber rafts and float them to sawmills. Black drivers directed most of this swamp lumbering. At the hundreds of sawmills across the South slaves performed most of the labor. Usually the only whites were the sawmill supervisor and the sawmen who actually operated the dangerous saw blade. Black "engineers" fired and operated the steam engines and hauled and stacked the lumber. Some lumbermen and sawmills employed over a hundred slaves, both owned and hired. The naval stores industry, centered in the Carolinas and Georgia, was another important forest business. North Carolina alone in 1850 supplied 88 percent of the nation's naval stores, consisting primarily of tar, turpentine, and turpentine products. Most of this work was performed by slaves, who girdled the trees, collected the resin, and manufactured it into turpentine. Planters with upwards of a hundred slaves operated turpentine plantations, harvesting the liquid crop of the long-leaf pines. Slaves and whites together worked in the distilleries and cooperages that serviced the naval stores industry and in the port complexes that shipped the goods to market.

Two types of industry—textile mills and tobacco factories—were directly related to the South's major agricultural products. Though the truly large-scale migration of the mills to the cotton fields was a postwar phenomenon, significant antebellum developments did occur in textile manufacturing, particularly in South Carolina and Georgia. There hundreds of slave operatives worked alongside white mill hands. Slave women and children were considered especially appropriate for such work because their smaller, more agile fingers facilitated handling the thread and bobbins. The tobacco manufacturing industry was centered in Richmond and Petersburg, where in the 1850s approximately 6,000 slaves worked in dozens of tobaccories producing chewing tobacco. Men predominated among the slave tobacconists, and as they performed their tasks they often worked in tempo to a slave singer or chanter who set the pace. In every link of the production chain of the South's great agricultural commodities, from planting to harvesting to transportation to initial manufacturing and subsequent marketing, slaves were involved.

Of all the industries in the antebellum South employing substantial numbers of slaves, the mining of iron ore and coal and the operation of ironworks had the longest history. By the early 1730s three major ironworks were established in the Chesapeake—the Virginia, Principio, and Baltimore ironworks—and all were operated by predominantly slave work forces. This tradition continued through the Civil War, culminating in Joseph R. Anderson's Tredegar ironworks in Richmond, which, employing slave workers, enabled him to become the "ironmaker to the Confederacy." Throughout the period as many as 7,000 slaves labored in the ironworks, most of which were in the various ore ranges of Maryland and Virginia—the Alabama ranges were developed only after the Civil War.

Slaves did the bulk of manual labor at the Chesapeake ironworks, but they filled many of the most skilled positions as well. Numerous separate tasks were involved in making iron. Iron ore had to be mined and brought to the site of the blast furnace; limestone was quarried to provide a fluxing material in the heating process; charcoal was manufactured to provide the heat. At every stage of production slaves supplied the labor, often supervised by a black driver who in this industrial context could more accurately be called a foreman. Another 2,000 or so slaves worked in coal mines, digging, running the tramways, firing the boilers, and serving as engineers for the steam-operated machinery ranging from elevators to water pumps. The coal mines and ironworks were often some distance from towns or even settled areas. The black workers, housed in cabins, often had to help grow their own food, provide firewood, and help in general ways the industrial camp to survive. Typically in both the ironworks and mines, the blacks worked alongside white laborers, both southern whites and immigrants from northern or European mining regions. Surprisingly little racial antipathy emerged, even when, as sometimes occurred, blacks supervised white workers.

There was an additional mining industry of some importance in the Old South—the mining of gold. The nation's first gold rush occurred in the South in the early 1830s, with significant success in Georgia, North Carolina, and Virginia. Panning the streams and utilizing placer mills, fortune seekers and hard-headed industrialists came south by the thousands. The production of precious minerals soon paled in comparison to the gold and silver riches of Sutter's Mill and the Comstock Lode, but before 1849 the South led the nation in gold production. And as in the mining of coal and iron ore, slaves by the hundreds labored in the mines. Some were even allowed on their Sunday free time to search for nuggets, sharing what they discovered with their masters.

A more mundane industry, and more important to thousands of average southerners of both races, was the antebellum salt industry centered in western Virginia in the Great Kanawha (River) Valley. Salt was essential to the food supply of the Old South for, because of the relatively mild winters, salting down pork was the safest method of preserving it. Salt pork was the favorite meat of southerners as much by necessity as by taste. Virginia was by far the leading salt-processing state, and by 1850 the Kanawha River Valley region was producing more than 3 million bushels annually. Steam-driven pumps raised brine water from deep wells, then huge coal-fired kettles boiled the water away, leaving the precious salt. In 1850 over a thousand slaves worked in the salt industry, and over half of them were hired, not owned. Again slaves performed work of every kind, ranging from the least skilled manual labor to operating the steam engines and overseeing the boiling kettles. Slaves dug the coal that fired the engines and kettles, ran the pumps, loaded the salt by the barrel on flatboats. The work was often dangerous as well as hot and hard, and slaves worked side by side with whites. Often the salt kettles were kept steaming around the clock, and the slaves, like the whites, were paid overtime for overwork.

No matter where a slave worked, no matter the industry or the nature of his skill or his remuneration, he was always a bondsman, never in complete control of his life. Even a slave like Simon Gray, who was accorded exceptional privileges, ultimately had no control over his employment. Yet industrial slavery in general provided more room for incentive, a greater degree of control over one's leisure time, more psychological living space, than slavery on a rural plantation. Because much of the industrial work was hard and dangerous and because often at isolated mining sites or ironworks there developed shortages of food and supplies—despite the best effort of owners and factors—some historians have been too quick to charge industrial slavery as the worst of a bad world for bondsmen. Especially because the majority of industrial slaves were hired, thus separating their immediate work supervisor from the owner whose investment they represented, critics have assumed the industrial supervisors had almost a license to underfeed, overwork, and generally take advantage of their temporary workers. Yet this was not the case; in spite of the dangers and the rigors of the job, most slaves who had the choice probably would have chosen industrial labor. Here they found more ways to gain self-esteem and opportunities to use to advantage their individual skills; they benefited from the various incentives offered; they enjoyed at the industrial site a degree of responsibility for and control over their lives that plantations seldom provided. Moreover, the divergence of interests represented by slave owners and slave hirers allowed slaves a mechanism to enlarge their privileges and gain better working conditions. White laborers were usually in extremely short supply, industrialists desperately needed and competed for the available slaves for hire, and slave owners had their economic investment to protect. The result worked out to the advantage of the slaves.

In the locales where industrial development occurred, there was always a shortage of slaves for hire, hence industrial employers had to compete with one another—not to mention with planters needing harvesters for the staple crops—for slaves. With the demand outrunning the supply, owners were extremely wary about hiring out their valuable property to industrialists who had a reputation for overworking, underfeeding, or otherwise mistreating slaves. Not only was the owner concerned about the physical well-being of his property, but he also feared that mistreated slaves might run away, a fear made more real by the usual isolation of the industrial sites. There is much evidence that slaves chose or avoided certain employers by letting their master know their feelings, and evidence that employers actively sought to prevent the kind of treatment that would gain them an unsavory reputation. The supply-demand squeeze thus ensured that hired industrial slaves were accorded treatment at least equal to that on plantations.

Employers also quickly learned that their profits increased if their work force was reasonably contented. Mistreated slaves malingered, feigned illness, sabotaged equipment, ran away—all in all, bad treatment was economically counterproductive. For their own benefit employers sought ways to improve the productivity of their slave workers, and they soon hit on the idea of paying bonuses for extra work. Industrial slaves, like plantation slaves, accepted as their reasonable duty a certain level of production, and in industry specified quotas of productivity were more easily set than in agriculture. So many cords of wood, or tons of coal, or bushels of salt, became mutually accepted as a day's or week's work; anything beyond was cause for reward. As early as the eighteenth century, for example, Virginia ironmakers began the trend of paying slaves extra increments for "overwork." Slaves—rented or owned—could earn overwork pay by extra productivity during the day or on holidays, or by doing extra work like cutting firewood, laboring in the camp garden plot, and so on. Slaves could also be docked for disciplinary reasons, and by keeping the accounts payable until the end of the contract period (usually a year), the employer had a method of controlling the slave.

Employers seldom abused the system because to do so would jeopardize their future supply of hired slaves; slaves on the other hand saw the system as a way of having their initiative rewarded. Over and over again bondsmen performed heroic feats of labor or skill, forgoing holidays and regular leisure time to earn extra money. With the funds thus gained they supplemented their diet and wardrobe, bought small luxuries for their wives and children, and at least one in Virginia opened a savings account in a Lexington bank. Thus slave industrial employment, through a process of compromise and mutual accommodation, allowed bondsmen enlarged freedom of action and incentive; the result was a system of labor and management that, while still slavery, had some of the overtones of modern capitalistic employment. The relationship between slave laborer and industrialist was more that of employee-employer than chattel-master. When, during the Civil War, the South was forced to industrialize to a greater degree than ever before, Joseph R. Anderson and others—for example, the managers of the Shelby Iron Works in Selma, Alabama—found that slaves adjusted quickly to the needs of the new industrial order. After emancipation many of the former industrial slaves continued their employment under the same management, working for wages. Their slave experience with the overwork system had prepared them for handling money, and their skills gave them ready employment. Here in industrial slavery perhaps to a degree found nowhere else, the antebellum slave experience proved to be an advantage in the postwar world. Of course, the postbellum South was overwhelmingly agricultural, so industrial jobs were limited.

As the successive adaptation of slave labor to tobacco and rice cultivation, then to cotton and sugar plantations suggests, the institution of slavery was flexible to a point. The multifaceted application of slave labor to a whole spectrum of industries from lumbering to salt manufacturing also indicates that slavery was a dynamic institution. Methods of control and incentive were available to allow the utilization of slave labor in every conceivable trade in the South. When labor needs shifted from the Chesapeake and the Carolinas to the Old Southwest, slaves were allocated to the region of greatest need. When slave prices increased in the 1850s, industrial employers shifted more and more to hired rather than purchased slaves. Nothing in the antebellum period suggests that the South's peculiar institution was rigid, moribund, obsolete, or disintegrating. Nowhere did the dynamic nature of slavery disclose itself more revealingly than in the region's cities, where in 1860 more than 140,000 bondsmen resided. Urban slavery proved a laboratory of experimentation and adaptation for both bond and free and offers solid evidence of the extent to which slaves were capable of carving out their own cultural community when any chance at all existed for doing so.

Half the urban slaves lived in the ten largest southern cities, with Charleston (13,909 slaves), New Orleans (13,385), and Richmond (11,699) having the largest number in 1860. The slave population in the various cities fluctuated in response to a number of factors, and while some cities saw their slave population peak in 1840 or 1850, others were still experiencing growth in 1860. The absolute number of urban slaves was higher in 1860 than in any previous census year, but in terms of their percentage of the total urban population, urban slavery was declining in 1860. The immediate cause of this relative decline was substantial white population growth in the largest southern cities, especially New Orleans, St. Louis, and Baltimore. There were several additional reasons for this apparent decline in the significance of urban slavery. As cotton prices climbed and remained high in the 1850s, planters simply out-bid urban employers for slave labor. With fortunes to be made in cotton (and in sugar too), capitalists invested in land and slaves. In a sense opportunities in the countryside pulled slaves out of the cities. In the rural areas when the labor demand went up, there were no alternatives to slave workers. However, as the urban regions enjoyed rapid white growth, fueled in part by the immigration of artisans and laborers from the North and Europe, employers in cities could substitute white labor for slave. And because in the urban milieu slaves, through a process of push, compromise, and accommodation, had successfully gained greater freedom of action and had regularized a system of bonus payments (moreover, for reasons of control urban governments required payment of license and badge fees for slave workers), the actual cost of a slave to a potential employer was sometimes more than that of a free white laborer. Consequently white laborers gradually began to replace slaves in nearly all positions except the most skilled and the domestic. The result was not only a relative decline in the number of urban slaves, but a slave population in which women increasingly outnumbered men. Richmond, the most heavily industrialized southern city, was the outstanding exception, for its slave population grew because of the labor needs of its factories, and this desire for male factory operatives gave it a male majority.

It was not that slavery did not work in cities; rather, the exceptional agricultural prosperity of the 1850s made it economically feasible to maximize crop production. Free white workers were incompatible with plantation labor when land was cheap and commodity prices high. White laborers could be substituted for urban slaves, hence the relative population shift. Had cotton prices declined (as they later would have, Civil War or no, because of a falling off in the rate of growth of the worldwide demand for cotton), there is no reason why urban slavery would not have again increased in statistical importance. Of course the Civil War did end slavery of all kinds, but freedmen flocked to the cities seeking employment in a variety of skilled trades. They met increased resentment from white artisans and laborers, and later stiff labor union opposition. Nevertheless, until about 1900 urban blacks in the South filed a far higher percentage of positions in the skilled trades than did their black counterparts in the North. The city was attractive to the southern slave (and later freedman), and for good reason. There, even more than in rural industrial employment, slaves found a degree of freedom and incentive. In the anonymity of cities, bondsmen developed a black counterculture that occupied a transitional zone between slavery and freedom.

A visitor to an antebellum southern city would have been quick to notice the high visibility of the black population, though he might have overestimated the slave presence because of the urban free black population of approximately 80,000 in 1860. Urban slaves and free blacks lived in such symbiotic relationship that it is almost an artificial distinction to discuss them separately, as we do here. Slaves in 1860 constituted 8.3 percent of the total population in the ten largest southern cities, free blacks 7.1 percent. Excluding the two large and in many ways atypical border cities of Baltimore and St. Louis, slaves represented 14.5 percent and free blacks 6.8 percent of the urban population in 1860. This represents a significant drop from the 26.3 and 13.3 percent respectively in 1840, but nevertheless in 1860 the South's largest cities were about 20 percent black. Charleston, Richmond, and Savannah were exactly one-third slave; with slaves and free blacks combined, the three cities were 40 percent black.

Everywhere an urban visitor might go in 1860 he would see a profusion of busy blacks. If he went to the bustling iron foundries, tobacco factories, or huge flour mills of Richmond, he would see hired slave laborers. If he visited the shipyards of Charleston he would see black carpenters and caulkers hard at work. If he traveled to Savannah, he would be impressed by the slaves operating the cotton presses and employed in various manufactories, and loading the ships with cotton and other products. In every city the visitor would note slave carriage drivers, wagoners, draymen carrying the goods of commerce. If streets or wharves were being built or repaired, there he most likely would see slave laborers; black carpenters and bricklayers, cabinetmakers and coachmakers toiled in every city. There were in addition slave painters and plasterers, tailors and tinners, barbers and bakers and butchers, porters and printers, washerwomen and fishermen. In

New Orleans slave blacksmiths made much of the ornate wrought iron balcony railings, window grilles, fences, and gates for which the city is famous. If the imaginary visitor went to the market, he would find most of the meat, fish, vegetables, fruit, and poultry products prepared, delivered, and sold by slaves—though here too, as in all the occupations, free blacks participated. Moreover, most of the buyers would be black women, sent out by their mistresses to do the marketing, and such a crowd of black faces would the visitor see and such a hubbub of black voices would he hear that he might momentarily wonder if he were in a black nation. The percentage of urban whites who owned one or more slaves was more than double the percentage of the entire South, though the typical urban dweller possessed only one or two women employed as domestics. Periodically urban whites worried about the large slave population in their midst and discussed their economic value in relation to their supposed potential for harm, but in every case the blacks' indispensability—particularly those who were highly skilled or those providing domestic labor—prevented permanent steps being taken to reduce their numbers appreciably. As slave prices shot up in the last antebellum decade, the percentage of whites who held slaves dropped, but the average size of holdings increased. Even the architecture of many of the cities—rear yards or patios enclosed with high walls and an absence of connecting alleys—was evidence of the ever-present slave population and a concern on the part of the owners both to confine them and minimize their ability to communicate with one another.

Their owners' efforts notwithstanding, urban slaves were able to meet, share ideas, and shape their own world beyond their masters' walls. Whether working with other slaves in factories and shops or on roadbeds and wharves, or mingling while at market or performing other domestic chores, slaves in the city never lived in isolation. If they were domestics, outside the master's house they found a network of slave and free black institutions, gathering places, even self-help organizations. Beyond his owner's door a slave could practically disappear temporarily in a black underground. This was far more true of those slaves employed in nondomestic occupations. Even more so than in rural industrial pursuits, urban slaves gained enlarged freedom of action. Employers increasingly utilized the overwork system of bonus pay—by the end of the period this became so standard that slaves sometimes refused to work where incentive pay was not given—and slaves grew to expect cash bonuses almost as a right. This incentive enhanced their self-esteem and allowed them to develop some control over their lives. With their extra funds they bought small necessities and luxuries. Grogshops and cook shops (small restaurants) emerged that catered to this black clientele. These were often run by enterprising free blacks, although there were always whites who for the sake of profits would violate the prevailing racial etiquette. In the large cities many industrial owners of slaves, seeking to avoid the expense and especially the disciplinary responsibility of housing them in company barracks, began the practice of giving each a cash payment in lieu of board and lodging. Though most whites objected, companies preferred this method and slaves greatly favored it. Bondsmen then had the freedom of choosing where they would live, and with whom. Black boardinghouses arose, and segregated black settlements developed on the outskirts of many southern cities. Prior to this, southern cities had been almost completely integrated residentially, and they remained more so than northern cities throughout the period. Buying their own food, renting their own often dingy rooms, competing for overtime work, urban slaves had a life far different from that of the majority of blacks on large plantations.

As the price of slaves increased, capital-starved entrepreneurs turned more and more to hiring slave operatives. Since the eighteenth century, slave hiring had been common in urban areas, but higher prices and the growing scale of industry accelerated the trend. Slaves were usually leased for one-year periods, though there were shorter contracts and they could be subleased. Cities developed certain sections that by tradition became the slave-hiring mart, and even slave-hiring agents emerged who mediated between owner and employer. In such owner-involved hiring arrangements, the slave's attitude toward his potential employer counted as much as it did in rural industrial slavery. Particularly in the larger cities, where an unhappy slave could disappear forever in the anonymity of the crowds, owners sought to avoid employers whom they feared would either harm their slave property or give them cause to run away. Employers of course sought to avoid reputations that interfered with their hiring needs, and they had early discovered that grossly mistreated slaves could by malingering, sabotage, or even arson easily retaliate. Hence the recourse to the overwork bonus system, which operated to the advantage of both the slave and employer.

In every southern city another process of slave hiring evolved that was even more to the advantage of the slave, that of self-hiring. Bondsmen were given authority by their masters to seek their own employer and strike a deal, returning to the owner an agreed-upon portion of the hire salary. Slave artisans—carpenters, bricklayers, engineers, and the like—were particularly adept at finding suitable employment, but less skilled laborers also often bargained with employers. Throughout much of the antebellum period there was a shortage of laborers for hire in the cities (a condition that population growth and immigration was beginning to change in the last years of the era), and slaves learned how to use the demand for their labor to good effect. Employers competed with each other for slaves, and this, more than any humane motives, caused the employers to avoid the worst labor abuses of which early industrialization was capable. There is evidence of slaves "shopping" for employers and even checking on those who offered them jobs. While masters may have doubted the wisdom of allowing their slaves such antonomy, they too recognized that it was to their advantage that their slave property be sufficiently fed, not overworked, and content not to resort to running away.

As with the overwork bonus pay and the boarding-out system, periodically criticism arose against the growing tendency of slaves hiring themselves out. Worried citizens saw all kinds of troubles hatching as a result of slaves making do for themselves, and crime and rebellion were often pointed to as the sure offspring of such lax procedures. Occasionally restrictions (usually temporary) were placed against one or another of these methods, and night watches were sporadically strengthened and then allowed to dwindle; special city courts—which were remarkably respectful of slaves' procedural rights—were organized with jurisdiction over black crime. But, everything considered, local government was too weak, and whites too comfortable with the system of black employment (and accustomed to being surrounded by slave laborers), to control effectively or limit significantly the quasi freedom that many urban slaves had gained for themselves.

There were also in every southern city a number of slaves, sometimes called "virtually free negroes," who might more accurately be called "free slaves." These persons, unsupervised by their legal owners, often ran their own businesses, accumulated property, traveled without passes, and lived virtually as though they were free. On occasion slaves were bought by patrons (or, in some areas, Quakers), then allowed to live unsupervised (and hence as free blacks) even though the laws usually required slaves actually freed either to leave the state or to post a substantial bond. On other occasions prosperous quasi-free urban slaves would buy their children or spouse, and then—without receiving official manumission papers, which sometimes required a legislative act— let them live as free (though technically slave). James P. Thomas, a free slave of Nashville who had been purchased by his mother, became a prominent and moderately wealthy businessman, and he associated with an entire community of "free slaves" in the city that numbered several hundred. Thomas owned a prosperous barbershop, and other unsupervised free slave entrepreneurs were hackmen with their own coaches and horses, ran various shops, or were skilled craftsmen. Such blacks were not really free, but their independence set them apart from other urban slaves whose lives were more closely regulated by their masters.

On the plantations owners often removed themselves from the harshest aspects of slavery by having the overseers or drivers handle disciplinary problems. In the cities employers set the slaves to work, and agencies were developed that for a fee whipped or otherwise disciplined slaves, saving the owner (or employer) from a distasteful task. Whites continued to regard urban slavery as a viable and convenient institution, and bondsmen knew they lived better lives in the cities and preferred their greater freedom there from white supervision. From the eighteenth century on, plantation runaways headed for the South's few cities, seeking not only the obscurity offered by numbers but the manifold advantages of urban life. And at least from the mid-eighteenth century the urban black community harbored runaways, helped them find an identity and livelihood in the city, or assisted them in passing through to another destination. Especially was this true for skilled plantation artisans, who occasionally disappeared only to emerge as a "free" black in some southern city. In ways only partially understood, the beckoning city served as a safety valve for plantation slaves who otherwise might have either committed suicide or killed their master. Troublesome urban slaves were sometimes sold to unsuspecting planters. As a result of abuses, slave traders bringing coffles of out-of-state slaves into a region were required by law to guarantee that the bondsmen were "well-behaved," but in practice the system of caveat emptor prevailed.

Urban slaves in cooperation with free blacks established several institutions of great cultural importance. In some cities schools were begun, though they had constant opposition from the legal authorities and were consequently short-lived. Other kinds of self-help organizations were founded, but the most important urban black institution was the church. Sometimes an adjunct to a white church, at other times a completely independent black entity, African churches (as they were often called) grew to enormous size, gave blacks ways of training leaders and exercising group discipline, provided for moral growth, and proved to be of immense social and cultural importance to the emerging black communities. As on the plantation, religion was a major factor in shaping the black character.

Yet despite all the advantages of urban living, slavery was still slavery. Laws were written to protect an owner's property, not a slave's rights. Whippings, treadmills, stocks, cages were employed to discipline the slave work force. By modern standards the working hours were long, the conditions often dangerous and unhealthy. Even the most advantaged urban slave was reminded daily of his bondage. Free slave James P. Thomas was once severely reprimanded for venturing a political opinion to a white customer in his barbershop. An urban slave could be sold and separated from his family; he could be sent to work at locations and at jobs he disliked; he could not testify against whites in court. While his situation was in general superior to that of his plantation brothers, it depended on the shaky ground of compromise and mutual accommodation where the master always ultimately had the upper hand. In terms of material well-being and perhaps even health care, the urban slave was often better off than an impoverished free black, maybe even a propertyless, unskilled white. But his greater autonomy, his glimpse of freedom and responsibility, made every relatively fortunate urban slave at least occasionally conscious of his fundamental lack of liberty. And that, in sum, was the essence of slavery.

From the very beginning of the black presence on the North American mainland, there had been some free Negroes. Before slavery hardened and became largely a matter of race, at least some blacks in the Chesapeake were freed after serving a set term of years. Others, by proving white ancestry or prior conversion to Christianity, were emancipated; still others were manumitted as a reward for a particularly meritorious act. By 1700 there was a small, struggling, free black community, numbering approximately 1,817 in Maryland in 1755 and 1,800 in Virginia in 1782. These figures grew both by natural means and by occasional manumissions. Now and then a white planter would free (usually by will) his black lover and the mulatto offspring of their miscegenational affair. Consequently the tiny free black community before the Revolution was noticeably more light-skinned than the slave population and contained more women than men, and, in part because mulatto children were often given special treatment, the free blacks as a group were more skilled, more likely to be of the artisan class, than the slave population as a whole.

Parenthetically, the amount of miscegenation in the Old South is as indeterminable as it is controversial. Certainly it occurred, perhaps more often on large plantations where overseers or the sons of the planter may have been the aggressors. Because in the Old South the whites were in the majority, there were enough white women for families to become the norm, and virulent racism as well as Christianity acted as restraints against interracial sex (which, after all, was often adultery), miscegenation was far less common than elsewhere in American slave societies. Sometimes true love was at the center of miscegenational affairs; sometimes black women initiated the affair in an effort to gain special favors for themselves or their children; sometimes unscrupulous white men forced themselves upon powerless slave women. Rape did not have to occur often to become a real threat and a constant fear to black women. Yet the antebellum South was not a giant brothel, as some abolitionists charged and as much trashy contemporary fiction portrays.

These characteristics of the pre-Revolutionary free blacks in the

United States were particularly true for the emerging free black population in French- then Spanish-held Louisiana. Because of a drastic shortage of European women, the French and Spanish soldiers and government officials mated with Indian and slave women. The resulting mulatto offspring were usually freed, often with the father openly admitting his paternity. A separate free black community emerged. For special historical reasons the free black population of Louisiana had more autonomy than did free blacks elsewhere, and they emerged almost as another caste in a three-tiered racial society: whites, "free people of color" (*gens de couleur*), and slaves. Under French rule there was a dire shortage of laborers, and with the slave population threatening to outnumber the white, the authorities respected the free black community and sought an alliance with it in case a slave insurrection erupted. Then when Spanish authorities took over Louisiana, they expanded the right of the free blacks in an effort to gain their support and thereby cement Spanish hegemony over the colony. The Spanish hoped to wean the free blacks away from their French sympathies and use them to control the slave population. When the Americans purchased Louisiana in 1803 they followed the same policy, implicitly acknowledging the power and influence of the free blacks. For example, Andrew Jackson in the Battle of New Orleans called upon free black troops to help defeat the British. The free blacks were especially numerous, wealthy, and influential in that city. As a light-skinned, skilled, and sophisticated—usually French-speaking, sometimes even European-educated—urban minority, the New Orleans free people of color were a distinct class that helped make the Crescent City the least American of U.S. cities.

The events of the era of the American Revolution had an impact on the national free black population that served to differentiate the Upper South's free black community from that of the Lower South. By the time of the Revolution, the agricultural economy of the Upper South was changing, moving from tobacco toward wheat and truck crops, neither of which required as intensive labor as "the stinking weed." One of the consequences of this crop shift was an apparent surplus of slaves in the Chesapeake, and for the three-quarters of a century, 1785-1860, there was a significant slave migration from Virginia and Maryland to the Deep South. The agricultural revolution in the Chesapeake influenced, and was in turn affected by, changing attitudes toward slavery. Many slave owners, caught up in the Revolutionary rhetoric about liberty and the rights of man, applied their principles to their bondsmen, recognized the contradictions involved in owning slaves and fighting for freedom, and moved forthrightly to liberate their slaves. (Many other slave owners, just as principled, had countervailing scruples against immediate emancipation, fearing a genocidal race war. They could countenance manumission only if it were accompanied by colonization of the ex-slaves outside the nation. In addition, perhaps others, like Jefferson, were also in debt and thus bound by law not to free their slaves. But the various reasons why emancipation sentiment was not unanimous belong to another book, not this one.) As a result of the Revolutionary desire of many slaveholders to liberate their bondsmen, the free black population soared in the two decades following the creation of the new nation. In the three censuses of 1790, 1800, and 1810, the South's free black population grew from 32,357 to 61,241 to 108,265, or an 89.3 percent increase between 1790 and 1800, and a 76.8 percent increase between 1800 and 1810. The bulk of this increase occurred in the Upper South, whose free blacks outnumbered those of the Lower South 98,000 to 14,000 in 1810. This largely Upper South principled manumission was indiscriminate, not confined to light-skinned "fancy girls" (mistresses) and their children. Instead many slave owners emancipated their entire work force.

This large-scale manumission changed the nature of the Upper South free black population: it became less urban, more equal in sex ratio, and darker skinned. In the Lower South, where slavery became more firmly entrenched in the 1790s, there was no widespread manumission. But the Haitian Revolution produced a flood of free mulattos who, having initially sided with the French, with the victory of Toussaint l'Ouverture were forced to seek asylum elsewhere. Most came to Charleston, Mobile, and New Orleans. Thus the free black population of the Deep South had a fresh infusion of light-skinned, highly skilled, urban dwellers. Hence the Upper South's free black population, much the larger, was darker and more rural; the Lower South's population was lighter and more urban. (The proportion of free blacks who were urban dwellers in

1860 was 32.3 percent in the Upper South, 53.2 percent in the Lower South; the proportion of mixed racial ancestry was 35 percent in the Upper South, 75.8 percent in the Lower South.) In part because as a group they were less skilled and more identified with their slave brothers, free blacks of the Upper South tended to be more harshly treated than their Lower South counterparts, who not only were more likely to be skilled and prosperous but also more often enjoyed the support of a white patron. After about 1820, with slavery ever more accepted as a permanent, profitable, and positive institution, the number of slave manumissions slowed to a trickle; the free black population increased primarily by natural means. No doubt many free blacks in the border states moved North, and in the cities throughout the region an indeterminable number of very light-skinned free blacks silently passed over the color line and emerged as free whites. Even so, the southern free black population in 1860 totalled 261,918, and in Maryland 49.1 percent of all blacks were free (in Delaware, the percentage was 91.7, in the District of Columbia, 77.8). In the entire South in 1860, 6.2 percent of all Negroes were free, with the proportion in the Upper South (12.8) eight times greater than in the Deep South (1.5).

Region-wide, about two-thirds of all free blacks lived in rural areas, and most were farmers. Some of course worked in the turpentine, lumber, and mining industries, but most were agriculturalists. Although free blacks were never prohibited from owning property, relatively few ever became landowners. In North Carolina, for example, less than 4 percent of the free Negroes possessed land. Most rural free blacks were tenants, hiring out their labor to white farmers and planters who used them to augment their work force in times of peak demand like harvest. A tiny minority of free blacks owned slaves, usually their wife or children, although a handful became planters with dozens of slave field hands and occasionally a white overseer. Periodically the white authorities would put restrictions on the freedom of movement of free blacks or limit their participation in certain trades, but these strictures usually came after slave insurrection scares and were seldom enforced. Free blacks could vote in North Carolina and Tennessee until the mid-1830s, perhaps controlling the balance of power in several counties. They apparently voted even later in some parts of Louisiana, but more because unscrupulous white politicians needed their ballots to stuff the boxes than out of any commitment to broadening the franchise. While most rural free blacks lived on the farms of their employers, in some regions small groups of them clustered together in crossroads communities. Scattered across the region, often working side by side in the fields with slaves, rural free blacks did not develop a separate culture and were often lumped together with slaves by whites. This was especially so in the Upper South, and especially in the last years of the 1850s, and helps explain why the laws regulating free blacks were harsher, more like slave codes, there. However, in the cities of over 10,000 population, where some 67,000 free blacks lived, real free black communities developed.

The cities were remarkably integrated residentially, though at the end of the period black shantytowns had begun to develop on the suburban fringes. Many prosperous free blacks ran thriving businesses, including hotels, restaurants, barbershops, cabinet-makers' shops, and the like. They often owned slaves or hired free black, and even white, workers. On good terms with their white clientele, some of the wealthiest free blacks—like the barber William Johnson of Natchez—socialized with whites, frequented the race tracks, exhorted their black employees to work hard and be thrifty, and even purchased a plantation in conscious imitation of the road to white respectability. Living in the most prestigious parts of town, such exceptional free blacks had fine houses that often overshadowed those of their white neighbors.

Of course most free blacks were poor though hard-working. Competing with southern whites, urban slaves, and, toward the end of the era, immigrant artisans, they had to scramble for a living. Often they lived on the margin of legality, trading surreptitiously with slaves and traveling and peddling their skills or wares in violation of increasingly harsh restrictions placed upon their freedom of action. The more skilled were dependent upon the support and patronage of whites and suffered the opposition of vocal white competitors; the less skilled caterers and grogshop keepers depended upon a slave clientele and were constantly criticized by those whites who feared the consequences of increasing black autonomy. The most skilled, prosperous, and influential free blacks, those who might have become the leaders of the united black community, were too aware of their privileges, and thus conscious of what they had to lose, to identify with the slaves. For that reason free blacks in the cities were often a conservative force and more likely to report rumored slave rebellions than, like Denmark Vesey, to lead one.

In a more subtle way the presence of free blacks may have defused potential slave rebellion by offering an escape for discontented slaves. The existence throughout the South, but particularly in cities, of a reservoir of free blacks allowed skilled, articulate slaves to escape from bondage and remain near loved ones. When discontent reached the boiling point, a slave could run away and emerge in a city or another rural region and with his slave-learned skills live as a freeman. Even though blacks were presumed to be slaves and the burden of proof of freedom lay with them, enforcement was so lax, and free blacks sufficiently skilled in forged documents and artful in subterfuge, that many successfully carried off their escape to freedom. Far more slaves probably achieved this kind of self-created deliverance than successfully followed the Pole Star via the Underground Railroad to freedom in the North or Canada. And with the harsh restrictions against free Negroes in the North, many free blacks may have preferred more familiar surroundings in which to live out their freedom.

Yet within their urban communities free blacks, to an even greater degree than urban slaves, evolved their own cultural life. Hemmed in by repressive laws and threatened with white competition and occasional demands that they be deported or reenslaved, they created separate black institutions that catered to their needs and allowed self-expression, individual growth, and enlarged self-esteem. Some prosperous free blacks, enjoying the benefits of their business and living in a fine house, shared in the city's larger cultural and intellectual life. In New Orleans the wealthy, educated free people of color had an intellectual and cultural life, replete with literary journals and opera, that rivaled the high cultural traditions of the whites. In other cities, however, it was the folk culture of the free blacks that dominated black life. In every city the autonomous black churches were the leading black institution. Quite often the largest religious establishments in the city, the churches set a moral tone that was quite consonant with white middle-class virtues. Usually urban slaves attended these churches, but positions of leadership were typically reserved for free blacks. The free blacks were also proud of their lighter color, and occasionally brown-skin organizations arose. In concert with the churches, though often independent of them, were various free black self-help organizations: grammar schools, fraternal orders, burial insurance programs, and the like. In their churches, their stores and grog-shops, their music and popular amusement, free blacks lived their own lives, with little reference to the white culture.

At times the upper-class free blacks consciously aped white society; at other times they remained truer to their slave sources. But ironically, as sectional tensions between North and South increased in the 1850s and white southerners grew more paranoid about the survival of the institution of slavery, they came to worry more about the living contradiction to slavery that the free blacks represented. If blacks were natural slaves, and inferior, whence free blacks, who often prospered because of their skills? The growing white population eased the urban labor shortage and produced white craftsmen who objected to black competition; calls were heard for colonizing all free blacks or pushing them back into slavery. This never happened, in large part because their economic contribution was too great, but it highlighted the precarious social and legal position they occupied. Categorized increasingly in the late 1850s with the slave masses, free blacks began to accept their racial identity. During the Civil War and Reconstruction, former free blacks emerged as the leaders of a remarkably united common black front. Class divisions existed, as did those based upon color, but they were minimal everywhere except New Orleans and Charleston. More important was the extent to which prewar free black leaders became the political, cultural, and business leaders of the freedmen. In the same way that antebellum urban whites, in their legal restrictions against urban slaves and free blacks, were unknowingly learning the rudiments of a later, more elaborate Jim Crow exclusionary system, antebellum free black craftsmen and businessmen were gaining experience for that day when segregation forced them to do business among and for a black clientele. Out of the prewar free black population largely came the postwar black middle and professional classes.

As the mere existence of industrial, urban, and quasi-managerial slaves suggests, much less the presence of more than a quarter-million free blacks, the institution of slavery in the Old South was more open, more flexible than is often recognized. Oppressive features were everywhere present, and slaves and free blacks as a group were nearly always at the bottom of the heap. Their lives were more restricted, their hardships more severe, their punishments more barbaric, than those of any other group in antebellum southern society. Yet the system never became so rigid, the control so complete, as to snuff out the human creativity and ingenuity of the slaves. We still have much to learn about the survival of human dignity and purpose under extreme conditions, but the culture and personality of bondsmen in the Old South speak volumes of the will to survive not simply physically, but with a remarkable degree of wholeness. Slaves never became simply victims; they were survivors. The values that allowed them to persevere, the culture they evolved and created in so doing, and their various responses to slavery, are our next subject.

6. Community, Culture, and Rebellion

Black cultural life before about 1720 in what is now the South was stunted because of the small numbers of slaves and their sparse distribution across an almost impenetrably wooded terrain. When scattered slaveholders owned only two or three slaves apiece, with few holding more than ten, blacks had little chance to create a community. It was difficult for them to find suitable marriage partners because of the imbalance in the sex ratio and the difficulty of communication and transportation on the southern colonial frontier. Family life was constricted, and the opportunities for talking, singing, sharing with other blacks were severely limited. Community by definition requires the presence of others, and culture becomes sterile and dies when its adherents live in isolation. In the seventeenth century and into the first decades of the eighteenth, when the relatively few black slaves lived interspersed with large numbers of white indentured servants, when slaves typically lived in the house of their master and worked and ate with him, when they seldom spent their leisure time with other blacks, not only was there little sense of a black community, but whatever African elements had previously existed in their world view were almost bleached out. Surrounded by whites, slaves' memories of African ways were not constantly reinforced. Rather, the white man's ways, at first strange and confusing, gradually came to replace much of the slaves' Old World culture.

After 1720 there was a huge upsurge in African imports, and in the next six decades about 60 percent of the total slaves imported from Africa arrived. At the middle of this period, the American

Slave population was more African than ever before or since. By this time, about mid-century, slaves who came to America before 1720 had become acclimated and had borne children. These creole youths—completely adjusted to the New World's climate and diseases, with a more equal sex ratio and the women reaching menarche by age 18—insured rapid natural population growth. The increase in the number of American-born blacks occurred at roughly the same time as the increase in African imports (the booming economy had an almost limitless demand for labor) and was more significant because it insured that slaves in the South, unlike those in other places in the New World, would be overwhelmingly American born.

The burgeoning numbers of American slaves, however, bore forever the impress of Africa from those who arrived during the 1720-80 peak in transatlantic imports. At the very moment when population growth was providing enough slaves for the beginning of a black community, when the average size of slaveholdings was increasing to the point that slaves could find mates and create families, when improved transportation along with swollen numbers meant slaves could develop ties of friendship and kinship that transcended plantation boundaries, a black culture was aborning. Into this proto-community with its developing culture came the African migrants with their fresh memories of African beliefs, rituals, customs, and styles of artistic and musical expression. The newcomers, mostly young males, were of neither the sex nor age to be optimum preservers of cultural traits, but what they carried with them was absorbed by the growing American-born slave population, which, because of its thriving family life, was an excellent receiver, preserver, and transmitter of culture. As the slave numbers increased in the eighteenth century, social tensions exacerbated the difference between the white society and the black community. Slaves felt this widening chasm as the more casual intermingling of the seventeenth century receded into history. Thrown more on their own, segregated from whites more than in the past, blacks began groping to create a better definition of who they were. African elements became a part of the emerging Afro-American culture of the mid-eighteenth century.

While these African seeds fell on fertile soil in the 1730s and 1740s, it was a field whose contours had in the preceding half-century been significantly shaped by European—specifically English—attitudes. The English or American contours helped to determine both which seeds took root and flourished and the shape and texture of the resulting growth. The initial slave community, having developed amidst a vastly dominant English culture with few recent African imports, was relatively Europeanized. Because of the difficulties involved in transporting a complete African world view to a new environment, those African elements that found some congruence with Euro-American (or American Indian) ways had a far better chance of taking root in the South. There was a tremendous diversity of West African cultures and languages, few ritual specialists with detailed knowledge of African ceremonies were imported, and the American flora and fauna did not provide obvious substitutes for African ritual ingredients. For these reasons specific African "survivals" were uncommon; rather, Europeanized American slaves borrowed more generalized African cultural styles and recast them in New World form. The result was a dynamic, evolving Afro-American culture that grew to be quite different from both its English and African roots. In art, in music, and in religion, the confluence of English and African styles produced in the nineteenth century a recognizable slave culture that in its very existence says much about the institution of slavery and the character of the slaves.

The labor demands on tobacco and rice plantations were not as harsh as those on West Indian sugar islands, and most owners lived on their plantations and approved of slave families. After foreign slave imports legally ceased in 1808, slave owners gradually realized that slave families and natural reproduction were absolutely indispensable to the region's economy. The number of slaves multiplied more than 600 percent in the seven decades after 1790, and the sex ratio of slaves in 1860 was more nearly equal than that of southern whites. This huge increase made possible the antebellum slave community and sustained a slave culture separate from the white culture.

Even without a constant infusion of fresh African influences the emergent Afro-American community kept alive and constantly reshaped its African heritage. African elements in the culture, however, were far less pronounced than elsewhere in the Americas. There was in the South a far higher percentage of whites than in the Caribbean or Latin America, and whites and blacks were much more intermingled. Consequently bondsmen in the Old South were much more influenced by European attitudes than were slaves elsewhere in the Americas. Had not the slave community developed in the mid-eighteenth century, southern slaves might have lost almost all their African heritage and been shaped much more in the mold of their owners. Yet a slave community did emerge in the late colonial period, combining African and American forms in new ways, with those elements of the two cultures that bore some resemblance to each other having a better chance of surviving in a revised form. Once the slave community had succeeded in forging a separate culture, that culture grew, evolved, and developed a life of its own, in many ways impervious to the changes in the surrounding white culture. For that reason Afro-American culture of the generation before the Civil War was more Africanized than scholars once thought, far more Europeanized than the culture in any other New World slave community, and more distinct than antebellum whites ever realized.

A generation or more ago it was academically fashionable to describe the results of the Middle Passage as the complete obliteration from the surviving slaves of any and all traces of African heritage. By implication the personalities of the newly arrived bondsmen were plastic and were to be molded by the white man, with only stray vestigial remnants of African culture remaining. Recent scholarship has corrected this view. Recognizing the impossibility of transplanting African cultural systems intact, historians and anthropologists have shown that underlying concepts, motifs, even styles of life, have persisted, albeit in different configurations. Folk art and crafts, music, folktales, and religious ideas have survived more successfully, in part because planters often discounted their significance and hence overlooked them, and in part too because often there were subtle resemblances between African and Euro-American folk practices that served to reinforce African memories and facilitate their survival in a revised, hybrid form.

In the same way that slaves preserved the core of African kinship systems in the New World by developing fictive kin networks and held on to African patterns of naming even while using European names, various folk arts adapted to local or Euro-American necessities kept alive a hidden, fundamental African principle of design or purpose. But because they were expressed in American garb, their Old World patterns have often been difficult to notice. By the first third of the eighteenth century, for example, and possibly earlier, South Carolina slaves in the rice-growing regions were weaving flat, coiled-grass baskets used as fanning trays to winnow the rice after it had been hulled. In shape, in design, in execution, these baskets were identical to those made and used in Africa along the Grain Coast, yet the South Carolina and Georgia baskets were made of pliable American grasses. The bondsmen may well have learned which grasses to use from American Indians who also wove coiled baskets, but if so, even while adopting a New World material they maintained Old World styles. Later, in Mississippi, for example, pinebelt slaves seem to have followed the Indians in making baskets from pine needles, but again the resulting baskets are recognizably different.

Similar adaptations to New World materials occurred in other realms of folk art and culture. Africans familiar with cane fifes made musical instruments from the switch cane that grew throughout southern bottomlands; the African stringed instrument, which Jefferson labeled a "banjar," developed into a squirrel (or raccoon) skin stretched across a cut gourd attached to a wooden frame or handle and, as the banjo, became an American folk instrument. An extant eighteenth-century watercolor depicts a black musician playing such an instrument, and architect Benjamin Latrobe described a handmade slave banjo he had seen in New Orleans in 1819. Woodcarving was another common folk art in Africa, and several surviving examples from the antebellum South suggest the preservation of African motifs and color patterns. A remarkably carved wooden drum from seventeenth- or mid-eighteenth-century Virginia, now on exhibit in the British Museum, reveals obvious African designs and shapes and yet is made of American cedar and deerskin. Women sewed quilts utilizing available materials, but the patterns (particularly the irregular squares) were definitely African in origin, and the parallels between slave and African textile designs are many.

Blacks were involved in ironworking, and slave blacksmiths often made artistic hinges, flatwork, and gates in addition to horseshoes and tools. As mentioned earlier, much of the ornamental iron scrollwork in cities like New Orleans was the product of slave craftsmen. A striking wrought-iron sculpture of a man, dating from before 1800 and discovered on the site of an Alexandria, Virginia, blacksmith shop and slave quarters, vividly suggests the ironwork of the Western Sudan. Most of the jobs turned out by slave blacksmiths obviously followed the styles and served the purposes of the white employer-owners, but now and again glimpses of an African heritage appear. The same was true for slave potters. There was, of course, a long tradition of pottery in Africa, but most potters were women. In this nation the potters were mainly men, and they had to learn the European techniques of the treadle-operated wheel (as opposed to completely hand-shaped clay) and kiln-baked ceramic glazes. Even so, many of the surviving vessels from antebellum potteries bear unmistakable African traits. The small "face vessels" made in South Carolina in the 1850s were stoneware cups and jugs with boldly sculptured faces recalling statuary in the Zaire-Angola region. The use of only one or two colors, with eyes of a separate material, are very reminiscent of African styles. In other words, slave potters using Euro-American techniques and ceramic forms produced a decorated face vessel that still possessed recognizable African traits. They were neither exactly African nor exactly American artifacts; they represented an emerging Afro-American culture. It was as though an underlying African grammar was being subtly expressed in a European vocabulary.

Blacks may very well have influenced southern vernacular architecture in important ways. The shotgun house—a rectangular structure with small rooms lined up one behind another, the short (gable) end facing the street—seems definitely related to the gabled rectangular huts of the African rain forest. Certainly the shotgun house represented an architectural concept different from either the log cabin of the frontier, whose dimensions were more square and whose gable ends were perpendicular to the road, or the more formal or Greek Revival styles. The shotgun house may have entered New Orleans via Haitian free blacks, and the style persists there today in a variety of decorated forms because the house lots are so narrow. Yet even in rural areas shotgun tenant shacks are still found, with the gable end facing the highway.

The front porch, so common today in the South, may also have been an Afro-Caribbean contribution to folk housing. Certainly the wide, open porch structures of the South are not found on

European homes, or in the architecture of the colonial Chesapeake, or the Carolinas. Porches and verandas seem first to have appeared about the time the Haitian refugees began to arrive at the end of the eighteenth century. Broad porches sweeping across the front (and even around the sides) of houses became common after the 1840s, and as a comfortable accommodation to the warm southern climate they came to be a hallmark of southern folk architecture.

The fundamental point, of course, is that the larger American culture is an amalgam of different influences. Europeans, Africans, and American Indians borrowed from each other, and the various heritages blended in complex ways. Each group was receptive to change, and one group would often take another's trait and reshape it and claim it for its own. The southern whites, for example, adopted the banjo of African origin, and it has emerged as a characteristic folk instrument of the rural white South. Eighteenth- and nineteenth-century blacks so adopted a European instrument, the fiddle, to their music that slave fiddlers became a stock character in the Old South. Now, however, the fiddle is almost completely absent from the musical repertoire of blacks. Blacks borrowed the trumpet from European-influenced brass bands in the Mississippi River cities, and it became the characteristic instrument of the black jazz bands of the early twentieth century. Indian foods, herbal lore, basket-weaving techniques, styles of dugout canoes, and so on, resembled many African practices, and with this New World reinforcement many African styles persisted. Because the planter did not care, for example, what pattern existed in the winnowing basket as long as the slaves worked at processing the rice, subtle African ideas about style and form continued under the noses of planters who otherwise consciously tried to eradicate all traces of African heritage.

Early travel accounts reveal a rich musical tradition in Africa, though to European ears the African music sounded exotic and decidedly non-Western. Because these early travelers were not trained musicologists and had no recording devices, they found it difficult to describe the peculiar character of the music they heard. The strangely complex rhythmic structure nearly always stood out, as did the evident role of improvisation, the strong beat, the communal nature of much of the singing, and the vigorous, even athletic dancing that often accompanied the music. Identical problems face the researcher who tries to understand slave music in the Americas. While there is abundant evidence of its difference, of its "African" qualities, the imprecision of the contemporary accounts renders sophisticated musicological analysis extremely difficult and tentative. One thing is clear: more than perhaps any other aspect of African culture, music survived the ordeal of the Middle Passage to play a significant role in the lives of American slaves and contribute greatly to indigenous forms of American music.

Slave traders often used music and forced dancing as a means of exercising slaves cooped up in coastal African barracoons or brought to the deck from the steamy holds of slave ships. Occasionally even African musical instruments were taken aboard the ships to provide a beat for the involuntary dances. We know practically nothing about slave music in the mainland colonies in the seventeenth and early eighteenth centuries, though we might imagine that there were either a few surviving African instruments or, more likely, American-made replicas. The slaves sang to pass the time and set a rhythm for certain repetitive tasks like rowing or pounding a pestle. For the first century after 1619, there were so few Africans and they were so intermixed with white indentured servants that much subtle, unconscious interchange of musical styles and songs probably occurred. Perhaps it was during this period that numerous slaves adapted the European fiddle to their own purpose and learned the many traditional English ballads and hornpipes that enabled black musicians later to become popular fixtures at white dances, parties, and weddings. Probably Africans borrowed more musical styles at this time than ever again, but the interchange must have been continuous. However, the upsurge of African imports from 1720 to 1770 caused a momentary African shift in the emerging Afro-American culture, and African music and dance styles were immeasurably strengthened in these years. Repeatedly contemporaries in the mid-eighteenth century remarked on the presence of strange (that is, African) music among the slaves, and the first published American mention of the banjo occurs in 1754.

Whites recognized the importance of music to the blacks and seldom interfered with slaves' singing or making music. Horns and drums were usually outlawed because they could conceivably be used to send messages about a planned slave uprising, but more innocuous black music was accepted. Planters realized that contented slaves were less troublesome and more productive, and if singing and musical entertainment in the slave quarters helped relieve the tensions and fatigue of the workday, then who was to object? Slave traders occasionally used fiddlers to accompany their slave coffles on their arduous overland treks. On numerous plantations toward the end of day, when slaves sat outside their cabins for a brief moment of rest and conversation, the local fiddler or banjoist would bring out his instrument and temporarily banish the cares of the world. The black "musicianers," as their fellow bondsmen called them, enlivened the social life in the slave quarters. Entertaining their fellows in the evenings, playing for their dances, adding a bit of zest and joy to cold winter nights and setting toes to tapping and hands a-clapping when the hot summer sun went down—here the fiddlers and banjo players enriched the lives of everyone in the black community. Music is a superb social medicine, soothing tired muscles and raw nerves, driving away for the moment resentments and frustrations. Solomon Northup, a free black musician who was captured and sold into bondage in Louisiana, left a moving account of how his fiddle, his music, helped him through many a weary night. Slave mothers, like all other mothers, sang songs to soothe their babies. When no drum was allowed, blacks tapped sticks together or against the door jamb, clicked spoons or bones, tapped their feet, or clapped their hands together and against their thighs and shoulders ("patting juba") in time with the music. Occasionally masters purchased musicians in order to control the other slaves, but even so, the slaves used the music for joyous escape and creative expression. Theirs was a life of bondage—the secret of survival was to find ways to endure and gain pleasure and fulfillment from an existence that promised little. Because musicians added so much to the well-being of their fellows, they stood high in slaves' esteem.

Every neighborhood seemed to have one consummate black fiddler appreciated as much by the white community as by the black. They were in great demand to play at balls and parties held by the great planters, and no dance or corn husking was held without the local slave musicians. Contemporary prints and woodcuts portray them entertaining at taverns, aboard steamboats, and around the verandas of their master's homes. Because their talent was in demand, black music-makers enjoyed an unusual position. Their masters commonly gave them permission to travel and time off from other chores; the slave instrumentalists contracted to play at balls, weddings, socials, and barn dances for a fee, which they customarily divided with their master. Like other slaves who had extra earnings, they purchased fancy clothes, extra food and drink, small luxuries for their families. Dressed up, able to travel within limits, a center of attention wherever he went, the slave musician had a special status. Masters prized them because of the additional money they earned and the entertainment they provided. Recognizing their value in the eyes of their owners, slave musicians often pressed for a greater degree of control over their lives and often won concessions.

Most of the slave music was communal and improvised. Whether the group was gathered around the slave cabin, or sitting in church, or working and singing in the fields, there was little solo singing. Rather, the group sang together, sometimes in response to a leader who lined out the verses (particularly when the song was a white-influenced religious one—frontier whites lined out their hymns too) and other times singing the chorus after verses sung out by the leader. While some songs had become standard and traditional, singers often took several familiar stanzas or a chorus and improvised additional verses to fit the circumstances. Special situations, individuals, and events thus entered the realm of song. Such impromptu compositions were communal, and listeners would add verses or snatches of a verse, and then the leader and the group would incorporate the newest ideas into the traditional song. Work songs, satiric songs, subtle protest songs, and especially spirituals were created in this fashion, having no one writer, no one text. Group singing was one way that the black community coalesced, with the individual drawn into identification with the group. This may very well have been a carry over from the African heritage, for in West African cultures no individual stood alone but instead conceived of himself as part of a larger kinship system. The blues, with its more individualistic focus, was a development of the post-Civil War American experience.

In Africa music was a constant part of life, for there were work songs, ceremonial songs, storytelling songs, songs for every occasion. In the antebellum United States we know far more about the spirituals, for by the time whites began systematically reporting slave music, the bondsmen had largely been evangelized into the South's Christian community. Witnesses have left accounts of slave workers in Richmond tobacco factories and black stevedores at dockside timing their work routines to the cadence of sacred songs. But slaves had a larger repertoire of song types than many strait-laced, "proper" observers noted, in part because slaves themselves apparently censored what they let whites hear. From at least the eighteenth century on there had been secular slave songs, with lyrics that were sarcastic, satiric (often directed at their masters), and even bawdy. Work songs varied with the occupation—field or industrial labor, corn husking, and so on—and the tempo and lyric were appropriate to the occasion. Boating songs, for example, had a slow, regular beat to which the oars were dipped, while the songs performed when shucking corn were rollicking and secular, prob-ably because of the whiskey, good food, and courting always associated with the harvest event.

The precise manner in which folk musical styles blend with each other and enter the musical mainstream is difficult to explicate. Surely the rhythmic complexity associated with Africa, along with the banjo and various rhythm instruments like the tambourine, became a part of the larger culture's musical tradition. Hand clap-ping in accompaniment to music may well have been a slave con-tribution, and fast-stepping dances like the jig probably represented an adaptation of African styles. The cakewalk of the slave may have been a caricature of more sedate, aristocratic white dances, as the frontier square dance of the white yeomen may have been a folk adaptation of more formal cotillion dancing. Semiprofessional black fiddlers and banjoists played for white dances, and whites often reported their pleasure in listening to slave singing; some-times plantation guests would be taken to the slave quarters to hear a folk "concert," and slaves would be brought to the big house to serenade listeners on the veranda. When blacks provided the musical accompaniment for white balls and parties, they of course played white tunes, but because of their skill at improvisation and rhythm, they might have produced "hotter," more jazzlike (to use a term not then invented) music than white musicians would have. We do not know for sure, though we are certain that in the antebellum South much musical intermingling of styles and influences occurred.

There was also among the slaves a rich tradition of folk tales and folk beliefs, and this folklore served functions far more important than simple amusement, though the tales were very entertaining. For a people prevented by law from attending schools or becoming literate (with occasional exceptions), some way other than the written word had to be employed to teach group values and preserve black identity. Children, for example, had to be socialized and taught survival skills and slave ethics. Coming from a region of the world where oral tradition was the prime repository of history and heritage, and largely cut off from the white society's literary mechanisms of culture transmission, slaves resorted to folk beliefs and tales to keep their culture alive. Life—the universe—was filled with danger, mystery, and caprice, and some means was required to explain, control, and understand the world. In the largest sense, of course, Christianity came to explain the purposes of life and suffering, as we shall see. But folk beliefs and tales not only helped one survive, they also offered insights and prescriptions outside the dominant society's comprehension. To the extent that slaves through their folklore were able to see the world in ways the whites were ignorant of, their folk beliefs and tales accentuated their cultural autonomy and provided role models and group values separate from the planters'.

Of course many slave beliefs about signs, superstitions, ghosts, and so on were similar to those held by the whites, for both accepted the legitimacy of the supernatural world. Both blended Christianity and superstitions, the result being theologically inconsistent but believable. Folk beliefs offered techniques to control the world in limited ways: one wore good luck charms, twisted one's pulled-out pocket to stop the call of a screech owl (whose voice signaled death), utilized certain rituals to distinguish liars from the truthful, administered potions to ward off disease and attract members of the opposite sex, even had "medicine" to prevent whippings from the overseer. Whatever the scientific efficacy of such beliefs, they often armed slaves psychologically to approach life more optimistically and with more zest than they would have done otherwise. Because they were in bondage and had little control over their daily lives, slaves put much store in semimagical folk beliefs that held out the promise of mastery of discrete parts of their life beyond the reach of the whites.

The question of origins is less important than that of function. Slaves held on to some vestiges of folklore from Africa, adopted some from those Euro-Americans with whom they had two centuries of contact, and both whites and blacks learned some folk beliefs and tales from the Indians, particularly in the frontier colonial days. But for whites with their hegemonic control of the society, folklore was more entertainment and less realistic (slaves had no place in their lore, for example, for fairy tales and tales of supermen like Mike Fink or Pecos Bill). Slaves utilized their folklore, syncretistic in origin as it was, for African-like functions, to explain, control, and understand their real lives.

The social uses of black folklore become clear when one examines the folktales, aphorisms, and sayings of the slaves. Black parents taught their children to watch their tongues, neither telling the master incriminating information about fellow slaves nor talking back in a manner likely to bring punishment. Folktales served this purpose, putting in memorable and often humorous form the wisdom and behavior necessary for survival. Slaves taught their children not to be too curious and to value the solidarity of the blacks and yet, paradoxically, in the ultimate sense to keep their own counsel—these lessons were taught by example and by retelling tales that made the point unforgettable: "A smart redbird don't have much to say." "De fox wants to know how de rabbit's gittin on." "Better not laugh too quick at de runt pig." The applicability of such sayings is obvious.

Many of the tales were long and involved, with humanized animals like Brer Rabbit and Brer Fox as the leading characters. (There was a rich tradition of trickster tales in Africa similar to Brer Rabbit stories, but American Indians also had trickster folktales specifically employing a rabbit as the protagonist. Here is probably another example of Old World memories finding reinforcement in the New World.) Much has been written of how Brer Rabbit— small and weak—and Brer Fox—larger and stronger—are symbols of slave and white, with the "helpless" rabbit defeating the powerful fox through wit and guile. Such tales gave slaves vicarious victories over their owners, further evidence that the experience of slavery did not psychologically emasculate bondsmen. Brer Rabbit stories were primarily escapist tales that allowed frustration and anger to be projected into another realm, where the weak did put down the powerful. They also included advice on how to act vis-à-vis the whites. In the animal tales Brer Rabbit was not always admirable, and his efforts were occasionally not in the pursuit of justice but of power. At times his overweening desires for food or control led to his downfall. Slaves knew they themselves were subject to such human faults—they stole from each other, fought with each other, competed for women and the master's favor. Some tales were warnings against such activities that harmed fellow blacks, as well as being ways to defuse hate and conflict within the slave community. But most of the animal tales, and the related John tales, where quick-thinking slaves outwitted their masters, served the positive function of projecting anger toward harmless substitutes and establishing the image of slaves mastering their owners in symbolic contexts. The confidence, the mental health, of the black community benefited from this folklore, which whites found only amusing and quaint, never sensing that the tales enabled slaves to reject inwardly their servile status and to preserve their self-worth.

As a system of ideas and practices that gave directions for living, symbolically marked significant turning points in an individual's life, and provided hope, fulfillment, and a special kind of freedom for persons mired in chattel bondage, religion was the heart and soul of the Afro-American's triumph over spiritual slavery. Though the importance and centrality of the slaves' religion has been widely recognized, the precise origin, nature, and function of their faith are still debated. West Africa, from which most slaves came, contained hundreds of different culture systems and an awesome variety of religious practices. But there were several underlying common assumptions and, even more important, some striking similarities to the kinds of Protestant evangelicalism Africans encountered in the American South. Generalizations, even though they risk over-simplification, can be made.

For the West African the world was infused with spiritual forces. Nature gods and ancestral gods gave a special value to one's kinship group and the physical environs of one's village. Every event—from cataclysmic natural disasters to minor personal misfortunes—had its roots in the realm of the spiritual. African societies in the seventeenth and eighteenth centuries appear to have been completely nonsecular; religion was all-encompassing, an aspect of every detail of life, an influence on every occurrence. Most Africans had a conception of time in which the present and the past were almost fused into one: ancestors were almost literally still present. But the future was extremely foreshortened, hardly conceivable except in the most limited, day-after-tomorrow sense. There was a triune conception of the supernatural, with ancestral spirits and nature spirits the most common, normally deemed responsible for the happenstances of life, and most often supplicated. Yet superior to these two reigned an omnipotent, omniscient god who could be appealed to when all else had failed.

Ordinarily in African societies the gods spoke to persons by sending a spirit, and possession—often frenzied—was the human evidence of communication with the supernatural. Throughout West Africa people considered themselves an organic part of the cosmos, and water had a special mystical, symbolic role. Streams, rivers, lakes, springs were often "aquatic temples," where various nature or ancestral spirits dwelt. Often springs gushing from the earth were thought to be symbolic of rebirth; still waters often represented creation; water in general suggested life, fertility, hope. Religious ceremonies often took place beside or even in water, were usually public, involved the community, and frequently were marked by participatory "congregational" singing. The religious ceremony provided the individual a sense of fellowship with his contemporaries, his ancestors, his natural environment; through spirit possession, one encountered the supernatural essence of the universe.

For reasons already discussed, the specifics of African religions—the ritual specialists, the religious language, the ritual paraphernalia—could not be transported intact to the American South, but the philosophical essence of the system was transplanted and slowly transformed. In the seventeenth century slaves were too few and too intermixed with whites to be able to maintain much more than a memory of African practices. Occasionally blacks were baptized as Christians, but the language barrier and the planters' lingering uncertainty about the slave status of a baptized bondsman minimized Christianization. Also there were few actively Christian whites in the seventeenth-century South. By the third quarter of the eighteenth century, however, Baptist, Methodist, and Presbyterian evangelicals had established themselves and begun the process of forming churches, recruiting ministers, and evangelizing that would eventually turn the Old South into a hothouse of religious orthodoxy and personal piety. The upsurge of African importations, the beginning of net population growth for American-born slaves, and the birth of Afro-American culture coincided with the commencement of the southern evangelical movement. Both were to have a major impact on the evolution of Afro-American Christianity in the Old South.

In 1774 a young Princeton-educated tutor to the family of Councilor Robert Carter encountered on the Virginia plantation an aged African-born slave, Daddy Gumby, who clearly had accepted the Calvinistic teachings of the Baptists. "God yonder in Heaven Master will burn *Lyars* with *Fire & Brimstone!* . . . Men are wicked." When the tutor, Philip Vickers Fithian, said it was too hot to attend church, the old slave admonished him. "Too hot to serve the Lord! Why I that am so old & worn out go on foot." Clearly some Africans who had mastered the English language had also adopted the Christian world view, and for every African like Daddy Gumby who did so there must also have been several American-born slaves who found comfort and purpose in Christianity: All three soon-to-be dominant southern evangelical denominations welcomed black worshippers and actively preached to bondsmen. Many planters were still skeptical of the utility and wisdom of converting the slaves, but the growing popular denominations, consisting primarily of non-slave-owning yeomen farmers, believed all were equal in the eyes of God. The early Baptists and Methodists especially were often critical of slavery and felt driven to spread the gospel message to all God's creatures. Most church services were integrated—and remained so throughout the antebellum period—but there were other factors besides the churches' welcoming black members that made evangelical Christianity attractive to increasing numbers of slaves.

If ever there was a situation in which Africans might feel that their lesser gods had failed them and as a consequence be disposed to approach their omnipotent god, then capture, the Middle Passage, and enslavement in the New World would evoke such sentiments. Increasingly after the mid-eighteenth century both newly imported and already acculturated slaves came into contact with fervent evangelicals who preached of a benevolent, all-powerful God who reached out to the lost and forlorn and provided deliverance. Such an idea was compatible with African views, especially when the Christian God was proffered by ministers (and congregational members) whose zeal and spirit-infused exhortations bore a comforting resemblance to African possession. The African concept of ancestral gods, nature gods, and an omnipotent creator god was transferable to the Christian trinity of God the Father, God the Son, and God the Holy Spirit.

As the density of slaves increased and slave families became common, blacks grew concerned with cultural values and religious services. After all, not only were their lives now more stable, but they also were having children, and families became, if not quite the norm, still an often realizable goal. With families came a desire to cement relationships ceremonially, to legitimate and maintain cultural values. Parents are always more concerned than young singles with religious traditions. At the same general time that demographic forces were pushing slaves in the direction of family formation and culture creation, Protestantism was penetrating the plantation South. The willingness of the evangelical churches to accept blacks as members and, by the use of such terms of address as *brother* and *sister*, to include them in fellowship gave slaves a sense of belonging and group identity that again resonated with African memories. The Baptist practice of immersion may very well have recalled African water rites, while the emotional intensity, the vigorous congregational singing, and the joyful sense of spiritual release common to the Methodists as well as Baptists appealed to the African sensibility. New World realities and Old World recollections formed the matrix out of which Afro-American Christianity emerged.

In the 1770s and 1780s, as pioneer churches were organized, black members participated in the acts of incorporation. The absolute numbers of black church members was small at first (of course, total church membership before the nineteenth century was only a tiny fraction of the population), but slaves were attending "white" churches, taking communion, being baptized and confirmed, listening to sermons, singing hymns, and gradually accept-

ing the Christian world view. The Great Revival at the beginning
of the nineteenth century established the mode of revival piety that
came to characterize the antebellum South, and at the birth of the
so-called bible belt during the climactic Cane Ridge camp meeting
of 1801, there was "a Black assembly, hearing the exhortations of
the Blacks; some of which appeared to be convicted and other con-
verted" (*An Account of an Extraordinary Revival of Religion in
Kentucky* [New York, 1802], p. 2.) Thereafter in steady, unspec-
tacular fashion the numbers of slaves worshiping in mixed congregations grew, despite the fact that sporadically before the 1840s
planters declared their unease about the potentially revolutionary
implications of the gospel. After the mid-1840s, when the three major denominations had splintered away from the national organizations and appeared "safe" on the issue of abolition, planters became
even more supportive of efforts to Christianize the slaves, in part
because they thought religion would make them better slaves. But
there were reasons unrelated to plantation efficiency for sponsoring
the gospel to the blacks. Ministers advocated missionary activities
both to rebut abolitionist charges that slaveholders left their bondsmen in heathenish conditions and out of genuine desires to enlarge
God's kingdom. Guilt and the urge to evangelize were both factors,
the relative importance differing from person to person and at
various times. By the eve of the Civil War perhaps as many as one
quarter of all slaves were members of biracial churches, yet one
should resist the temptation to interpret the resulting slave Christianity simply as an example of successful social control exerted by
whites over blacks.

Slaves avidly accepted Christianity and made it their own because it served their purposes so well. As the white ministers often
said and the Bible proclaimed, slaves understood that in the eyes
of God all men are equal, bondservant and free alike. Likewise
salvation was available to everyone who had faith in Christ, and
slaves found Jesus particularly attractive in his role as the suffering
servant with whom they could identify. With salvation came the
promise of a better life after the earthly travail was finished, but,
just as important, the Christian faith provided a moral purpose for
day-by-day living. As a child of God, one's life was not meaningless or of little worth. And because God was just, many slaves
expected recompense in Heaven for the injustice of their present

lives in bondage. The concept of the Chosen People was widely
adopted by bondsmen as descriptive of their own situation; for like
the people of Israel they were enslaved, mistreated, downtrodden,
but if they kept faith with God they could look forward to eventual
triumph. Again the effect was to inject a healthy dose of self-respect
into the slave community, and the identification with the people of
Israel gave a certain sense of moral grandeur, even feelings of moral
superiority vis-à-vis haughty masters, to the slaves struggling to
maintain their essential humanity amidst an institution that clas-
sified them as mere property. In the churches black men and
women found persuasive reason to live as morally responsible
adults, discovered arenas for the practice of black leadership, and
experienced a far greater degree of equality with the surrounding
whites than anywhere else in southern society. No wonder the
church was the dominant institutional force in the lives of so many
black southerners throughout the antebellum period and into our
own time.

Historians have sufficiently recognized neither the role of the
slave in the so-called white churches nor the role of those churches
in the lives of the slaves. From the very inception of institutional
church life, and particularly among the soon dominant Baptists and
Methodists, slaves were active church members. Of course the
percentage of black members varied according to their percentage
in the local population, but in every region blacks and whites worshiped together. Blacks commonly represented 20 to 40 percent of
the congregation of Baptist churches; often they were the majority.
Generally blacks sat segregated in benches reserved at the rear of
the church, or in the balcony, or in a lean-to addition to the church.
Blacks and whites heard the same sermons, took communion at the
same service, were baptized or confirmed together, were buried in
the same cemeteries. On occasion, when the white members built
a new church building, the blacks were given the old building and
allowed virtual autonomy over matters in the "adjunct" church. A
white committee would be appointed to supervise the black congregation, now called, for example, the Stamping Ground African
Baptist Church to distinguish it from the parent, now "white"
Stamping Ground Baptist Church; such supervision appears to
have been nominal. The slaves so separated were both the victims
of segregation and the beneficiaries of whites' recognition that

bondsmen had special needs and special interests best served by their own leaders. In the far more common biracial churches black deacons and elders served alongside whites, and it was not unusual, when no white minister was available, for the whole congregation to listen with approval to black preachers.

Across the South particularly skilled black preachers gained great fame as pulpit orators. Slaves had a well-developed oral tradition whereby the spoken word was the repository of the history and folk wisdom of their culture. Many black preachers whose gifts of oratory enabled them to perform verbal symphonies of religious expression captivated white audiences as well as black. Most slave ministers preached exclusively to blacks, though white supervision was usually required by laws that were observed in the breach. White ministers considered slave preachers a valuable adjunct, and slave ministers customarily had special passes that allowed them to travel and witness. Here and there famous black preachers like John Jasper of Virginia achieved such renown that whites flocked to hear them and were thrilled by their moving depictions of God's grace and miracles.

Talented slaves rose to various positions of leadership in the integrated churches, serving often as elders and deacons and occasionally as preachers. Black worshipers usually showed a clear preference for black preachers, men whose natural eloquence and familiarity with the Scriptures gave them extraordinary influence in the slave community. While slaves no doubt took vicarious pride in the attention given Jasper and Black Harry, who often accompanied Methodist Bishop Francis Asbury, bondsmen especially looked up to their black preachers, who exhorted them weekly in church, in Sunday afternoon slave religious meetings, and at camp meetings. In order to live like humans in situations of extremity, persons must generate a powerful will so to live and discover self-worth and purpose. The slave preacher was the key figure in this struggle, and the Afro-American Christianity that he professed morally rearmed the slaves for their lives in bondage. A giver of purpose, a source of meaning, an example of human triumph over chattel slavery, an example of leadership, character, and self-direction, the slave preacher enjoyed a special position in the eyes of the black community. He was one of their own to be looked up to, a role model and plantation leader who by his moral authority enabled slaves to hold on to their humanity and not let themselves be consumed by cynicism, nihilism, or bitterness. Masters understood the position the preacher occupied and at times had to bend their rules to accommodate him. Some masters did so because they believed religious slaves were more obedient and hardworking and less unruly. They probably were, but what was important to the black community was the contribution slave preaching made to that sense of purpose and human worth that over and over again allowed bondsmen to triumph over their situation and avoid being enslaved psychologically.

There was more nearly a biracial community in the antebellum Protestant churches than in the society as a whole. Standards for admission to and dismissal from churches were essentially the same for both races. A measure of spiritual equality was accorded blacks even in the language of address: "brother" and "sister" were affixed to their given names as with white co-members. Church clerks wrote to home churches to obtain letters of dismissal for slaves recently sold away, and when the letter arrived attesting to the slave's good standing he or she would be admitted to the new church. Bondsmen clearly took pride in their name and good character; after all, it was one thing masters could not take away from them. The relationship of the church to slavery was filled with irony and contradictions. Even while churches had slave members and accorded them relative equality in the spiritual realm, they were always careful to recognize the realities of the slave society of which they were a part. Churches generally obtained the slave owner's permission before accepting slave members.

An even more impressive example of how slaves entered into the life and spirit of the churches, and vice versa, is provided by the way the churches functioned as moral courts. The three dominant evangelical churches took seriously and tried to put into practice Jesus' directives as outlined in Matthew 18:15-18. The different denominations had differing procedures. The Baptist churches, for example, at least once a month on Saturday or Sunday afternoon met in a "business" session where the major business was the moral supervision of its members. Each member was expected "with love and charity" to watch over other members and counsel them to mend their ways if they had been seen to transgress some moral law. When there was a dispute or no quick confession, charges would be brought against the offending parties at the business sessions. Most transgressions consisted of such human failings as drunkenness, profanity, Sabbath-breaking, fornication, adultery, stealing, lying, and so on. Charges were made, witnesses heard and testimony taken, and the defendant was judged either innocent or guilty. If found guilty, the person either confessed and promised reformation or was excommunicated. Such activity was a significant part of religious life and responsibility in the Old South, and slaves participated in the whole process voluntarily and to a surprising degree as the equals of whites.

Blacks were held by whites—and apparently by the other Christian slaves themselves—to substantially the same moral standards as whites. Testimony was taken from and about slaves in the same way it was for white communicants. When whites brought charges against a black member, the accused was not automatically assumed to be guilty. Rather, he or she was brought to trial, witnesses heard, the case decided apparently on its merits. For example, Baptist church minute books in Mississippi reveal several occasions when white charges against slave members were dismissed and the slave deemed innocent. In like fashion slaves bore testimony against whites, and the whites then underwent moral examination. All this happened in a society in which slaves could not testify against whites in civil courts. In 1819 William West was denied a letter of dismissal from the Hephzibah Baptist Church in East Feliciana Parish, Louisiana, because the church had concluded he had unjustly whipped a "black brother of the church." Three years later another white member, D. Edds, was excommunicated after charges that he had abused one of his slaves were substantiated by examination. The church records show that masters frequently brought charges against slaves for lying, stealing, even running away, but in every case slaves were accorded a reasonable semblance of due process and often were judged innocent. That masters would utilize the church in an attempt to maintain plantation discipline is not surprising, but that they accepted the authority of the church—where black testimony was given—suggests a social complexity not always appreciated by historians.

Moreover, slaves brought charges against one another, defended themselves, and in general stood before their fellow members as free moral agents. Clearly whites and blacks accepted the same

moral code, identifying the same "sins" to be overcome. The
churches' position on black adultery is highly significant. In a society where slave marriages were not legally recognized and were
breakable at the master's convenience, evangelical churches held
slaves strictly accountable for adultery. Hence in the eyes of many
southern churchgoers, the slave marriage was sacred and its com-
mitments firm (though allowance was made to enable slaves sold
and separated against their will to remarry). None of this indicates
that the South was not racist, for in subtle ways whites were always
in the ascendant position and blacks literally and figuratively at the
back of the church. Nevertheless, despite the necessary qualifications, what is more remarkable is the degree to which there existed
a biracial religious community in the Old South.

As the antebellum period drew to a close, all white denominations were moving toward trained ministers, sedate worship, and
short services, while black Christianity remained true to the early
revival style. Even so, commonalities in belief, sermon structure,
and worship style persisted. Remnants of these shared practices
were visible in the clear affinity between Baptist presidential candidate Jimmy Carter and urban black church members in 1976.
Historians have been too prone to emphasize the differences between white and black religion in the Old South, contrasting joyful, emotionally demonstrative black services with stereotypical
images of arid, lifeless, white services. Of course, most white
southerners, Baptists or Methodists, enjoyed fervent worship with
spirited preaching and participatory singing. Predominantly white
rural church services were more like black services than the
Episcopal ceremony or the more sophisticated urban churches.

Although it was illegal to teach slaves to read, there were literate
bondsmen and black preachers in all areas of the South. Often they
had been taught by God-fearing masters or mistresses so they could
read the Bible, though occasionally white children or other literate
slaves were their tutors. When black preachers spoke to mixed congregations they trod softly lest the gospel theme of liberation raise
the hackles of the whites; but when unsupervised, most black
ministers apparently preached of the freedom provided by redemp-
tion. No doubt the described "freedom from sin" and "spiritual
liberty" often came near to being a double entendre for freedom
from slavery, at least to mistrusting whites especially after insurrec-

tion scares. But it would be a mistake to interpret slave religion simply as either an opiate for passive slaves or a training ground for rebel activists. This conclusion becomes increasingly evident when we consider the variety of institutional forms slave religion took.

While the overwhelming majority of slave worshipers practiced their faith with whites in the mainline Protestant churches, in most fair-sized southern towns and cities there were independent black churches under the control of free black leaders. St. James African Episcopal Church in Baltimore is a good example of such autonomous churches, many of which benefited from white patrons. Occasionally— as in Richmond and Louisville—the major black Baptist church was the largest congregation in town. Although only free blacks held the leadership positions in such churches (the church charters discriminating against slaves), bondsmen found the all-black churches meaningful and uplifting. White visitors often noted the decorum, the eloquent sermon, and the marvelous singing that characterized the black temples of worship. The theology preached was little different from that in racially mixed "white" churches, though by the 1830s the old camp meeting kind of fervor was practically absent from the urban white churches. Except that services were usually longer and more overtly emotional, the ritual and organization of the black churches closely resembled that of the white. Independent black churches added much to the cultural life of urban blacks, providing a sense of order and direction, opportunity to hone leadership skills, a variety of self-help organizations, and—most important—visible proof to all blacks, slave and free, that they could govern important aspects of their lives. Sometimes, as when the black church was a mission church funded by a predominantly white church, a white minister officiated, but the usual pattern in these influential citadels of black cultural life was total black leadership, a secular as well as religious leadership that continued well into the postbellum period.

An insufficiently understood and greatly exaggerated aspect of slave religion was the so-called underground church, the invisible institution of covert worship services held deep in the woods or secretly in slave cabins and urban cellars. Certainly the religious lives of slaves extended beyond the church structures, beyond the formal services where whites were present. Devout bondsmen in

the privacy of their quarters certainly had prayer meetings, sang
hymns and spirituals of their own composition, and pondered the
dilemmas of trying to do right in a world that did them so wrong.
Weather and master permitting, slaves on Sunday afternoons often
met together for songs and preaching to supplement what they had
heard in the morning worship hours. In these informal settings,
black preachers could preach with less constraint. While this could
mean they exhorted their listeners to rebel, it probably more often
freed the slave ministers to preach the gospel with greater ebul-
lience, enlivening their messages with colorful imagery and weaving into their texts stories of Old Testament heroes and New Testament miracles that magnified the awesome power of God and love
of Christ. Black ministers proclaimed the terrors of hell and the
joys of heaven with a concreteness of detailed description that few
whites could match. In the manner of the rich African oral tradition, the spoken word moved people, transmitted the heart of their
culture from one generation to the next, and entertained them in
the process. With consummate oratorical skills Afro-American
preachers utilized an African medium to spread and maintain a
Euro-American message. As might be expected, black Christians
magnified the role and importance of the preacher. Nowhere were
their verbal skills given more license than in the Sunday afternoon
and night-time meetings where they were not inhibited by the presence of whites. Here black preachers developed their characteristic
and distinctive homiletic style.

There were other occasions—as perhaps when a master prohibited his slaves from attending church or when the white minister
at church showed scant respect for the true religious feelings of the
blacks and preached little but self-serving doctrines of "slaves obey
your masters"—when slaves sought in their own special "brush ar-
bor" services to explore and proclaim the full gospel message of
repentance and joy. Extant testimony shows the slaves' dissatisfaction when ministers foreshortened the Christian message. In situations where slaves were repeatedly subject to such truncated
preaching, they slipped away, held secret services (often turning a
pot upside down in the belief that it would capture the sounds of
their ceremonies and not betray their presence to white patrollers),
developed black leaders, created secret churches largely invisible to
prying whites. The very attempt to do this, of course, indicates

how false was the belief by some earlier scholars that slaves had no role models, no cultural norms, other than those provided by their masters.

In two small and isolated geographical regions, the sea islands of Georgia and South Carolina and the sugar-producing areas of Louisiana and New Orleans, where the percentage of blacks to whites was extremely high, African (or, in Louisiana, Caribbean) admixtures were strong enough to give slave religious services a decidedly un-European cast, as with the frenzied "shouts" of the sea islands and the voodoolike practices sprinkled through South Louisiana. With these two exceptions, perhaps in no other aspect of black cultural life than religion had the values and practices of whites so deeply penetrated. After all, black folklore, dance, art, basketry, and other practices flourished during those hours "from sundown to sunup" when white supervision was least, and most readily identifiable Africanisms occurred in those areas of slave life whites found of marginal importance. Of what concern to a planter were the kinds of stories slaves told in evenings on their cabin stoop, or the kind of motifs they wove into their baskets or sewed into their quilts? In this cultural twilight zone that supposedly had no effect on the plantation work routines or the society's racial etiquette, blacks carved out a surprising and important degree of cultural autonomy. From this beachhead slaves resisted dehumanization and expanded control or at least influence over aspects of their life ranging from food supply to clothing styles.

With religion it was different. Whites did care what blacks believed, in part because the whites felt the gospel truths were too important to be left to "untutored" and "superstitious" slaves, in part because the masters correctly sensed the potentially liberating and even revolutionary implications of several scriptural doctrines. Whites worshiped with blacks, listening to the same sermons. Apparently slaves sat through the entire worship service, hearing the same theology the whites heard; only at the conclusion of the services, when the minister turned his special attention to the slaves and addressed them in a short homily that was an addendum to the main sermon, did slaves have to endure the message of social control. Exhortations of obedience and repeated admonitions not to lie and steal both made religion seem safe to whites and made many slaves doubt the intentions of the preacher. But the substance, the heart of the sermon was understood by the bondsmen, and that message of life-affirming joy, a message that obliterated one's worldly status and placed supreme value on steadfast faith, was more revolutionary than planters ever suspected.

Christianity taught that in the eyes of God slaves were the equals of their earthly masters; Christianity taught slaves that their souls were precious; Christianity provided a context wherein slaves along with their masters struggled against the evil forces within themselves. Christianity was life affirming for slaves as well as whites; it infused individuals of both races with joy and confidence. Strong emotions and fervent belief characterized the worship of free people as well as the enslaved. In a social institution that defined them as no more than property, slaves found within the church powerful reassurance of their humanity. Within the church earthly status was less important than one's spiritual status, and so armed with faith slaves discovered a profound guarantee of their worth as persons.

Passivity and cynicism alike were overcome as bondsmen struggled to purify their lives through the discipline offered by the church. Slaves recognized the harmful effects of lying, stealing, violence against one another, drunkenness, and promiscuity, especially when fellow slaves were hurt. Consequently they labeled such practices sinful, and when conversion promised to help them reform their lives, they, like all evangelicals, spoke of being freed from sin. Eloquent black preachers and devout laymen gave testimony to slaves' sense of responsibility, providing role models of enduring strength. The prototype of the Chosen People kept faith in a final retribution alive, and Jesus as a personal friend and savior offered daily encouragement to lives filled with suffering and toil. Often religious slaves felt themselves morally superior to their masters, and the whites' disproportionate wealth and power had no effect on such self-confidence. Experiencing hope, joy, and purpose in their faith, Christian slaves found more than a will simply to survive physically. They survived as a people who amidst chattel slavery could find within themselves the power to love and care, the strength to forgive, and the patience to endure with their souls unshattered.

Psychologically most slaves appear inwardly to have repudiated the dehumanizing implications of chattel slavery and to have been emotionally strong. Certainly there were those whose sense of worth was gnawed away by constant abuse, and these became "Sambos"—spiritless, unresisting, conforming to the whites' desires. A life of monotonous labor in frontier regions of the South drove some whites and blacks alike to near insanity. Other bondsmen projected their anger at the institution of slavery on to those weaker than themselves and mistreated their spouses, or children, or the farm animals. Slaves occasionally fought among themselves, taking out their anger in blows against available enemies. Some committed suicide or struck out blindly against offending whites and were killed as a consequence. Yet the remarkable fact is not the aberrant social pathology but the degree to which slaves succeeded in maintaining their families, their honor, and their sense of individual worth. Perhaps more than any other factor, Christianity in several forms—the "white" church, the independent black church, or the "invisible" church—provided slaves with a purpose and a perspective with which to overcome slavery psychologically and spiritually and survive as humans.

As some critics have charged, in one sense much slave religion was otherworldly and escapist. In part because their life in this world was frequently broken by separation and hardship, and in part because the African heritage of an extremely foreshortened view of the future made the expansive Christian view of the hereafter exhilarating, slaves in their songs and sermons often reveled in blissful descriptions of heaven. To a degree such raptures were compensatory, but elements of the descriptions—where all God's children have shoes, where there is no more work, where families and loved ones are united never to be torn apart again—were telling comments on life in this world. Moreover, the clear implication that slaves were destined for, and deserved, "a home in glory land" reveals a profound rejection of images of degradation and worthlessness. Belief that in the end they would occupy seats in Heaven spoke volumes about their sense of God's justice, and their sense of eternal reward again raised the uplifting theme of identification with the Chosen People. Such beliefs no doubt worked against suicidal assaults against bondage, but the belief immeasurably armed slaves for a more profound inner repudiation of the bonds of slavery.

There is also some truth in the view that slave religion was primarily a staging ground for revolt by blacks. Surely slave Christians saw the paradox between the gospel view of equality and freedom on the one hand and the preached injunctions that slaves should obey their masters on the other. Throughout the history of Christianity, oppressed peoples have been inspired by its teachings to attack their oppressors and repudiate their earthly rulers. No one can deny that Christianity holds forth the possibility of rebellion for conscience sake, and slave owners certainly knew the potential. Church participation, moreover, gave slaves a chance for developing leadership skills, for communicating with one another, for developing the common sense of purpose and injustice that could stimulate insurrection. For some slaves in particular situations religion did precisely that—motivate and facilitate rebellion. Most slave revolts in the United States, those only planned and those actually undertaken, had a religious dimension, from the Stono Revolt in 1739 to Nat Turner in 1831. There was a fateful ambiguity at the heart of the slave response to Christianity, and the fervent rebel and the passive, long-suffering servant were equally authentic expressions of black religion. Yet in the Old South the overwhelming majority of slaves internalized rebellion, recognizing the imbalance of power that made armed insurrection sheer futility.

The submission to bondage was, in many instances, merely a conscious way of coping with the exigencies of life in a slave society. Submission was not total but controlled; it reflected the limited possibilities for overt action and sublimated moral rebellion. For the huge majority of slaves, folk Christianity provided both spiritual release and spiritual victory. They could inwardly repudiate the system and thus steel themselves to survive it. This subtle, profound spiritual freedom made their Christianity the most significant aspect of slave culture and defused much of the potential for insurrection. Repeatedly the narratives tell of slaves having their souls "freed." One aged ex-slave even remarked that she often heard her mother say, " 'I am so glad I am free.' I did not know then what she was talking about. I thought she meant freedom from slavery." It was precisely this belief that one was in the ultimate sense "free" that allowed countless slaves to persevere so eloquently. In ways masters never suspected, the Christianity of blacks mitigated against slave uprisings and supported the essential humanity of a people defined as property.

In part because slaves' religion, along with other manifestations of cultural independence, provided them a safe way of revolting against psychological enslavement, more physically risky kinds of rebellion were far less common in the Old South than in any other New World slave community. Yet many other factors entered into the equation of slave rebellion. Rebellion itself consists of a broad spectrum of activities ranging from subtle efforts to maintain individual cultural autonomy to armed insurrection. The many forms of slave revolt, and their relative frequency in the antebellum South, have constituted a topic of sustained research in southern studies. Human struggles for freedom are intrinsically interesting, but in the case of southern slavery the subject is especially worthy of close examination for what the frequency and form of slave rebellion reveal about the nature of the peculiar institution itself.

One of the difficulties in making broad generalizations about slave rebellion, as with other aspects of the slave experience, is that the institution changed dramatically over time. Most discussion of rebellion has centered on the period after about 1800, when the slave population was greatest, yet the very factors that served to set the Old South apart from the Caribbean and Latin America situations were most prominent in the final half-century of slavery in the United States. Particularly after 1808 when the foreign slave trade to the United States was closed, planters realized that slave living conditions had to be such as to allow population growth. For this and various other reasons, including, after 1831, abolitionist charges of planter brutality, paternalistic slave owners gradually ameliorated some of the worst abuses of the institution. Periodically reformers urged that planters respect the marriages, families, and religious needs of slaves. In general slaves were better fed and housed, received better health care, and were physically better off in the nineteenth century. At the same time, Afro-American cultural development and the strengthening of black family structures and kinship systems gave slaves increased defenses against the psychological ravages of slavery. All these conditions helped to minimize the frequency of armed slave rebellion and to shift resistance to more subtle forms. But of course slavery in the South had been very different in the seventeenth and eighteenth centuries from the way it was in 1850, and resistance in the earlier period had been more akin to the Latin American experience.

In the first half-century after blacks were introduced to Virginia, slaves were so few and so intermingled with white indentured servants that black rebellion was not a category separate from servant rebellion. The handful of slaves, relatively acculturated from their West Indian sojourn, tended to identify in class terms with their fellow workers, and blacks and white indentured servants ran off together. Presumably they hoped to emerge as free in another location, or else hire out their time at a better rate to another employer. Some may very well have disappeared into the West, intermarrying with the Indians. But as the number of blacks began to increase in the 1680s their color slowly separated them as a category distinct from whites. By the 1690s and early 1700s slaves were far more numerous and, coming directly from Africa, were perceived as more alien, more threatening. Race now segregated blacks from white workers, and racism forced slaves when running away to avoid all whites.

The population density was not yet such as to discourage the hope of establishing maroon (runaway) settlements, and the backcountry was not yet filled with white yeomen, though Indians already were willing to capture slave runaways and return them for a reward. The upsurge in African imports, with their characteristic unbalanced sex ratios, meant that the slave work force was male dominated, young, and potentially rebellious. Cultural defenses and families had not yet had time to form. Consequently there were relatively more attempts by African slaves to run away in the early eighteenth century. Not yet acculturated and carrying with them strong memories of African group identity, these "outlandish" (as African-born slaves were called) bondsmen often ran away in small groups. Knowing Africa was unreachable, they would run toward wilderness areas and attempt in their secret hideouts to re-create or restore some semblance of the life they had known in the old country. Slaves running away in groups were obviously less likely to avoid being seen or caught, and soon obliging Indians and race-conscious whites minimized the possibility of successful maroon settlement. Slaves were also more apt to use violent means to redress their grievances in the eighteenth century, with arson, poisonings (a common African way of seeking revenge), and shootings more common, as well as proportionally more insurrection attempts.

By the final quarter of the eighteenth century, complex changes were already well under way that would significantly affect black-white relations. Indigenous population growth led to a balancing of the sex ratios; population increase, the expansion in average plantation size, and improvements in transportation made mate selection easier and led the way toward the restoration of the black family. These developments also allowed the creation of an Afro-American cultural life. As conditions for slaves improved incrementally, they had more to risk and consequently became more cautious. Not only had white numbers and relative power grown enormously, but the fears and social strains resulting from the enlarged black presence had produced a network of legal restraints called slave codes, backed up by a variety of patrol systems. At the same time as the slaves' social and cultural opportunities were improving, the regulatory dimensions of the institution were hardening.

This dual movement was suddenly interrupted by the American Revolution. Thousands of slaves, both voluntarily and involuntarily, were swept up by the call to arms. Tens of thousands of bondsmen, realizing the stiffening of the slave codes and hearing the promises of freedom, also sensed that the presence of British troops offered the best opportunity for liberty. No demographic profile of those slaves who fled to the British side is available, but we can imagine that even cautious ones, with families to protect, seized the precious moment when freedom seemed obtainable. Others with similar motives, who calculated their chances differently, aided the colonists. While 50,000 or so slaves were eventually evacuated by the British, with consequences still incompletely understood, and hundreds who joined the patriot cause were rewarded with emancipation, the majority of slaves after the Revolution remained locked in chattel bondage. Perhaps those who engaged in the Revolutionary combat had been the more adventurous slaves, leaving the great bulk of blacks after the war without their admixture of courage and experience. Following the Revolution a goodly number of slave owners, motivated by Enlightenment or evangelical ideas about the brotherhood of men (at least in the eyes of God), freed their slaves, tripling the free black population by 1810. But emancipationist ideas declined shortly thereafter as the Revolution faded into the past and ameliorationist ideas became dominant, prefiguring the coming age that historians call the Old South (to distinguish it from the colonial South).

The one overriding fact about slave rebellion in the Old South was the almost complete absence of large-scale armed insurrection such as occurred in Latin America and the Caribbean and lay like a horrible specter in the back of the minds of countless southern planters. Explaining nonoccurrences is always difficult, and this case is no exception. But even a partial explanation does shed light on two important components of any historical analysis, the comparative and the temporal. The situation in the South after about 1800 was significantly different from that elsewhere in the Americas. Moreover, one must remember the wide variety of rebellious acts that stopped short of insurrection, rebellious acts as diverse and individualized as the planter-slave confrontations themselves. Yet during the heyday of the Old South, in the final decades before the Civil War when cotton was king and the slave population was at its highest, the broad surface of the plantation society was remarkably smooth and stable despite the many small eddies of unrest and the strong, deep current of slaves' cultural and psychological rejection of enslavement. That apparent calm, experienced even by those acute observers who suspected the swirling torrents underneath, has helped perpetuate many myths about the Old South and its two peoples, black and white.

Many factors mitigated against successful armed insurrection by slaves in the Old South. Unlike the situation in Latin America, in the Old South as a whole whites far outnumbered slaves, and of course totally controlled the police power of the states. (As described in Chapter 3, nonslaveholding whites almost unanimously supported slavery as a method of controlling blacks even if slave ownership was not their personal goal.) In certain regions like the sea islands of South Carolina and Georgia and the sugar districts of Louisiana, blacks were in a significant majority, yet even there the distance between individual plantations and the maze of unbridged estuaries, rivers, bayous, sloughs, and swamps made communication and travel between plantations difficult. The geography of the Old South conspired with demography to complicate still further slave attempts at rebellion and escape. Slaves in Brazil and in the Guiana region of northeastern South America, for example, had the huge, unexplored jungle fastness of the Amazon River basin in which to escape; similarly, plantations were located on the perimeters of the West Indian islands, whose interiors offered sure havens for runaways. In both regions slaves escaped to the interior and in maroon settlements often managed to survive for years, occasionally fighting white authorities to a standstill and achieving treaty recognition of their status (often in exchange for returning newly escaped slaves).

This kind of escape from slavery was never possible for the overwhelming majority of bondsmen in the Old South. Except for those few who lived near the Dismal Swamp on the eastern Virginia-North Carolina boundary, and some in Florida and Georgia near the Okefenokee Swamp and the trackless Everglades, there was no safe hinterland where maroons could survive. Moreover, cold winters, particularly in the Upper South, made the prospect of hiding out in the woods uninviting. In the early decades of plantation development, the Indians in the backcountry quickly learned they would be rewarded for capturing and returning slave runaways. The Indians were replaced in later decades by yeoman farmers who either returned the runaways for the reward or kept them. For most slaves the freedom territory north of the Mason-Dixon line or the Ohio River was simply too far away, and while several thousand bondsmen in the last half-century of slavery did escape by way of the Underground Railroad, most of them came from the border states of Maryland and Kentucky.

In Latin America and the Caribbean Islands, where hundreds of slaves lived on huge plantations, the owners were absent, and the working conditions were far more harsh than those typical in the South, desperate slaves, often plagued with famine as well as overwork, occasionally struck out against their brutal oppression and escaped to preexisting maroon communities. The working conditions on the tropical sugar plantations drove slaves to rebellion, and the example of successful escape offered by the maroon settlements in the backcountry emboldened otherwise hesitant bondsmen to act. There was, in other words, a heritage of insurrection in the Caribbean and Latin America that offered slaves not only incentive to rebel but the expectation of success. No such vital spark of hope was possible in the Old South. The few insurrections were small, localized, and quickly and brutally suppressed, with many innocent slaves usually punished and the general restrictions against all slaves made temporarily more harsh.

After 1808 the foreign slave trade to the United States ended, but in the slave societies to the south the transatlantic trade in humans continued. As always, the African imports were disproportionately young males, maintaining the highly unequal slave sex ratios in Latin America and the Caribbean. This, combined with the rigorous work routines, the cruelty of managers on absentee plantations, and the disease-induced high death rates produced a degree of despair that seldom obtained in the Old South. A work force of mostly young males, with neither wives nor families to be concerned about, with expectations of a life that could only be "nasty, brutal, and short," with an almost inpenetrable backcountry beckoning them and the ever-present example of successful maroons suggesting that escape was possible, and with the number of superintending whites tiny in proportion to the black population—there is no wonder that out of this unstable situation slave resistance and insurrection were constant realities. Yet by the time there were significant numbers of blacks in the antebellum South, the demographic situation was so different as to provide in effect a check on potential slave unrest.

During the era of the cotton kingdom most slaves were American born, the sex ratio was practically equal (more so than the white ratio), and slaves typically lived in family groupings. As a result the slave family became the single most important bond holding members together, and as we have seen, naming practices and kinship systems evolved to cement relationships made fragile by the possibility of sale or removal. This demographic development also prevented slave insurrection.

While a population composed mostly of unattached young males can be very explosive (especially when faced with harsh conditions and the possibility of escape), a population where males and females are equally present, family relationships have been formed and there are small children to love and care for, is far more conservative. The possibility of an entire family escaping was practically nil, and parents were loath to forsake their children to save themselves. Likewise few men would leave their loved ones for an escape attempt with little chance of success. If family attachments lessened runaway efforts, so much more did the ties of family affection reduce the possibilities of insurrection. Few male slaves would risk almost sure death when to do so would leave their families fatherless. Moreover, the knowledge that family members and innocent bystanders would be pitilessly punished and their rights severely circumscribed in the aftermath of a rebellion attempt must have restrained many discontented slaves.

In the Old South, where family structures, leisure time, and fairly good living conditions prevented most slaves from being driven into utter desperation, slaves usually found less risky avenues of countering the dehumanization of chattel bondage. Because hunger and abject hopelessness were less common in the Old South, slaves calculated their options more carefully, waiting— sometimes all their lives—for good chances for successful rebellion. Thousands did not find the right moment to strike until the Civil War and the presence of Union troops profoundly changed the balance. Then no one was more shocked than complacent planters when droves of their seemingly most devoted, most responsible slaves "deserted" and chose freedom.

The realities of power and geography in the Old South also minimized the kind of slave rebellion that often occurred in the other New World plantation societies. In the antebellum South, slaves were very seldom driven to mindless, suicidal acts of outrage and rebellion. Fully aware of their situation, they learned, socialized, and passed on to their children a wide range of behavior— voice intonations, facial expressions, feigned illness, purposeful laziness and slowness of motion, dumb-like-a-fox incomprehension—that combined equal portions of insubordination and minor rebellion to produce a constant undercurrent of resistance to psychological bondage. Although never completely giving in to authority, most slaves were able, at least in the eyes of their master, to acquiesce in their state of servitude and thus survive with their essential humanity intact. In the most fundamental sense, racial slavery as it existed in the Old South was premised on the assumption by whites that blacks were inferior, either a subhuman or a permanently childlike race. Planters' everyday experience, of course, gave the lie to this assumption, and therein may have been the cause of the guilt that some historians believe troubled many whites, particularly those who constructed elaborate proslavery

defenses. Had slaves in general accepted this racial subordination
and aspired to be only what the white man prescribed, then blacks
would have been total slaves, and all resistance—except occasional
outbursts of violence—would have disappeared. But the rich pano-
ply of Afro-American culture, their tales, music, art, and religion
protected bondsmen from complete capitulation. Out of the inner
reserves of their humanity slaves in measured ways resisted servitude and defended the limited rights that had become, through
mutual accommodation, accepted by whites. The black community
evolved a culture from which proceeded all forms of slave resistance other than rebellion.

Owners were most concerned with their slaves' labor output,
and for that reason bondsmen developed a repertoire of techniques
to gain a modicum of control over the amount of work required of
them. While some slaves were downright lazy, a low-incentive
labor system like slavery obviously gave them few reasons to
overexert themselves. Even the application of force soon became
counterproductive. Slaves realized they had to work at a moderate
pace, for their physical well-being and the stability of their family
relationships depended on the success of the plantation. While
there was never enough incentive or mobility to turn bondsmen into competitive men-on-the-make, they did accept a responsibility
to work at a productivity level that eventually came to be accepted
by master and slave alike. Often there was a perpetual low-grade
war of wills between the two, with masters cajoling, threatening,
and occasionally whipping and slaves complaining, moving at a
deliberate pace (though the nature of the crop culture required
careful labor that outside observers apparently misunderstood at
times for indolence), and even practicing minor agricultural
sabotage like breaking tools, "accidentally" plowing up crops,
"carelessly" letting the teams get out of the barn-lot, and so on. To
what extent owners realized what was going on is problematical;
usually they ascribed such behavior to the accepted irresponsibility
and childishness of slaves, but surely they at times must have comprehended the guerilla resistance under way. (It should be said that
such sabotage had a negligible effect on the total agricultural
system.) Slaves frequently acted dumb, carefully "misunderstood,"
and—in earlier days—confessed ignorance of English as effective
ways to minimize the demands placed on them.

When a master or overseer tried to force slaves to work harder, or longer hours, than convention had come to establish as the norm, slaves were quick to protest. Not only did the war of the wills heat up, but slaves were sometimes quite bold in their insistence against being pushed beyond endurance or general practice. Particularly if an overseer was the offending taskmaster, slaves did not hesitate to take their case to their masters. Whether the overseer was the culprit or not, aggrieved and protesting slaves complained and shuffled along, slowed their pace, and feigned illness. On any plantation at any given moment there were always several laid up for sickness, real and pretended, a tactic planters were ultimately helpless to counteract. If conditions persisted, or when personal relations between a slave and his owner or overseer became extremely strained—as when a slave felt himself unjustly punished—bondsmen often ran away.

Slave runaways were a perennial problem for southern planters. Over the course of the slave-plantation system in the South the nature of runaways and their destinations changed, but in the antebellum period, after the spread of cotton and sugar cultivation, bondsmen ran away for three general reasons. Probably most common and of least worry to owners were those who in response to a real or felt injustice ran away for a short period simply to deprive the owner of a portion of the slave's labor. After all, here was a way for a slave to exert himself, to thwart his owner's intentions, to make a statement about his rights even if it came at some eventual cost to himself. Periodically when an owner or overseer forced slaves to work too hard or on the accepted weekend off (usually Saturday afternoon and Sunday), punished one unjustly, blamed one unfairly, or insulted a specially favored or skilled slave, the offended bondsman would disappear for several days or for three or four weeks.

Masters sometimes came to accept with a shrug this type of protest, knowing the absent slave would soon reappear, having in the meantime been living probably on the fringes of the plantation, maybe even slipping back to the quarters at night for food. Usually when the runaway did return he would receive a whipping or some other punishment, but occasionally owners disregarded the infraction of their rules and welcomed the runaway's return without disciplinary measures. This kind of commonplace running away was not a threat to the institution of slavery. The runaways themselves were protesting less the institution itself than invasions of their perceived rights as slaves. Owners seldom hunted for, probably never advertised for, such absent—not escaped—slaves. Because such limited running away was an accepted if unconscious method for aggrieved or angered slaves to work out their feelings in a bold but, from the owner's view, safe and harmless form, it no doubt relieved tensions, allowed resentments on both sides to cool, and incidentally reduced the possibility that hidden or suppressed rage might build to explosive levels.

While temporary running away was in effect a safety valve, a second common reason for running away represented a longer-term threat to slavery. The separation of slave families caused many bondsmen to leave their plantations in an effort to reunite with loved ones. Even if runaways of this kind eventually returned to their owners, the absence was often long enough to persuade the owner to place advertisements for their return in local newspapers. These advertisements, written as accurately as possible in hopes that the described slave would be located, frequently included hints that the runaway had joined his spouse or children at a certain location. Perhaps there is no stronger indication of the strength and resiliency of family ties among bondsmen than these efforts against all obstacles to see once again kin separated by distance. Even when runaways like these were recaptured and returned to their owners, the more realistic owners frequently would sell them to someone living in the vicinity of the loved one, knowing full well that the bonds of affection were stronger than discipline. Certainly many callous sellers and buyers of men disdained any human sympathies, but just as many—for reasons of practicality if not humanity—tried not to separate families unless in their view economic necessity required them to do so. Slavery's defenders as well as its critics recognized that the separation of families was a moral sore spot in the theoretical justification of bondage, and for that reason very seldom were small children parted from their mothers. Nevertheless, the trauma associated with sales of whatever nature forced many slaves to risk great danger and even greater hardships to see once more the faces of dear ones stolen away from them.

Despite the various factors that minimized slave rebellion and running away, there were nonetheless always situations, personality clashes, misunderstandings that drove slaves to cast aside their doubts and fears and escape to freedom. Often slaves who could not endure their bondage any longer but recognized the futility of individual violence or the inhospitableness of the countryside simply ran away to southern cities where they blended into the sizable free black population and disappeared. Skilled, articulate slaves, well-versed in the ways and expectations of their masters, were at the same time those most able to direct a potential slave insurrection and those most able, and likely, to succeed and even prosper as free blacks in Richmond, Charleston, or New Orleans. In yet another way southern cities, by offering a refuge to highly skilled slave runaways, helped defuse the potential for rebellion that might destroy the institution of bondage. Permanent slave escapees, then, whether they fled north or to southern cities to gain their freedom, had the ironic effect of making the existing system of slavery more stable by depriving the larger population of bondsmen of their most vocal, most able leaders.

While slave owners often convinced themselves that the possibilities of large-scale slave insurrection were remote and failed to recognize the intent of resistance present in malingering and short-term running away, they realized that there were lethal individualistic ways of rebelling. Slaves were often suspected of arson and poisoning, in part because the causes of destructive fires and fatal diseases were so often mysterious. There are of course recorded instances of bondsmen using either of these to strike back at their owners, and surely both were successfully employed occasionally without raising undue suspicions. Contemporaries seem sometimes to have become almost hysterical over the imagined presence of vindictive slaves behind every unexplained fire or death. It would be a mistake, however, to follow the lead of overwrought, guilt-ridden slave owners. Sparks from fireplaces, poorly constructed chimneys, accidents associated with the smoking of meat or drying of tobacco, spontaneous combustion, and a lengthy list of barely understood and misdiagnosed diseases were probably more often at the bottom of sudden fires and unexplained illnesses.

The absence of a tradition of armed slave uprisings in the Old South in no way supports the old myth of Sambo, the contented slave. Certainly there were passive, fawning, irresponsible, childlike Sambos, but they must have been but a fraction of the slave population. Far more common were the realistic slaves, men and women who knew they had to accept at least the physical constraints of bondage, who had a healthy sense of the possible and for whom family concerns were restraints against self-destructive rage. Whether it was understood or not, the vital Afro-American culture protected realistic slaves from being dehumanized; their culture provided them alternative ways of viewing life and did not allow the white man to control their inner world of values and dreams. By having something of their own to hold to, most bondsmen survived slavery, bending when survival dictated but not letting their spirit be broken.

They learned by necessity to cope with their existence, being by turns passive and assertive; knowing when to fawn and dissemble and when to protest; knowing how to get by guile what they had to have and how to avoid punishment. This indispensable knowhow was transmitted from parents to children in a variety of ways. Whites, who seldom could see beyond their slaves' black faces, comprehended them all as Sambos, but again and again, when pushed too far, slaves resisted with a firmness and forthrightness that surprised their masters. To suppress their guilt over slaveholding, most southern whites tried desperately to convince themselves that blacks were a permanent child-race who needed and preferred slavery. When time after time slaves reacted with a maturity and boldness that should have called the racial stereotype into question, whites instead suspected outside forces—abolitionists, the example of free blacks, emancipationist literature—at work.

These realistic slaves represented the huge middle range of character types; at the opposite end of the spectrum from true Sambos were an equally small number of true rebels who with every fiber of their being rejected enslavement. Slave parents, knowing the consequence of attitudes of this kind, would try to dissuade their children from conspicuous rebellion. If the warnings were of no avail, sooner or later rebels were usually killed or suffered such brutality that their spirit was permanently broken, with suicide or self-mutilation sometimes the ultimate result. Too much attention has been focused on Sambos and rebels; most slaves were neither, though they could be a little of both as the occasion required.

With the invention of the cotton gin in 1793, the closing of the foreign slave trade in 1808, and the opening of the Old Southwest to the expansion of slavery after 1815, the political and economic foundations of the cotton kingdom were laid. The Revolutionary era imperceptibly merged into the Old South, with the institution of slavery like a giant black glacier inexorably spreading across the land, grinding down the rocks of resistance along the way and changing the entire social and cultural landscape in its wake. Nothing and no one remained untouched across the face of the South. Only a cataclysmic civil war could wrench blacks out of bondage and transform even incompletely a land so marked by natural beauty and human tragedy.

7. An Unfinished Ending, 1861-1869

In what proved to be a momentous miscalculation, the southern states seceded from the Union in two interconnected stages during the winter and spring of 1860-61. Brimming with bravado and confidence, some southerners spoke of easy victory and a great Confederate future. Others, often large planters, had entered the war with less gusto and silently feared for the continuation of their slave-based prosperity. Yet no one knew the shape the conflict would eventually assume, no one could foresee the changes wartime necessity would demand. Slowly, almost imperceptibly at first, the institution of slavery began to crumble. Neither black nor white at first understood the process underway, and tensions, embarrassing situations, conflicting pressures occasionally brought hesitation and even confusion to nearly every actor in this unscripted drama. In the end a mighty revolution had been worked by forces complex and contradictory, chattel slavery was finished, new human relationships were painfully worked out, and one whole phase of southern history ended and another began. The past, however, dies slowly, if at all. No clean break with slavery occurred; despite far-reaching changes, human attitudes evolved and old habits persisted. The era of the Civil War and Reconstruction is all the more important because many of the issues it raised were only imperfectly resolved, and we still live with the consequences.

The Civil War had courage and bloodshed and gallantry aplenty, and both sides shared in the glory and the gore. Yet cavalry charges and assaults repulsed do not exhaust the drama of the war. In many ways the most interesting stories occurred unnoticed on isolated plantations between masters and slaves, for at the individual human level a great change was unfolding. Basically the war was fought over slavery; slavery continued amidst the war, and slaves were used by both sides for military purposes. Approximately 100,000 ex-slaves fought as soldiers for the Union cause, and perhaps 500,000 or more fled their plantations and as refugees sought aid from Union armies. But that undeniable evidence of slaves' dissatisfaction with their bondage stood in contradiction to the slaveholders' persuasion that blacks were content in their "natural" position as human property. As though to push this discrepancy from their consciousness, white southerners after the war cast "the loyal slave" as a stock character in their mythical recreation of the Confederate crusade. For many white Americans even today, the faithful black retainer burying the master's family silver as the Union troops come over the horizon is the only image they have of black participation in the Civil War.

Of course all myths and stereotypes have some grounding in fact, and this one is no exception. Slaves had a wide range of reasons for remaining loyal to their old masters. In many instances a personal bond of friendship or love transcended race, and in others a strong sense of duty overrode other calculations. Defenders of the Old South could find examples of such devotion, which they found admirable in an age when freedmen all around them were rejecting deference to whites. Some house slaves who had lived most of their lives in intimate contact with whites found that the attachment to their "white" family loomed larger than commitment to an abstraction like freedom. There are true tales also about the personal slaves of white military officers who served their Confederate masters in combat with courage and fidelity, even to the point of bringing their wounded masters home, and then—duty having been done—returning to the front to join the Union troops. Some slaves did protect white women and children from assault by federal troops; did stay to help aged or wounded masters or widows when escape to the Union army was possible; did continue to work on the plantation long after the old constraints of force and discipline had disappeared.

But love or duty were not the only motivations that could lead a slave to "loyal" activity. Forced by their position to be prudent, slaves were cautious in calculating the risk of opting for "freedom." Even though Yankee troops might be nearby or rumored nearby, experience soon taught slaves that military fortunes waxed and waned. A decision to flee one's master and seek freedom at the hands of invading troops could leave one dangerously exposed to the master's wrath if the Union forces suddenly withdrew. Many slaves possessed an uncanny sense that emancipation was coming in God's good time, and years of wariness schooled them to avoid precipitately bold behavior. They would simply bide their time, serving their masters with apparent loyalty, until the opportunity for seizing freedom was certain. Still other bondsmen, particularly in isolated regions where the slave grapevine was inefficient, were skeptical of the Yankees' intentions. Told repeatedly that northerners were devils who would work them harder or sell them to Cuba, some slaves feared Union troops and clung to the familiarity of their situation. There are reports of slaves who were actually surprised to discover that Yankees did not have horns, of others who quite naturally called their eventual emancipators "damn yankees" because they had never heard them referred to otherwise. Slave loyalty springing from caution or misinformation was hardly testimony to the beneficence of the peculiar institution.

Whatever the incentive behind slave loyalty, real or apparent, most bondsmen chose freedom when the opportunity allowed. Actually only a minority of slaves had to face a stark showdown between fidelity to master or escape to liberty, for a variety of factors insulated most of them from such a dilemma until the latter stages of the war when freedom seemed merely a matter of waiting out Confederate defeat. In those regions along the Atlantic coast and the Mississippi River where Union troops quickly won control, slaves decided overwhelmingly for freedom. Much of the interior of the South was remote from northern military advances, and there slaves seldom had a chance to choose liberty. Along the battle routes slave owners fled from the Union troops and took their slaves with them. Thousands of bondsmen were consequently uprooted and relocated in the up-country. The roads to Texas were crowded as planters from Louisiana and Mississippi moved their chattel away from the emancipating armies. This forced migration, often called "running the niggers," caused severe dislocations within the slave community: families were split; unfamiliar work routines were imposed; the quality of food and shelter deteriorated. Much of the often discussed roving about of ex-slaves after the war was a result of freed people attempting to find war-separated spouses and children and to return to old homeplaces. In addition to the obvious hardships imposed upon slaves, the widespread fleeing of planters and their work forces caused a serious decline in agricultural output, one of the reasons, in addition to an inadequate transportation network, for food shortages in the Confederacy.

Despite planters' efforts to frighten slaves away from the Union troops with horror stories of Yankees harnessing blacks to plows like oxen or selling them to the death-camp-like sugar plantations of the Caribbean, or planter efforts to remove slaves from proximity to northern armies, many bondsmen had the experience of living on plantations caught up in the maelstrom of war. For those slaves in the theater of battle, where invading northern troops were nearby and the "secesh" forces were clearly defeated or at least on the defensive, the critical moment of decision had arrived. Paternalism and deference are useful terms when describing the antebellum slave community, but wartime realities destroyed all pretenses that slaves generally were contented with their lot. When presented with a genuine option for freedom, bondsmen overwhelmingly chose liberty, not loyalty to their masters.

Few things disconcerted slave owners more than their slaves forsaking them and fleeing to the Union armies. Many planters genuinely believed *their* bondsmen were tied to them by cords of need and affection. If some "foolish" slaves did choose to leave the security of the plantations for the imagined glories of freedom, planters reasoned that they must be either the dupes of abolitionist propaganda or crude field hands who barely knew and thus did not truly love their masters. Yet, in one of those momentous developments that foreshadowed the collapse of the Confederate dream, the myth of the satisfied Sambo was shattered by tens of thousands of slaves dropping all appearances of contentment with the status quo and seeking the unknown condition of freedom. Again and again it was not the field hands who left first, but rather the house-servants—the cooks, valets, and maids the whites most trusted. Perhaps because in their slightly elevated status they better appreciated the virtues of freedom or because their forced closeness to their white masters bred contempt more often than devotion or perhaps because their position allowed them earlier notice of the possibility of escape—or a combination of all three reasons— privileged slaves were frequently the first ones to reject bondage. Whites were usually thunderstruck, alternately frustrated and confused, then angry at the supposed ingratitude of their runaways. No other event showed more clearly how little whites really understood the blacks among them, nothing else so starkly highlighted the discrepancy between white expectations and black desires. The whole basis of Confederate civilization disintegrated as countless blacks, individually and in groups, chose to risk liberty when it seemed to be within their grasp.

Two sets of events allowed slaves to choose freedom. The military advances of Union troops, first along the perimeter of the South then into the heartland of Dixie, offered visible support for the aspirations of freedom-minded slaves, even though the Union position toward runaway slaves was initially ill-defined. Also, severe dislocations were caused by planters removing their slaves to interior locations and by the wartime conscription that sent thousands of slave owners to serve the Confederacy. As increasing numbers of planters, overseers, planters' sons, and other white men who in normal times controlled slave labor exchanged the agricultural life for the military, the whole regimen of slave discipline broke down. Despite futile attempts to regularize the slave patrols and the use of militia for social control, the vital nexus between planter authority and slave obedience weakened precipitately. Women, young boys, and old men simply could not replace the practiced eye and hand of the planter. (By the so-called twenty-slave rule, many large planters were legally exempted from conscription, but patriotism led numbers of them to take up arms for the Confederacy.) Finding weak discipline on the plantation and strong inducements to flee, thousands of slaves filtered through the cracks in the plantation system and repudiated their bondage. Before the war most slave runaways had been males acting alone, but now success seemed within reach and whole families went, with infants and mothers and white-haired grandparents taking the risk along with those better able to run. They came in such numbers as almost to overwhelm the Union armies and pose a profound dilemma for federal commanders and an opportunity for the cautious Abraham Lincoln.

War is a powerful social engine that often forces governments as well as men and women to do things that they would never consider in peacetime. War can accelerate social change. The Civil War proved to be such a revolutionary agent, and North and South were pushed by necessity into actions unthinkable in 1860. Nowhere was this more apparent than in the Union's relationship to slavery, for the migration of freedom-seeking bondsmen simply demanded a series of epochal decisions on the part of Lincoln and the Congress. The Republican party platform of 1860 had made clear that it did not advocate destroying slavery where it already existed, and in his speeches Lincoln had consistently disavowed any intention to use governmental power to end slavery in the South. In his inaugural address President Lincoln continued to disclaim any policy of abolishing slavery in those states where it was legal. Lincoln had constitutional scruples that held him back from forthrightly attacking slavery, and his own relatively mild racism precluded him from visualizing a biracial America; nevertheless, he personally abhorred slavery and pushed for colonization. The major factor in his decision to be cautious on the slavery issue was his fear that bold action might irrevocably tilt the border states toward the Confederate cause. After all, Union victory was not a sure thing in 1861, and Lincoln knew that overhasty action would lose him much of his northern support too. When the time appeared ripe in late 1862, Lincoln, despite what had seemed much temporizing, acted boldly to end racial bondage.

No sooner was the war begun than practical dilemmas began to intrude themselves in the midst of safe political compromises. In late May 1861 three slaves escaped to the Union lines at Fort Monroe, Virginia, only a few miles from where the first blacks had been introduced into Virginia in 1619, and asked to be received. General Benjamin F. Butler accepted them and put them to work. Because the Confederates had been employing the slaves as war laborers, Butler declared them contraband and refused to return them to their owners as the normal operation of the fugitive slave laws would require. No national policy had been established by Butler's decision, however, and Lincoln, despite his private feelings about slavery, had not yet been shoved from his conservative position with regard to government action. For several more months contradiction, confusion, and delay marked the administration's program, with commanders improvising in the field. In June General Henry W. Halleck decided to return all fugitive slaves, but on July 9 the House resolved that it was not the duty of federal troops either to capture or return them. Then a week later General Winfield Scott requested permission to allow the owners of slave runaways to seek and recover their claimed property behind Union lines.

The Halleck-Scott position seemed to be ratified by Congress on July 22 by the Crittenden resolution, which declared that the war was not being waged for the purpose "of overthrowing or interfering with the rights or established institutions" of the seceded states. On August 6, however, Congress passed the first Confiscation Act, which gave the federal government authority to seize any property used to aid the rebellion and to free slaves employed either as soldiers or workers against the United States. Lincoln signed the bill but intended to use very gingerly the powers granted him and the government, for he was determined to give the border states no reason to leave the Union. Yet events in the field provided Lincoln the opportunity to move toward recognizing the military potential of slave emancipation even as he continued to doubt the desirability of a biracial society. On August 30, 1861 barely three weeks after the Confiscation Act was passed, General John C. Frémont declared Missouri under martial law and proclaimed that all the slaves of persons resisting the Union were free. This obviously went far beyond the intentions of the framers of the Confiscation Act, and Lincoln quickly ordered Fremont to confine emancipation to the parameters set by the act.

The steady stream of slave refugees complicated the task of field commanders. Morality would not let them be turned away, but their numbers hindered the mobility of the Union armies and strained their supplies. Since it was apparent that the Confederate army was using slave laborers to spare white soldiers the most onerous work and, by so doing, effectively augmenting the number of men ready for combat, northern officers pushed at the restraints laid down by Lincoln. In October 1861 General Thomas W. Sherman was authorized to "employ fugitive slaves in such services as they may be fitted for," yet the acting secretary of war was careful to ensure that this was not construed as a general arming of slaves for military duty. The following March, General David Hunter issued a proclamation freeing slaves in Georgia, Florida, and South Carolina, but Lincoln quickly countermanded it.

By this time Lincoln seemed willing to allow the army to use fugitive slaves in noncombat duty, but not to have general emancipation discussed, for with the war stalemated he was ever mindful of the divided northern support for abolitionism and the need to keep the border states in the Union. When in May 1862 General Hunter, elaborating on the authorization given to General Sherman eight months earlier, began calling upon Negroes to form what he called the First South Carolina Regiment, Lincoln again objected, and the black troops were disbanded. Meanwhile Congress was addressing slavery both because of growing emancipationist sentiment in the North and because the fugitive slaves flocking to the Union armies in the South were simply forcing action. On March 13, 1862, Congress passed an act prohibiting the use of military force to effect the return of runaways. Lincoln had earlier proposed that Congress jointly resolve to aid any state that adopted a plan for gradual emancipation, including compensation of the former slave owners, and this was adopted on April 10. Within a week slavery was abolished in Washington, D.C., and, as the tempo picked up, a treaty was negotiated with England on May 20 pledging the two nations to cooperate in suppressing the international slave trade. Then, on June 19, 1862, Lincoln signed a bill abolishing slavery in the territories. On July 17 Congress, in a strengthened Confiscation Act, proclaimed free all those slaves belonging to disloyal masters who found themselves, either because the slaves had escaped to the Union lines or because the advancing army had occupied the region where they lived, within territory controlled by northern troops.

This was more an empty gesture than an effective act of emancipation, but it represented the slow advance of congressional sentiment to the point of recognizing that slavery had become the crux of the war. Somehow the basic purpose of the war had to be readjusted to take into account the emerging determination that slavery must be ended. This revolution in war aims did not occur solely as the result of northern moral growth. Free black protests above the

Mason-Dixon line and especially the tidal wave of fugitives below it made the revolution a practical and military necessity. Lincoln, a superb politician with his eye equally on the homefront and the battlefront, knew when to be cautious and when to act boldly. The war was not going well for the North; morale was sinking; troops were becoming frustrated, weary, angry at the heavy use of slaves as military laborers by the Confederates; international opinion questioned northern purposes. The border states were cool toward Lincoln's emancipation-colonization schemes. Something had to be done.

By early July, despite continuing public remarks about the war's being fought to preserve the Union, not to free the slaves, Lincoln's views about the feasibility and propriety of government action to end slavery shifted. He remained unconvinced of black equality and may have doubted to the very end of his life the practicality, much less the desirability, of a racially integrated society; moreover, his constitutional scruples allowed him no feasible way to change existing institutions without a constitutional amendment. But as an emergency war measure, extraordinary action could be taken. On July 13 Lincoln told Secretary of State William H. Seward and Secretary of the Navy Gideon Welles that he had nearly decided that an emancipation declaration was necessary in order to save the Union. The following week, on July 22, he announced at a cabinet meeting his decision to declare free all slaves within rebellious states on January 1, 1863. The cabinet members were not enthusiastic; only Seward and Secretary of Treasury Salmon P. Chase actively supported the plan, and Seward persuaded Lincoln to wait until a more favorable military situation before making the proclamation. Otherwise it would smack of desperation.

In late summer 1862 General Robert E. Lee began an invasion of Maryland, hoping to isolate Washington. A series of skirmishes followed with inconclusive results. Then in mid-September General George B. McClellan caught the Confederates, 40,000 strong, near Sharpsburg, and there followed the single bloodiest day of the war. After more than 23,000 casualties, nightfall mercifully came with the opposing forces at a draw, but on the next day, September 18, Lee retreated to Virginia, handing McClellan and the Union an important victory. By cutting short Lee's Maryland plans, the Union aborted a potential European intervention and paved the way for Lincoln's announcement. Consequently, on September 22, 1862, the president issued his preliminary Emancipation Proclamation, serving notice that on January 1, 1863, he would officially proclaim "all persons held as slaves within any State, or designated part of a State, the people whereof shall then be in rebellion against the United States, shall be then, thenceforward, and forever free."

It has often been pointed out that in a technical sense the Emancipation Proclamation freed no slaves (except in those Confederate-held regions where the Union had no power to effect any change), but the impact of the act was far-reaching nevertheless. Europeans were electrified by the notion of bondsmen being freed, as they imagined, by the stroke of a pen; southerners were frightened and incensed at what they guessed the consequences might be; abolitionists were disappointed that Lincoln didn't go further; slaves were cautiously optimistic when and if they heard about the Proclamation. But in a subtle though profound way Lincoln's pronouncement changed the purpose of the war, for without being completely aware of its impact (and in fact categorically denying that the military aim was now abolition) he opened the way for the war to be seen as a struggle to end slavery.

After Lincoln had decided to issue the Proclamation, it was harder to continue the restraints against freedmen serving as military laborers and even soldiers. During the autumn of 1862, therefore, Lincoln began to permit the enlistment on a limited basis of Negro troops. General Butler in New Orleans promptly mustered a troop composed supposedly of free men of color, though ex-slaves served too. General Rufus Saxton reconstituted the South Carolina regiment that General Hunter had formed and then disbanded in the face of Lincoln's disapprobation. By late fall the numbers of fugitive slaves coming into Union lines increased as northern forces pushed deeper into the South. In November General U. S. Grant attempted to deal with the problem in Tennessee by appointing Chaplain John Eaton, Jr., to be in charge of fugitives. A camp was established at Grand Junction, and later moved to Memphis, where shelter, food, and a modicum of medical attention was supplied. Able-bodied freedmen were hired out to whites who had leased abandoned plantations. Henceforth the emancipators were to deal with the refugee problem by adjusting the plantation system to the new realities of wage labor. This technique had been pioneered earlier in 1862 in the vicinity of Port Royal, South Carolina, and the prospects of combining social control of the blacks with the profitable production of staple crops proved too enticing for northern reformers to resist. Seeing therein a way to teach newly freed slaves middle-class Yankee habits of self-discipline and industry, hard-headed military commanders and visionary do-gooders agreed on the utility of this gradual transformation of dependent slaves into independent farmers. But as we shall see, Yankee notions of efficiency clashed with black notions of autonomy, and utopian dreams foundered as misunderstanding flourished. Freedmen in general were never given the wherewithal to prosper, and racism put limits on the patience of whites. In several locations—like the Davis Bend, Mississippi, properties of Jefferson Davis—freedmen were allotted land directly, planted food and cotton, and practiced virtual self-government under the watchful authority of army-appointed superintendents of Negro affairs. Despite localized success stories, most freedmen who farmed behind the Union lines did so as wage laborers on white-leased property. Such conditions were more nearly an apprenticeship for sharecropping than for real freedom. That freedmen were provided no solid economic footing was to be the ultimate failure of Reconstruction.

The war, however, had to be won before Reconstruction proper could commence, and the Emancipation Proclamation added a new dimension to the conflict: black soldiers. From the very beginning of the war northern free blacks had volunteered to fight for the Union and the freedom of their slave brothers, but their initial overtures were rejected. The Union forces had quite early in the conflict learned how to utilize for military purposes those slaves who escaped to their lines, but blacks were restricted to noncombatant roles. Even so they made an important contribution, building fortifications, constructing roads, scouring the countryside for food, transporting thousands of tons of military supplies by wagon over the wretched roads of the South. Moreover, ex-slaves who knew the terrain guided Union troops, piloted their vessels through the mazelike estuaries of the coastal regions, served as effective spies whose network of informants spread across the war-torn territory. Yet Union armies were hesitant to expand black participation beyond these functions.

On those occasions when field commanders decided for military or political reasons to arm blacks as Union soldiers, Lincoln had countermanded their orders. Lincoln was careful not to get too far ahead of public and congressional opinion on the issue, and through both leading and pushing he slowly helped educate the North in the cause of freedmen. The same slow process that culminated in the Emancipation Proclamation also changed governmental and eventually popular attitudes toward black soldiers. There had been a few blacks among the Union troops before mid-1862, but only afterward did the propriety of having black soldiers become widely accepted by the North. The Enlistment Act of July 17, 1862, tacitly acknowledged their existence by providing a differential wage for white and black troops, with the blacks receiving significantly less pay. Five weeks later, on August 25, 1862, the War Department authorized General Saxton to accept "volunteers of African descent" into the army. The Union army was obviously moving toward full-scale black participation in the war. Lincoln's Emancipation Proclamation of January 1, 1863, declared that the freed slaves "of suitable condition, will be received into the armed service of the United States to garrison forts, positions, stations, and other places, and to man vessels of all sorts in said service." Thereafter black soldiers became commonplace, eventually numbering 178,895, of whom 133,000 came from the former slave states.

Lincoln and most northerners were in the beginning uncomfortable with the idea of arming black soldiers to fight against white southerners. There were worries about border state sensibilities and about hardening the southern resolve, and of course there was a degree of racism involved. The discrimination against blacks in pay has been mentioned, but there was also concern that they had neither the habit nor the temperament for command. Consequently Negro troops were generally placed under white officers, several of whom, like Thomas Wentworth Higginson and Robert Gould Shaw, were considered representative of the flower of New England manhood. Black troops had inferior equipment and medical care and were expected to perform disproportionate amounts of backbreaking fatigue labor, but many proved themselves superb fighting men. In fact, their courage on the battlefield in a number of spirited engagements changed the low estimate most whites initially held of black military capabilities. Even Lincoln, ever circumspect, praised their martial accomplishments. Prejudiced white soldiers underwent a similar transformation. As the war dragged on, with casualties mounting and morale flagging, the potential of a vast reservoir of black troops slowly began to enter the white consciousness. Many northern whites had borne smoldering anger toward slaves for somehow causing the war and would not even think of serving with Negro troops. But with the purpose of the war evolving beyond merely saving the Union and with the visible evidence of blacks suffering and eager to sacrifice for the higher cause of freedom for all in bondage, racist Billy Yanks began to undergo a shift in opinion. Black performance on the field of battle opened the eyes of such doubters, and, out of self-interest as well as higher principles, white soldiers came to accept black comrades in arms. The military heroics of black soldiers helped transform the meaning of the war itself, lifting the act of emancipation from the dead level of military necessity to the lofty heights of a moral crusade.

Negro troops saw action in every theater of the war, serving with distinction in most southern states. At Battery Wagner in Charleston Harbor, at Milliken's Bend in Louisiana, at Vicksburg and Savannah, black soldiers shed their blood along with whites in the cause of union and freedom. The Confederate government and Rebel forces were infuriated, however, at the northern use of "slave" soldiers. In the eyes of the Confederates, black troops were slave insurrectionaries, and thus if captured subject either to reenslavement or death for treason. Lincoln responded by stating that a rebel soldier would be executed for every black Union soldier killed in violation of the commonly accepted laws of warfare, and that for every act of reenslavement a Confederate captive would be sentenced to hard labor. Since neither side officially retaliated against the other, Lincoln's forthright response may well have prevented widespread barbarities against black troops. Even so, there were clearly incidents where Confederates killed blacks in violation of the code of war and where they refused to take Negro prisoners; and at Fort Pillow, Tennessee, on April 2, 1864, southern troops in the heat of battle massacred almost 300 black Union soldiers who had surrendered. In total more than 38,000 black soldiers died from all causes in the Civil War, a mortality rate almost 40 percent higher than that of white troops. Within the limits of possibility open to them, blacks fought manfully (to use a nineteenth-century phrase filled with meaning in this context) for their freedom. Emancipation was not simply given to the slaves; they fought for freedom and, by their actions, both pressured Lincoln into formulating the Emancipation Proclamation and gave him the opportunity to do so. No one could have foreseen in 1861 what changes would occur in northern aims and black deportment.

Neither could anyone have envisioned the revolutionary changes that war wrought on the South. Without doubt the ultimate reason for secession had been the desire to preserve slavery, and southerners perceived that a Republican president threatened the peculiar institution. Even most large planters of Whiggish background and Unionist sentiment who opposed secession did so to preserve black bondage, for they thought secession would surely lead to war, which would cause the demise of slavery. Alexander Stephens, Confederate vice-president, stated the southern position on slavery with great candor in a notable address in Savannah on March 21, 1861. "Our new government is founded," he proclaimed, ". . . its corner-stone rests upon the great truth, that the negro is not equal to the white man; that slavery—subordination to the superior race—is his natural and normal condition."

Yet no sooner had the war commenced than the institution of slavery slowly began to dissolve like sugar cubes stirred in hot coffee. In the turmoil and social upheaval, patterns of discipline and structures of control collapsed. Migration of whites and removal of slaves from the theater of war brought irreparable upheaval to the once supposedly stable institution. Slaves were requisitioned by the army and reassigned to military commanders, breaking down the old power of the masters and giving black military laborers a glimpse of a larger world. Slavery simply disintegrated in the crucible of war. The logic of wartime necessity finally forced Jefferson Davis and Robert E. Lee to make the fundamental decision against slavery in a critical choice between sure defeat and possible success. With the northern edge in men and material bearing ever heavier upon southern forces, with the Union tapping deep reservoirs of black support via the Emancipation Proclamation, wearied and desperate men in the South dared to think the unthinkable. With defeat would come the certain end of slavery, and subjection to the victorious North. Why not offer to slaves who would volunteer to fight for the Confederate cause their freedom in return? While Confederate victory on such terms would mean the end of slavery, the victorious South would at least be an independent nation.

At first hardly anyone risked contemplating such a rash decision, for it represented a transformation of southern war aims (from the winning of national independence and preservation of slavery at all costs to preservation of independence at the cost of giving up slavery) as fundamental as the shift in northern war aims (from preservation of the Union even if slavery had to be left intact to ending slavery). But in the South as well as in the North, the realities of wartime forced each side to do what previously it could not have accepted. By early 1865 the Confederate establishment, led by Robert E. Lee and Jefferson Davis, was promoting emancipation of slaves and utilization of black soldiers for the southern cause. How their decision to emancipate slave soldiers evolved is the story of the declining military fortunes of the Confederacy.

As the months unfolded after Lincoln's Emancipation Proclamation on January 1, 1863, southern hopes for victory and independence began to wane. First Vicksburg fell, then Lee's bold thrust into Pennsylvania ended at Gettysburg. With Lincoln and the Union taking the moral high ground, Confederate attempts to gain support from France collapsed in midsummer. Almost imperceptibly the futility of southern struggle against the more powerful, more populous North began to enter the consciousness of southerners. Even more imperceptible was the gradual realization that slavery, "somehow," in Lincoln's phrase, the cause of the war, might be turned into a Confederate asset if slaves could be enlisted as soldiers in the cause of southern independence. Following the successful introduction of black troops by the North, scattered individuals broached the idea of Confederate Negro soldiers, and even the legislature of Alabama suggested the use of black troops. But it was an officer in the army of Tennessee, General Patrick Cleburne, who first made a careful analysis of the potential of slave troops, and he outlined on January 2, 1864, his detailed plans for enlistment of slave soldiers and emancipation of loyal bondsmen.

Although there was spirited debate in the officer corps over Cleburne's plan, his idea was officially scotched. When Jefferson Davis learned of the plan from a disgruntled Georgia general, he ordered suppression of all discussion of the suggestion. Davis knew how explosive the issue might be, but he clearly recognized the merit of Cleburne's proposal. In fact, Davis apparently had reasoned his own way along the path of logical arguments that supported Cleburne's conclusion. In his message to the Confederate Congress on November 7, 1864, Davis asked that the government be authorized to purchase 40,000 slaves, who in return for their military service would be emancipated. As was to be expected, Davis's request engendered animated debate, and the Confederate Congress sidestepped the issue. There was support, and support from unexpected quarters, but for many southerners, to arm slaves was to repudiate their entire world view. As General Howell Cobb argued in January 1865, "If slaves will make good soldiers our whole theory of slavery is wrong."

Yet the Confederacy was collapsing around them at the end of 1864. Savannah had fallen, and in desperation Davis sent Duncan F. Kenner to France and England promising emancipation in exchange for diplomatic recognition. Napoleon III said he would do what England did, and Lord Palmerston bluntly refused the offer. In early February a secret peace meeting between Lincoln and Seward and southern spokesmen aboard a steamboat in the waters off Hampton Roads fell apart when Lincoln refused to budge on his demand for reunion. A week later the Davis administration introduced a bill to arm the slaves, and the critical issue hung in the balance awaiting General Lee's opinion. On February 18, in an open letter to Representative Ethelbert Barksdale, Lee wrote that "with reference to the employment of negroes as soldiers I think the measure not only expedient but necessary." Moreover, he believed that the slaves would "make efficient soldiers," and furthermore he felt that "those who are employed should be freed." Following Lee's announcement, the Congress narrowly voted to arm the slaves but not to free them.

However, when President Davis acted to implement the law via General Order Number Fourteen of March 23, 1865, he went beyond Congress's authorization and in effect offered freedom to those bondsmen called upon for military duty. Two days later black troops were being formed into a company, but the great experiment came too late to have any military effect. Eight days later, on April 3, with his city surrounded by Union troops, the mayor of Richmond surrendered the city. Within a week Lee met General Grant at Appomattox Courthouse, west of Richmond, and told his war-weary men to lay down their arms. On April 9, 1865, at long last, the great war was over.

If it had gone on for several more months, if thousands of slaves had fought for the southern cause and gained not only their freedom but possibly also the respect and appreciation of white Confederates who saw their antebellum theories exploded as General Cobb had suggested—but history is not written in the subjunctive. The South was defeated, soundly whipped, her peculiar institution effectively dismantled by outside forces. Among the far-reaching results of the process of emancipation was a significant increase in white racial animosity toward blacks. Northern leaders knew that military necessity had spurred emancipation and were suspicious of southern intentions once the war was concluded. The Thirteenth and Fourteenth Amendments were pushed through Congress (January 31, 1865, and June 16, 1866, respectively) and ratified by a complex and controversial process (December 16, 1865, and June 20, 1868, respectively) to guarantee that ex-slaves would remain free and be citizens protected by due process of law. The Reconstruction Acts of March 2 and 23, 1867, gave southern blacks the right to vote. Despite the failures of Reconstruction and all the missed opportunities of the immediate postwar years, these two amendments, along with the Fifteenth (ratified in 1870), which gave northern blacks the right to vote and confirmed constitutionally the Reconstruction Acts' enfranchisement of southern blacks, eventually proved to be the foundation upon which greater justice could be achieved.

Yet many contemporary southerners interpreted the amendments as a slap in the face, a rubbing of Confederate noses in the dirt. Careful Confederate decisions about freeing loyal slave soldiers were one thing, but forced black citizenship, following military defeat, economic collapse, and Union occupation strained to the breaking point southern conceptions of the nature of civilized society. The newly emerging racial reality was evolving faster than the ability of most white southerners to adjust, and former rebels reacted with a sullen resistance that only proved their insolence in the eyes of northerners. The anger of white southerners was aimed almost equally against occupying northern troops, Republican congressmen, and the freedmen in their midst—who were least able to protect themselves from vengeance.

Widespread reports of violence and brutality greeted blacks' introduction to freedom in the South, but black violence in return was limited. On some occasions, as in the case of the planters' townhouses in Beaufort, South Carolina, blacks wreaked vengeance for two centuries of bondage by ransacking homes and taking away what they deemed usable, but this was an exceptional occurrence. Freedmen typically avoided doing damage to their plantation homes, in part because they realized the planter's mansion had been built by their sweat and toil, because they identified with and even took a kind of pride in their plantations, and because, practical even in the euphoria of newfound freedom, they realized how powerful the grasp of the landowning whites, their erstwhile masters, still remained. No matter how much had changed, the whites still owned the land, still controlled the government, and the blacks had only their labor to offer. As it turned out, whites needed black labor as badly as blacks needed white-owned land, and gradually, as in the days of slavery, by push and shove, give and take, mutual accommodations were worked out that resulted generally in a system of agriculture called sharecropping.

Newly freed blacks had no experience with freedom, but they intuitively sensed its major components. Nothing meant freedom more tangibly than having the leisure to move around, to travel about without the mandatory pass and ever-present fear of patrollers. Consequently many freedmen tried out their freedom shoes by rambling, but this migration was less pervasive and more purposeful than most contemporary whites realized. There was a degree of aimless wandering as some experimented with freedom, but most blacks were seeking loved ones previously sold away or separated by wartime dislocations, or they moved to towns and urban areas where personnel of the Freedmen's Bureau (technically the Bureau of Refugees, Freedmen, and Abandoned Lands, established by Congress on March 3, 1865, to handle "all subjects relating to refugees and freedman") could offer them protection from unrepentant Confederates and provide food, blankets, and other emergency supplies; or, most important, they moved about in search of better employment. The black population of southern towns and cities grew very rapidly, as significant numbers of former slave artisans moved to cities to try to practice their crafts, but the overwhelming majority of freedmen remained in rural areas.

Most southern whites misinterpreted this black mobility as confirmation of their belief that blacks were irresponsible and would not stay put and work productively unless coerced. The result was strong proscriptions against black "vagrancy" in the oppressive black codes passed by the southern state legislatures in 1865-66, proscriptions that northern observers saw as a stubborn rebel effort to reject the outcome of the war. White overreaction to black mobility only served to strengthen the resolve of northern liberals that slavery not be reinstituted under another guise. As the *Chicago Tribune* editorialized on December 1, 1865, "We tell the white men of Mississippi, that the men of the north will convert the State of Mississippi into a frog pond before they will allow such laws to disgrace one foot of the soil in which the bones of our soldiers sleep and over which the flag of freedom waves." Southern stubbornness and northern arrogance did not bode well for the future, and regrettably much Confederate anger fell upon the more convenient and relatively defenseless ex-slave.

If anyone needed further evidence that slaves were not childlike, fawning Sambos by nature, then the cautious persistence with which freedmen asserted their personhood in the face of the entrenched white animosity should prove the point. Blacks in the postwar period were to push for greater control over their leisure time and for more autonomy as a family unit, as will be discussed below. The strength of the freedmen's desire to cement their marriages—legally nonexistent and in practice often fragile during slavery—revealed itself as thousands of black couples came to Union army chaplains to have their vows solemnized.

There was also an almost pathetic desire on the part of freedmen to gain an education, a rejection of the restrictions against slaves being taught to read. Hundreds of northern schoolteachers came south and found that blacks, children and adults alike, were eager to learn. After all, segregated schools were better than no schools at all. These northern schoolmarms met vicious southern resistance, and as soon as military occupation was over and southerners controlled southern politics again, funds for public black schools were severely reduced. Illiteracy imposed by whites continued to plague freedmen, and not until the 1950s, with the separate-but-equal (always in fact separate and unequal) doctrine threatened, did southern legislatures make any serious effort to provide a high-quality education for their black citizens. Not until a century after Reconstruction did southern blacks receive equal and integrated schooling in the South, where ironically it is now more common than in the North.

In many areas of everyday life, blacks progressed from being excluded (from schools, health and welfare services, and public accommodations) to being granted admission to segregated facilities, but in religion the change went in the other direction. In the antebellum South most black Christians had worshipped with whites in biracial churches, where, even though to be sure there was discrimination and slaves were second-class members, they had gained more privileges and received more equal treatment than anywhere else in southern society. Northern churchmen, however, saw the South after the war as a fertile mission field, with four million freedmen as possible converts. Northern churches rushed to establish southern branches of the African Methodist Episcopal Church, the African Methodist Episcopal Church Zion, and the Methodist Episcopal Church North, for example. Tens of thousands of ex-slaves withdrew from their biracial churches and joined these new all-black churches. (Some white missionaries and scattered white northerners who had recently settled in the region were also members, but in the South churches affiliated with northern denominations quickly became almost exclusively black.) After the formative stages when northern missionaries were founding the churches, freedmen who had been slave preachers and exhorters led the new denominations. These men and their fervent congregations were part of the delayed harvest of slave Christianity.

Across the South many thousands of freed people also withdrew from their biracial churches and formed black versions of the southern denominations. The National Baptist Convention and the Colored Methodist Episcopal Church were the two largest denominations to result. In all the black churches the theology, the ritual, and the organization were very similar to those of the white churches from which their membership was drawn. The numbers and devotion of the black worshipers and the adeptness of their ministers suggest the vitality of slave Christianity. Even though slave members had not been accorded complete equality, they had practiced leadership roles, nurtured their sense of self-worth, and grown in faith. Slave participation in antebellum southern "white" churches had been a critical proving ground for black survival skills and cultural growth. The burgeoning of black churches after the Civil War points back to the centrality of Christianity in the slave community.

It should be pointed out that the blacks withdrew from their old churches; they were not initially excluded. Many whites tried to persuade the freedmen not to separate, both because whites feared losing still more control over them and because many sincerely doubted the ability of blacks to preach the Gospel "pure and undefiled." Still others genuinely hated to see a racial division in the church, believing with Saint Paul that in Christ there was neither bond nor free. But freedmen had chafed under white control—even well-intentioned white paternalism—for too long. Black faith was strong, black leaders were able, and the black need for self-direction and autonomy was manifest. Consequently southern churches became significantly more segregated after the Civil War, and the move away from joint worship was instigated by blacks though the separation was later applauded by the whites. Despite the similarities in theology and organization, the two races have continued down separate paths ever since. The differences between white and black Christianity—especially the expressed emotion, sermon style, music, and length of service—were ironically greater in 1960 than they were in 1860.

The changes required by their altered status went beyond things of the spirit, as blacks well knew. Inexperienced as they were with the reality of freedom, the freedmen nevertheless understood the necessity of land ownership if they were to have real liberty. "What's de use of being free if you don't own land enough to be buried in? Might just as well stay slave all yo' days," said one freedman. During the war the Freedmen's Bureau had settled several thousand blacks on land abandoned by southern planters, particularly in the coastal regions of South Carolina and Georgia, and throughout the South the federal government had gained control of hundreds of thousands of acres of abandoned land (and of course there also was public, government-owned land in the South). On a limited scale, in isolated regions, freedmen were granted ownership of small parcels of land. Partly because of this, and partly because of a much-discussed speech by Thaddeus Stevens advocating that ex-slaves be given forty acres, the "forty acres and a mule" rumor spread across the South. Yet never was there an explicit plan to confiscate and redistribute the property of wealthy planters. Even the relatively small-scale efforts undertaken by the Freedmen's Bureau with abandoned land were aborted by President Andrew Johnson, who ordered all property returned to the Confederates whom he pardoned with abundant generosity. Johnson's actions ended the last best hope most freedmen had for genuine financial independence. Yet the wrenching economic conditions in the postwar South were so severe that land ownership would probably not have made a substantial difference in the long run unless blacks had opted for a peasantlike existence outside the market-crop economy.

One final attempt was made to provide the freedmen with land, the Southern Homestead Act, which was passed by Congress and signed by President Johnson on June 21, 1866. This act set aside approximately 45 million acres of public land in five southern states for homesteading; the land was available in plots with a maximum size of 80 acres; it was free except for a $5.00 registration fee due after five years' settlement; and it was reserved solely for freedmen and loyal refugees until January 1, 1867. Yet this apparent windfall was of little consequence, for practically no newly freed slaves had the capital to move, buy supplies, seed, implements, draft animals, and feed themselves while waiting for the first crop. Moreover, much of the land was of inferior quality. Hence the freedmen's dream of free land in return for their two hundred years of previously unrequited toil remained a dream unfulfilled. Even if freedmen had the money to buy good land in familiar areas with adequate transportation, few whites would sell to blacks—indeed in Mississippi it was illegal to do so for a time. For most freedmen, then, the beginning of the age of liberty saw them landless, uneducated, untrained, and faced with white animosity and only a very grudging white willingness to accept the new dispensation of black freedom.

No part of the new dispensation was more upsetting to white southerners then and for long after than black participation in politics. One of the results of Reconstruction was that blacks voted, were elected to office, and became active members of a national political party. Nothing angered former Rebels (some of whom were temporarily disfranchised) more than the "spectacle" of blacks voting. Charges of "barbarism overwhelming civilization" and "Negro supremacy" were bandied around, and these accusations have been surprisingly tenacious in their hold on American historical mythology. In fact, while about four-fifths of southern Republican voters were black, whites dominated party policy making and positions of influence. Blacks never controlled the South politically, never even held the percentage of offices their population entitled them to. No black ever became governor of a southern state, and only in South Carolina from 1868 to 1876 did blacks hold a majority in the lower house. Less than 20 percent of southern political offices at the height of Reconstruction were held by blacks, and many of those office holders were clearly qualified. Only two blacks were elected to the Senate, both from Mississippi, and both were well prepared for the position. Blanche K. Bruce was northern-educated and had attended Oberlin College (1865-67), and Hiram R. Revels was a graduate of Illinois's Knox College. Fifteen blacks were elected to the House of Representatives from the entire South during the whole period. Negro rule was more in the minds of white southerners than in reality.

A disproportionate number of Negroes elected to national and local offices had been free blacks before the Civil War, and many were light-skinned. Often the ex-slaves who rose to political prominence had held privileged positions even as slaves. Also many black politicians had been either preachers in antebellum times or, immediately after the war, teachers in Freedmen's Bureau schools; in other words, they were natural leaders. Many were relatively well-to-do, and they often had white patrons, were upwardly mobile and middle-class in attitudes, and were markedly moderate in their racial and economic policies. As with all people, there were some corrupt, incompetent black officials, but as a group, especial-

ly given their educational and economic disadvantages in the antebellum South, freedmen handled their political responsibilities
remarkably well. In no other aspect is the old "angry scar" version
of Reconstruction more false than in its indiscriminate condemna-
tion of black politicians in the postwar South.

The unwillingness of southern whites to accept the changed
status of blacks led to their efforts to control blacks in ways clearly
reminiscent of slavery. Some whites wanted to avoid all relationships with the "ungrateful" former slaves and toyed unsuccessfully
with imported Chinese and later Italian laborers. Despite harsh
feelings, black and white were forced to work out mutual accommodations because without black labor the white-owned land was
useless, and without the whites' land (and to some degree, managerial and marketing skills), the blacks' labor was meaningless.
Both races had to make difficult adjustments.

Whites had no experience in managing blacks as legal equals, as
independent free men and women; whites expected still to control
their black laborers' life-style, to discipline them by whipping, to
dictate their wages and working hours; whites especially expected
to be responded to in the same deferential manner they had known
in the era of slavery. Blacks' moving about—and mobility was normal for free labor in the mid-nineteenth century—was interpreted
as irresponsible behavior; every slight infraction of the old slave
etiquette was seen as evidence of blacks "not staying in their place."
While freedmen had long been schooled in the arts of deference and
dissembling, they were now cautiously willing to express their
freedom. This seldom meant much more than no longer stepping
off the sidewalk to let whites pass, or no longer performing the
obligatory tipping of the hat, or perhaps no longer even practicing
such a subtle act of deference as averting the eyes, but whites saw
every infraction of the old decorum as proof of Yankee-inspired
Negro insolence.

Antebellum white society had contained a muffled undertone of
fear that slaves might rebel, a fear legitimated by such rare occur-
rences as Nat Turner's 1831 insurrection and kept alive by rumor.
In the months following Appomattox, with Union troops visibly
present, often with black soldiers on active duty, southern whites
felt a resurgence of the old terror that had haunted antebellum
days. They saw freedmen growing more bold and arrogant every

day, and they feared that when the ex-slaves realized there was not going to be a government gift of land and livestock they would rebel in anger and disappointment. Southerners across the region in late 1865 imagined a great Christmas Day insurrection plot. Frustrated over the collapse of the Confederacy, filled with anxiety about the future, white fears and tensions built up to fever pitch, and near hysteria reigned in dozens of counties across the South. As so often in the past, the rebellion existed only in the overwrought imaginations of the whites; Christmas Day passed peacefully. But after the panic subsided white southerners were even more unified, Union authorities were put on the defensive, and blacks were vividly reminded that white fear and white power were two interlocking facts that could still inflict great injury on blacks who strayed too quickly and too far from old patterns of behavior.

In that sense blacks had as difficult an adjustment to make as did whites to the new conditions of freedom. For while whites had no experience managing freedmen, blacks had little in acting as free agents in their dealings with whites. Most blacks wanted to stay on the safe side of expected behavior, but most at the same time wanted to assert their changed status in subtle but clearly recognized ways. There was a tentativeness, an uncertain tone, a nervous sense of experimentation as blacks tried out new patterns of relationships with whites. Racism was still rampant, even growing in the aftermath of Appomattox, and white southerners were determined to find new ways of maintaining their sense of racial superiority now that slavery was legally dead. Nevertheless, as in the days of slavery, blacks pushed against white restraints, tugged at new opportunities, and succeeded in working out an expanded arena of autonomy in the face of white suspicions and recrimination. For example, freedmen insisted on being farmers, not wage slaves, and the result was a reshaping of southern agriculture.

In some ways black emancipation was a mighty revolution, but in others, the more things changed the more they stayed the same. The South was not a blank slate upon which could be written a new society. The same actors were present, carrying their old attitudes with them, the climate and soil were unchanged, cotton still loomed as the great money crop, and the power relationships between black and white were essentially the same. With the war over, persons of both races had to turn their thoughts to making a living, which meant a return to the old staple-crop standbys of the past: rice, sugar, tobacco, and especially cotton. Convinced as they were that blacks would not work unless forced to, whites began to experiment with methods of exploiting them in ways reminiscent of slavery. They accepted with resentment that freedmen now had to be paid wages, but landowners expected the blacks to dwell once more in the former slave quarters bunched together near the big house and to work the fields in gangs under close white supervision. Sometimes wages were paid monthly in cash (about $10 per month for an adult male), but usually half the wages were payable at the end of the year after the crops were harvested.

The system of monetary wages did not work out well for either party. Whites required their agricultural workers to sign contracts severely limiting their freedom of movement, specifying the landowner's right to control their working hours and arrangements, and requiring "strict obedience" to the landowner. The contracts also contained some guarantees of the rights of blacks, and for that reason Freedmen's Bureau personnel helped to persuade or force reluctant freedmen to sign them and live up to their contractual obligations. Even some whites reluctantly admitted that in this important matter, the despised Freedmen's Bureau aided the interests of the whites. Blacks obviously resented the heavy overtones of bondage associated with such labor contracts and resisted by shopping around for landowners who gave them better terms.

In the postwar labor shortage, this limited ability of blacks to choose their employer gave them considerable leverage, and they used it to gain greater autonomy. After all, they knew far too well the cost of having one's practical freedom controlled by another. Freedmen pushed for the right to live apart from the old slave quarters, out from under the landowner's watchful eye; they wanted their houses on separate acreage, so they could grow their crops as an independent family unit. This insistence was eloquent testimony of the persistence of the black family during slavery and the blacks' desire to strengthen it. Moreover, because landowners devised numerous methods of shortchanging often illiterate blacks when payday came—even sometimes dismissing freedmen for some minor infraction after the harvest was in and telling them they had thus forfeited their wages—freedmen preferred payment in the form of a share of the crop. In a sense blacks then were paying a portion of their share of the crop as rent, rather than receiving a wage from the landowner. By receiving a specified percentage of the harvest their skill and hard work would be rewarded.

Landowners too were dissatisfied with the wage system that first evolved, in part because, since it gave freedmen no incentive to work hard, a great deal of irksome supervision was required. Occasionally blacks would leave in midseason, with or without their wages, and the landowner was then precariously short of manpower to harvest his cotton at the most labor-intensive period of the entire crop year. Primarily, however, white landowners—the former planters—desired a shift away from wages because there was a desperate shortage of money in the postwar South. Planters, even wealthy ones, were land poor and simply had no ready cash with which to pay wages. For that reason they welcomed the development of a system of payment in crop shares, for not only did that lessen their cash requirements, but it also placed an equal share of the crop risk on the freedmen. Moreover, without really ever openly acknowledging it and despite all their fears of black laziness and irresponsibility, they discovered that blacks could and would work productively without substantial supervision when they and their families were allowed a degree of independence, which gave pride and incentive free play. Ironically, what blacks desired and pressed for, whites began to accept too as the best compromise. Sharecropping emerged as another form of mutual accommodation.

Most freedmen, without an opportunity to possess their own land in fee simple, came to see their assigned sharecropper's "farm" as the next best thing, for at least they had more control over their own work schedules and had privacy in their home life. In addition to their greater freedom, the ex-slaves in the years immediately after the war received more than twice as high a proportion of the agricultural output of the large agricultural units (an aggregate of many sharecroppers' plots, the new form of the old plantation) as they had in the days of slavery. In fact, considering the total standard of living, the basic material income of these blacks increased by about a third as a result of emancipation. But what freedmen apparently valued most was the increased control over their own lives, over their patterns of consumption, over their leisure time.

On their individual agricultural units, black families could choose to maximize output by keeping the women and children in the fields as during slavery, or they could accept a somewhat lower output (and material standard of living) by withholding a portion of the family members' labor. On the whole black families preferred to withdraw the mother from the field except at periods of most intense labor needs and let her perform more the role of mother and housewife than that of field hand. Similarly children were exempted from some labor when public schooling was available.

Blacks now had the freedom to choose more leisure for their families, and they chose to enhance the maternal role of the wife. In part this represented an adoption of white cultural norms, where the farm women were primarily housewives and mothers and only secondarily field workers; in part it was a conscious rejection of white capitalistic ethics that deemed output maximization the highest value. Freedmen had their own ideas about the proper mix of work and leisure, a carryover from bondage, and their alternative attitudes about work habits persisted into the new age. Whites, especially northern capitalists come south to take advantage of cotton opportunities, found black work discipline irrational if not incomprehensible, but blacks simply did not value work in and of itself and had little reason to expect significant gain from additional increments of labor. Given the ultimate plight of the postwar cotton economy, the blacks may have been wiser than they knew.

Sharecropping never became the exclusive system of agricultural organization in the postwar South. A variety of systems existed: plain renting of land, work for cash wages or wages paid in crop shares, and so on. Some blacks, utilizing the entrepreneurial skill they had developed as slaves through their ownership of livestock, fowl, boats, wagons, and their growing of garden produce, combined hard work, skill, and luck to scrape together enough money to buy small parcels of land, and by 1880 about one-fifth of the black farmers in the South owned their land—a miraculous accomplishment, even though the average size of the farm was less than half the size of those owned by whites. But for the majority of blacks, some variant of sharecropping was their lot. Those who owned their own mules, plows, and enough capital to provision themselves for the year needed a landowner to supply the actual land, a house, and usually firewood. In return the blacks, called in this case share tenants, would pay the owner one-third of the corn and one-quarter of the cotton; this was called "working on thirds and fourths."

Most freedmen, however, were in no position to provide themselves with draft animals, implements, and provisions. Instead they could offer only their labor. The landlord supplied everything else but food and clothing and for his efforts received one-half the cotton and grain production. For their essential food and clothing the sharecroppers had to find a supplier who would extend them credit, the balance being due when the cotton was picked. Thousands of small country stores mushroomed across the cotton South in the years immediately following the war to perform this service, and many large landowners also began to offer their sharecroppers store supplies on credit. The "furnishing merchants" charged the sharecroppers "credit" prices that included interest rates averaging about 60 percent per annum on the provisions bought.

The stores were able to charge such rates because the sharecroppers usually had no alternative supplier. Stores were sparsely scattered across the rural South, and there was little competition. The merchants justified the charges by the high risk of offering credit to penniless farmers dependent upon an unreliable crop affected by the vagaries of climate and the selling price of cotton. Moreover, the large northern wholesale houses that supplied the local stores on credit charged them enormously high interest rates because of the risks involved in their business. Even well-disposed furnishing merchants had no choice but to pass their interest rates (often camouflaged as higher prices) on to the consumers. Because of the inflated prices of necessary provisions, hundreds of thousands of sharecroppers found that their one-half of the cotton would not even cover their debt at the local store. So at the end of the year, after the landowner took his share and the storekeeper settled up his accounts, the sharecropper family had no choice but to ask for credit for another year in the futile hope that an extraordinary crop yield would finally boost them over their debt hurdle and allow them to buy a little patch of land. Another year's labor, another middling crop, left them deeper in debt. This situation explains the use of the pernicious crop lien.

Merchants quite understandably required collateral from the sharecroppers for the credit extended them, but the landless farmers had no assets except the expectation of a crop. In the first postbellum years the state legislatures passed crop-lien laws, which allowed merchants to require that the sharecroppers given credit sign a lien bond that legally bound the future crop to the merchant, and the merchants often stipulated (if not in writing then by a plain understanding) that cotton be grown almost to the exclusion of grain crops. The lien laws had several effects. First, of course, the croppers were tied to the merchant by the legal promise of the next year's harvest, and the merchant had first claim to the crop. If the sharecroppers' harvest did not cover what they owed the merchant, they ended the year further in debt. They had to get credit for the following year, often having to take a reduction in the amount loaned (and hence a further reduction in the standard of living), and by the lien that secured the credit were tied once more to cotton and farming on the shares. There simply was no escape; every year many slipped further behind, locked ever more firmly into an endless circle of cotton, credit, and economic catastrophe. Secondly, since the merchant demanded that they maximize cotton production because he received his payment from its sale, farmers on shares had to reduce the labor and acreage given over to food crops, thus forcing them to buy more canned goods from the store, pushing them still further in debt. For hundreds of thousands of sharecroppers, black and white, King Cotton had become a tyrant from whose grasp there was no escape.

The net result of the far-reaching changes in how cotton was grown, financed, and marketed in the South was both a tremendous increase in bales harvested and a sobering increase in southern poverty. Because the freedmen valued a modicum of leisure and withheld some of the labor of their wives and children, there occurred immediately after the war about a one-third drop in the number of hours worked per capita; this of course resulted in a substantial drop in cotton output per capita. But as persons of both races in the war-prostrated South turned almost exclusively to cotton as a way to get on their feet and perhaps prosper, cotton acreage skyrocketed and so did the total output. The crop lien system further aggravated this trend, as well as causing an equally distressing decline in the production of foodstuffs. The South as a whole had been basically self-sufficient in 1860, but by 1870 its food output had declined by half.

To make matters worse, as the South produced more cotton, so did other regions in the world, and the opening of the Suez Canal made Indian cotton more competitive in price. At the same time global demand for cotton had declined from its antebellum rate of growth, and worldwide overproduction caused the price to fall. For example, in the twenty years after 1869, southern cotton production doubled and the price fell almost 50 percent. Individual sharecroppers, sliding deeper into debt, simply arranged another credit line and did what seemed rational—planted still more acres of cotton in hope of one good year that would allow them to pay out. But every sharecropper did the same, production increased, prices fell, and the poor suffered most. The crop lien tied the sharecropper to cotton, and the merchant, who bought his goods on credit from northern wholesalers, had to insist that his creditors plant the sure money crop. The system could not be budged off center.

Hundreds of thousands of white farmers, including many who began the postbellum era owning their land, lost money, then their farms to the falling cotton market; they too became sharecroppers. Even had blacks been given forty acres and a mule, since they had had little experience with money management and credit arrangements in slavery times, chances are that they, like so many white yeoman farmers, would have backslid into sharecropping. Almost no one in southern agriculture, except perhaps some furnishing merchants, really prospered. The South's great lack of capital linked sharecropper to merchant to northern wholesaler, with enormous though often hidden interest rates extracted at each successive stage. Profits flowed north, poverty flourished in the South. In 1880 the per capita income of the southern states had plummeted to about one-third that of the rest of the United States.

Mired in such a situation, freedmen often found the fruits of liberty to be less bountiful than they expected. Even though their antebellum experience often left them skilled agriculturalists, their inexperience with ledgers and credit often made them easy game for unprincipled landowners and storekeepers. Even more debilitating was the virulent racism that infected the postwar South. Whites, even before the withdrawal of Union troops at the end of Reconstruction, always controlled the region, and the bitter racial feelings that emerged from Confederate defeat and the end of slavery if anything worsened amidst the debilitating poverty that struck whites as well as blacks. With laws and the authorities against them, with woefully inadequate educational opportunities, with increasing disenfranchisement and their mobility limited, freedmen found the New South no promised land.

Perhaps the ultimate tragedy of slavery and Reconstruction is that it prepared neither the blacks, nor the whites, nor the southern economy for a changing market system. Just as with slavery, no one escaped the implications of poverty, racism, and, ultimately, hopelessness in the postwar South. There was a brief moment of protest near the end of the century, a farmers' rebellion that even held promise of limited biracial political cooperation. But the tyranny of King Cotton was not really lessened until the twentieth century, when the boll weevil, farm mechanization, the automobile, paved roads, and World War II finally forced the South out of its one-crop, labor-intensive farming, its rural isolation, and its paucity of capital. Not until almost a century after the Civil War began did southern blacks really begin to move beyond racism and poverty and into freedom.

When the grandchildren and great-grandchildren of former slaves finally achieved the real beginning of liberty, they were led by fellow descendants of former slaves. Despite all its deprivations and brutality, slavery never completely erased that spark of humanity and thirst for freedom from the souls of its victims. When they were able to find the opportunities, in the midst of the Civil War, in the early fluidity of postwar agricultural readjustments, in the early twentieth-century migrations to the North, in the 1960s struggle for desegregation, blacks strode toward freedom. The history of the blacks, those other southerners who have lived and died and struggled in Dixie for over 350 years, is so intertwined with that of their white brothers that both are quintessentially southern. Neither group's past can be understood without that of the other, and both are so bound by the tie of related historical experience that perhaps it will be in the South after all that racial harmony and justice will first take deep root and prosper.

Bibliographical Essay

The earliest comprehensive scholarly history of slavery in North America is Ulrich B. Phillips, *American Negro Slavery: A Survey of the Supply, Employment and Control of Negro Labor as Determined by the Plantation Regime* (New York: D. Appleton and Company, 1918), now available in paperback (Baton Rouge: Louisiana State University Press, 1966) with a perceptive and appreciative foreword by Eugene D. Genovese. Phillips's obvious racism mars the book, but it nevertheless contains much detailed information and remains the indispensable beginning point of slavery scholarship. It was replaced as the basic textbook by Kenneth M. Stampp's even more widely researched study, *The Peculiar Institution: Slavery in the Ante-Bellum South* (New York: Alfred A. Knopf, 1956) which, among its other virtues, contains a racially liberal answer to Phillips. With slavery's malevolent nature established, Stanley M. Elkins in *Slavery: A Problem in American Institutional and Intellectual Life* (Chicago: University of Chicago Press, 1959) showed that it was essential to go on to the other questions: what was slavery really like and what was its effect on slaves themselves? Elkins proved the necessity of utilizing the techniques of the behavioral sciences, comparative history, and model building to understand the nature of slavery. If his major conclusions, even his basic historical assumptions, have not stood up well to subsequent inquiry, his immensely provocative book asks the right questions and has inspired a generation of fruitful scholarship. Even more than Phillips, Elkins set the agenda for slavery studies, and most students of the subject since 1959 have found themselves, consciously or unconsciously, addressing Elkins's theses.

The 1960s brought a proliferation of scholarship on slavery, with important monographs on its many aspects. Representative titles are sprinkled throughout the following pages. The decade ended with a seminal work by Philip D. Curtin, *The Atlantic Slave Trade: A Census* (Madison: University of Wisconsin Press, 1969), that in terms of slavery in the United

States was more important for what it implied than for what it actually said. Census figures for African importations to the mainland of North America were surprisingly low, especially considering the resident black population in, say, 1830. Perhaps physical conditions and, by extrapolation, maneuvering room for black family and cultural life, were better in the United States than in Latin America. Such proved to be the case, as exemplified in two important studies published in 1972, George P. Rawick's *From Sundown to Sunup: The Making of the Black Community* (Westport, Conn.: Greenwood Press) and especially John W. Blassingame's *The Slave Community: Plantation Life in the Ante-Bellum South* (revised and enlarged; New York: Oxford University Press, 1979). Not only did these two volumes exemplify the shift from viewing slaves as hapless victims to seeing them as individuals who creatively coped with their plight, but they also introduced more historians to black sources. Blassingame skillfully used ex-slave autobiographies and memoirs, and Rawick showed how immensely valuable the WPA-gathered ex-slave interviews could be. Rawick's book introduced an eighteen-volume set of reproduced interviews with former slaves, *The American Slave: A Composite Autobiography* (Westport, Conn.: Greenwood Press, 1972), a set extensively augmented recently by two series of supplemental volumes and a detailed index compiled by Donald M. Jacobs, *Index to The American Slave* (Westport, Conn.: Greenwood Press, 1981). Blassingame's bibliography lists the major black autobiographies and memoirs, and he includes a perceptive essay on how to read such sources. The slave narratives that Rawick brought to the attention of the scholarly world have frequently been put to careless use and have themselves become an object of study. See Blassingame, "Using the Testimony of Ex-Slaves: Approaches and Problems," *Journal of Southern History* 41 (November 1975): 473-92; David Thomas Bailey, "A Divided Prism: Two Sources of Black Testimony on Slavery," *ibid.*, 46 (August 1980): 381-404; and Paul D. Escott, *Slavery Remembered: A Record of Twentieth-Century Slave Narratives* (Chapel Hill: University of North Carolina Press, 1979).

The surge of scholarship on slavery continued, even increased, in the 1970s. Almost every year at least one major monograph appeared, and two very significant general studies were published. Eugene D. Genovese had first attracted attention with *The Political Economy of Slavery: Studies in the Economy and Society of the South* (New York: Pantheon Books, 1965), but his mature book, *Roll, Jordan, Roll: The World the Slaves Made* (New York: Pantheon Books, 1974) is a distinguished work that, along with Stampp's *Peculiar Institution*, stands as the best introduction to the broad subject of slavery. Deeply researched, carefully attentive to religion and culture, and containing innumerable apt examples and rich quotations, *Roll, Jordan, Roll* repays several readings. Equally distinguished, though less widely know, is Lawrence W. Levine's *Black Culture and Black Consciousness: Afro-American Folk Thought from Slavery to Freedom* (New York: Oxford University Press, 1977), with its sophisticated use of anthropological and folkloric methodology. In many ways Levine presents the most satisfying depiction of the slave world view. Leslie Howard Owens's *This Species of Property: Slave Life and Culture in the Old South* (New York: Oxford University Press, 1976), is solidly grounded in manuscript sources, and Nathan Irvin Huggins's *Black Odyssey: The Afro-American Ordeal in Slavery* (New York: Pantheon Books, 1977) is a brief, almost poetic evocation of the black experience. Willie Lee Rose, *Slavery and Freedom*, edited by William W. Freehling (New York: Oxford University Press, 1982), offers an important corrective to much slavery scholarship in her emphasis on how the institution changed over time.

In addition to these general histories, several exceptionally well-edited collections of documents provide the reader with representative sources. Willie Lee Rose's *A Documentary History of Slavery in North America* (New York: Oxford University Press, 1976) has meaty excerpts from the documents, substantial introductory remarks for each, and a very useful bibliographical essay. Michael Mullin's edited volume, *American Negro Slavery* (New York: Harper & Row, 1976) is distinguished by its perceptive introduction and his attention to the pre-1800 period, which is often neglected in the rush to the era of the cotton kingdom. The Rose and Mullin collections both contain numerous documents written by whites. John W. Blassingame's edited volume, *Slave Testimony: Two Centuries of Letters, Speeches, Interviews, and Autobiographies* (Baton Rouge: Louisiana State University Press, 1977), consists entirely of sources by blacks. In addition, his very lengthy introduction offers cautionary advice about the use of black documents, especially those elicited by white interviewers. Aubrey C. Land has edited a book of documents focused on the colonial period, *Bases of the Plantation Society* (Columbia: University of South Carolina Press, 1969), which concentrates more on the plantation system than on slavery itself. Travel accounts are also an important source of information about the South. Probably the most famous and often cited is by Frederick Law Olmsted, whose works are available in a number of editions. To put his observations in context, the reader should consult the introduction by Charles E. Beveridge to *Slavery and the South, 1852-1857*, volume II of *The Papers of Frederick Law Olmsted*, edited by Beveridge and Charles Capen McLaughlin (Baltimore, Md.: Johns Hopkins University Press, 1981) and the introduction by Lawrence N. Powell to Olmsted's *Cotton Kingdom* (New York: Alfred A. Knopf, 1983).

The rise of the study of slavery to a premier position in American historical scholarship has resulted in a number of useful books either collecting important articles previously published in specialized journals or presenting new essays. Good representatives of collections of reprinted articles are Laura Foner and Eugene D. Genovese, editors, *Slavery in the New World: A Reader In Comparative History* (Englewood Cliffs, N.J.: Prentice-Hall, 1969); Randall M. Miller, editor, *The Afro-American Slaves: Community or Chaos?* (Malabar, Fla.: Robert E. Krieger Publishing Company, 1981); Elinor Miller and Eugene D. Genovese, editors, *Plantation, Town, and County: Essays on the Local History of American Slave Society* (Urbana: University of Illinois Press, 1974); and Allen Weinstein and Frank Otto Gatell, editors, *American Negro Slavery: A Modern Reader* (New York: Oxford University Press, 1968; with subsequent editions), which contains a good bibliography. Useful collections of original essays are Sidney W. Mintz, editor, *Slavery, Colonialism, and Racism* (New York: W. W. Norton, 1974); Stanley L. Engerman and Eugene D. Genovese, editors, *Race and Slavery in the Western Hemisphere: Quantitative Studies* (Princeton, N.J.: Princeton University Press, 1975); Harry P. Owens, editor, *Perspectives and Irony in American Slavery* (Jackson: University Press of Mississippi, 1976); and Nathan I. Huggins, Martin Kilson, and Daniel M. Fox, editors, *Key Issues in the Afro-American Experience*, volume I (New York: Harcourt Brace Jovanovich, 1971).

Many of the above books have valuable bibliographical essays, and the footnotes of most of the general texts offer tantalizing leads to the industrious reader. Other indispensable research aids are: James M. McPherson, Laurence B. Holland, James M. Banner, Nancy J. Weiss, Michael D. Bell, *Blacks in America: Bibliographical Essays* (Garden City, N.Y.: Doubleday, 1971); Dwight L. Smith, editor, *Afro-American History: A Bibliography* (Santa Barbara, Cal.: ABC-Clio Press, 1976), with signed, annotated entries; Joseph C. Miller, *Slavery: A Comparative Teaching Bibliography* (Waltham, Mass.: Crossroads Press, 1977); and Bennett H. Wall's excellent essay, "African Slavery," in Arthur S. Link and Rembert W. Patrick, editors, *Writing Southern History: Essays in Historiography in Honor of Fletcher M. Green* (Baton Rouge: Louisiana State University Press, 1965), pp. 175-97. The most widely used textbook on Afro-American history, which of course includes far more than the history of slavery, is John Hope Franklin's *From Slavery to Freedom: A History of Negro Americans* (New York: Alfred A. Knopf, 1947, with many subsequent editions); it contains extensive bibliographical notes.

1: A Tentative Beginning

Here, as for each subsequent chapter, no attempt will be made to offer a complete bibliography. Rather, those books and articles that I found particularly useful for my purposes will be discussed. For general African background, see Robert W. July, *A History of African People* (New York: Charles Scribner's Sons, 1970); Basil Davidson, *The Growth of African Civilization: West Africa 1000-1800* (London: Longmans, 1965), and John D. Fage, *A History of West Africa* (London: Cambridge University Press, 1969 edition). A classic statement on the importance of the African background is Melville J. Herskovits, *The Myth of the Negro Past* (New York: Harper & Brothers, 1941), and a brief, anthropologically informed survey is Paul Bohannan and Philip D. Curtin, *Africa & Africans* (Garden City, N.J.: Doubleday, 1971). For slavery in Africa, the best single volume consists of the original essays collected by Suzanne Miers and Igor Kopytoff, editors, *Slavery in Africa: Historical and Anthropological Perspectives* (Madison: University of Wisconsin Press, 1977). For slavery in the ancient world and in Arabia respectively see Frank M. Snowden, Jr., *Blacks in Antiquity: Ethiopians in the Greco-Roman Experience* (Cambridge, Mass.: Harvard University Press, 1970), and Bernard Lewis, *Race and Color in Islam* (New York: Harper & Row, 1971). The legacy of slavery in Europe is made vivid by David Brion Davis in his magisterial *The Problem of Slavery in Western Culture* (Ithaca, N.Y.: Cornell University Press, 1966) and by the long introduction in C. Duncan Rice, *The Rise and Fall of Black Slavery* (New York: Harper & Row, 1975). A perceptive recent essay is A. J. R. Russell-Wood, "Iberian Expansion and the Issue of Black Slavery: Changing Portugese Attitudes, 1440-1770," *American Historical Review* 83 (February 1978): 16-42. The literature on the Caribbean is extensive; the best introduction remains John H. Parry, *A Short History of the West Indies* (London: Macmillan, 1963). I have also profited immensely from Sidney W. Mintz, *Caribbean Transformations* (Chicago: Aldine Publishing Company, 1974).

For English attitudes toward slavery and race there luckily exists Winthrop D. Jordan's impressive study, *White Over Black: American Attitudes Toward the Negro, 1590-1812* (Chapel Hill: University of North Carolina Press, 1968). Jordan places the evolution of black servitude in a broad cultural context. For a brilliant examination of the rise of slavery in colonial Virginia, with concern for both the English cultural background and the immediate social context, consult Edmund S. Morgan, *American Slavery/American Freedom: The Ordeal of Colonial Virginia* (New York: W. W. Norton, 1975). A spirited historical debate has continued for several decades over the evolution of slavery in Virginia. The reader can follow the argument as it runs through the following important articles: Oscar and Mary F. Handlin, "Origins of the Southern Labor System," *William and Mary Quarterly* 3d series 7 (April 1950): 199-222; Carl N. Degler, "Slavery and the Genesis of American Race Prejudice," *Comparative Studies in Society and History* 2 (October 1959): 49-66; and Winthrop D. Jordan, "Modern Tensions and the Origins of American Slavery," *Journal of Southern History* 28 (February 1962): 18-30. Several recent articles were more useful for my interpretation, particularly George M. Fredrickson, "Toward a Social Interpretation of the Development of American Racism," in the previously cited collection by Nathan I. Huggins, Martin Kilson, and Daniel M. Fox, editors, *Key Issues in the Afro-American Experience*, vol. I (New York: Harcourt Brace Jovanovich, 1971) pp. 240-54; Russell R. Menard, "From Servants to Slaves: The Transformation of the Chesapeake Labor System," *Southern Studies* 16 (Winter 1977): 355-90, and Menard, "The Maryland Slave Population, 1658 to 1730: A Demographic Profile of Blacks in Four Counties," *William and Mary Quarterly*, 3d series 32 (January 1975): 29-54; Allan Kulikoff, "Black Society and the Economics of Slavery," *Maryland Historical Magazine* 70 (Summer 1975): 203-10; Timothy H. Breen, "A Changing Labor Force and Race Relations in Virginia, 1670-1710," *Journal of Social History* 6 (Fall 1973): 3-25; Warren M. Billings, "The Cases of Fernando and Elizabeth Key: A Note on the Status of Blacks in Seventeenth-Century Virginia," *William and Mary Quarterly*, 3d series 30 (July 1973): 467-74; Alden T. Vaughan, "Blacks in Virginia: A Note on the First Decade," *ibid.* 29 (July 1972): 469-78; Jonathan L. Alport, "The Origins of Slavery in the United States; the Maryland Precedent," *American Journal of Legal History* 14 (July 1970): 189-221; and Ross M. Kimmel, "Free Blacks in Seventeenth-Century Maryland," *Maryland Historical Magazine* 71 (Spring 1976): 19-25. Wesley Frank Craven's *White, Red, and Black: The Seventeenth-Century Virginian* (Charlottesville: University Press of Virginia, 1971), though largely superceded by Morgan's *American Slavery/American Freedom*, still contains important information. Also useful is T. H. Breen and Stephen Innes, *'Myne Owne Ground': Race and Freedom on Virginia's Eastern Shore, 1640-1676* (New York: Oxford University Press, 1980).

For South Carolina the student has another monumental book, Peter H. Wood's *Black Majority: Negroes in Colonial South Carolina from 1670 through the Stono Rebellion* (New York: Alfred A. Knopf, 1974). This should be supplemented with M. Eugene Sirmans, "The Legal Status of the Slave in South Carolina, 1670-1740," *Journal of Southern History* 28 (November 1962): 462-73; Daniel C. Littlefield, *Rice and Slaves: Ethnicity and the Slave Trade in Colonial South Carolina* (Baton Rouge: Louisiana State Univ. Press, 1981); and Philip D. Morgan, "Afro-American Cultural Change: The Case of Colonial South Carolina Slaves," paper presented at the Organization of American Historians meeting, April 13, 1979.

There are of course many older state studies of slavery that I have not listed; the best of these, and still a very useful book, is Charles Sackett Syd-

nor, *Slavery in Mississippi* (New York: D. Appleton and Company, 1933).
Three important articles have broad geographic focus: William M.
Wiecek, "The Statutory Law of Slavery and Race in the Thirteen Mainland
Colonies of British America," *William and Mary Quarterly*, 3d series 34
(April 1977): 258-80; Ira Berlin, "Time, Space, and the Evolution of Afro-
American Society on British Mainland North America," *American Histor-
ical Review* 85 (February 1980): 44-78; and Berlin, "The Slave Trade and
the Development of Afro-American Society in English Mainland North
America, 1619-1775," *Southern Studies* 20 (Summer 1981): 122-36. Two
books focused on the Chesapeake, but with far broader implications, in-
dicate well the current sophistication of scholarship on the colonial South:
Aubrey C. Land, Lois Green Carr, and Edward C. Papenfuse, editors,
Law, Society, and Politics in Early Maryland (Baltimore, Md.: Johns
Hopkins University Press, 1977), and Thad W. Tate and David L. Ammerman, editors, *The Chesapeake in the Seventeenth Century: Essays on
Anglo-American Society* (Chapel Hill: University of North Carolina Press,
1979). For an introduction to the subject of white indentured servitude, the
labor system that slavery gradually replaced, see Abbot Emerson Smith's
standard treatment, *Colonists in Bondage: White Servitude and Convict
Labor in America, 1607-1776* (Chapel Hill: University of North Carolina
Press, 1947), and, among the many revisionist articles, David W. Galen-
son, "British Servants and the Colonial Indenture System in the Eighteenth
Century," *Journal of Southern History* 44 (February 1978): 41-66.

2: The Crucial Eighteenth Century

The Atlantic slave trade has been the topic of many writers; a good
place to begin is the popularly written *Black Cargoes: A History of the
Atlantic Slave Trade, 1518-1865* (New York: Viking Press, 1962), by
Daniel P. Mannix and Malcolm Cowley. See also Basil Davidson's moving
account, *Black Mother: The Years of the African Slave Trade* (Boston: Little, Brown, 1961). Kenneth G. Davies, *The Royal African Company* (London: Longmans, 1957), details the rise and decline of the monopolistic
British trading company. A remarkable study of the trade from the African
point of view is Philip D. Curtin's *Economic Change in Precolonial Africa:
Senegambia in the Era of the Slave Trade* (Madison: University of Wisconsin Press, 1975). Portions of Herbert S. Klein's volume, *The Middle
Passage: Comparative Studies in the Atlantic Slave Trade* (Princeton, N.J.:
Princeton University Press, 1978), are focused on trade to the North Amer-
ican mainland. Elizabeth Donnan's four-volume compilation, *Documents
Illustrative of the History of the Slave Trade to America* (Washington,
D.C.: Carnegie Institution, 1930-35), is essential reading. There are many

significant articles on different aspects of the slave trade; several of especial value are Philip D. Curtin, "Epidemiology and the Slave Trade," *Political Science Quarterly* 83 (June 1968): 190-216; Walter Rodney, "African Slavery and Other Forms of Social Oppression on the Upper Guinea Coast in the Context of the Atlantic Slave Trade," *Journal of African History* 7 (1966): 219-46; Herbert J. Foster, "Partners or Captives in Commerce? The Role of Africans in the Slave Trade," *Journal of Black Studies* 6 (June 1976): 421-34; W. Robert Higgins, "The Geographical Origins of Negro Slaves in Colonial South Carolina," *South Atlantic Quarterly* 70 (Winter 1971): 34-47; Darold D. Wax, "Preferences for Slaves in Colonial America," *Journal of Negro History* 58 (October 1973): 371-401; and two essays in Martin L. Kilson and Robert I. Rotberg, editors, *The African Diaspora: Interpretative Essays* (Cambridge, Mass.: Harvard University Press, 1976); Christopher Fyfe's "The Dynamics of African Dispersal: The Transatlantic Slave Trade," pp. 57-74, and W. Robert Higgins, "Charleston: Terminus and Enterpôt of the Colonial Slave Trade," pp. 114-31. A representative first-person account of the trade is offered by Captain Theophilus Conneau, *A Slave's Log Book, or, 20 Years' Residence in Africa*, introduction by Mabel M. Smythe (Englewood Cliffs, N.J.: Prentice-Hall, 1977). The central role of Rhode Island in the import of Africans to the North American mainland is portrayed in Jay Coughtry, *The Notorious Triangle: Rhode Island and the African Slave Trade, 1700-1807* (Philadelphia: Temple University Press, 1981), while the most recent estimates of the volume of the trade, along with an analysis of the business aspects of the enterprise, are presented by James A. Rawley, *The Transatlantic Slave Trade: A History* (New York, N.Y.: W. W. Norton, 1981). Philip D. Curtin's *The Atlantic Slave Trade: A Census* (Madison: University of Wisconsin Press, 1969), remains the most important quantitative study of the trade, with significant implications for other aspects of the American slave experience.

There is an emerging literature on the social history of eighteenth-century slavery, long neglected by scholars. A pioneer work is Thad W. Tate, *The Negro in Eighteenth-Century Williamsburg* (Charlottesville: University Press of Virginia, 1966), and Peter H. Wood's previously cited *Black Majority: Negroes in Colonial South Carolina from 1670 through the Stono Rebellion* (New York: Alfred A. Knopf, 1974) is the best study of colonial slavery with the emphasis on the black experience. Gerald W. Mullin's *Flight and Rebellion: Slave Resistance in Eighteenth-Century Virginia* (New York: Oxford University Press, 1972) has several wonderful chapters on the plantation world of colonial Virginia, with an imaginative use of newspaper sources. Sidney W. Mintz and Richard Price offer a brilliant interpretative overview of the problem of African acculturation in *An*

Anthropological Approach to the Afro-American Past: A Caribbean Perspective, ISHI Occasional Papers in Social Change, No. 2 (Philadelphia: Institute for the Study of Human Issues, 1976).

My understanding of the development of Afro-American society and cultural life in the eighteenth century has been largely influenced by a series of pioneering articles by Allan Kulikoff: "A 'Prolifick' People: Black Population Growth in the Chesapeake Colonies, 1700-1790," *Southern Studies* 16 (Winter 1977): 391-428; "The Beginnings of the Afro-American Family in Maryland," in Aubrey C. Land, Lois Green Carr, and Edward C. Papenfuse, editors, *Law, Society, and Politics in Early Maryland* (Baltimore, Md.: Johns Hopkins University Press, 1977), pp. 171-96; and "The Origins of Afro-American Society in Tidewater Maryland and Virginia, 1700-1790," *William and Mary Quarterly*, 3d series 35 (April 1978): 226-59. Two other extremely significant articles are Russell R. Menard, "The Maryland Slave Population, 1658 to 1730: A Demographic Profile of Blacks in Four Counties," *ibid.* 32 (January 1975): 29-54; and Ira Berlin, "Time, Space, and the Evolution of Afro-American Society on British Mainland North America," *American Historical Review* 85 (February 1980): 44-78. See Also P. D. Morgan, "Afro-American Cultural Change: The Case of Colonial South Carolina Slaves," paper presented at the Organization of American Historians meeting, April 13, 1979.

The material on slave-naming practices is derived from Herbert G. Gutman, *The Black Family in Slavery & Freedom, 1750-1925* (New York: Pantheon Books, 1976); and Cheryll Ann Cody, "Naming, Kinship, and Estate Dispersal: Notes on Slave Family Life on a South Carolina Plantation, 1786 to 1833," *William and Mary Quarterly*, 3d series 39 (January 1982): 192-211.

In addition to those already cited, there are other immensely helpful articles on slavery, indentured servants, and colonial society in Land, Carr, and Papenfuse, *Law, Society, and Politics in Early Maryland* and Thad W. Tate and David L. Ammerman, editors, *The Chesapeake in the Seventeenth Century: Essays on Anglo-American Society* (Chapel Hill: University of North Carolina Press, 1979). Four special issues of historical periodicals should also be consulted: the "Chesapeake Society" issue of *William and Mary Quarterly*, 3d series 30 (January 1973); the "St. Mary's City Commission Special Issue" of the *Maryland Historical Magazine*, 69 (Summer 1974); the "Special Issue on Colonial Slavery" of *Southern Studies*, 16 (Winter 1977); and the "Blacks in Early America" issue of *William and Mary Quarterly*, 3d series 35 (April 1978).

3: The Maturation of the Plantation System, 1776-1860

The indispensable starting point for all study of the black role in the War for Independence is Benjamin M. Quarles's judicious volume, *The Negro in the American Revolution* (Chapel Hill: University of North Carolina Press, 1961). Three more recent books place slavery in the larger political context: David Brion Davis, *The Problem of Slavery in the Age of Revolution, 1770-1823* (Ithaca, N.Y. and London: Cornell University Press, 1975); Donald L. Robinson, *Slavery in the Structure of American Politics: 1765-1820* (New York: Harcourt Brace Jovanovich, 1971); and Duncan J. MacLeod, *Slavery, Race and the American Revolution* (Cambridge: Cambridge University Press, 1974). A visually stimulating study is Sidney Kaplan, *The Black Presence in the Era of the American Revolution, 1770-1800* (Washington, D.C.: New York Graphic Society / Smithsonian Institution Press, 1973), written to accompany an art exhibit. For black soldiers, see, in addition to Quarles, Pete Maslowski, "National Policy Toward the Use of Black Troops in the Revolution," *South Carolina Historical Magazine* 73 (January 1972): 1-17, and James W. St. G. Walker, "Blacks as American Loyalists: The Slaves' War for Independence," *Historical Reflections / Reflexions Historiques* 2 (Summer 1975): 51-67. For the effect of the Revolution on the black, from the black perspective, see Ira Berlin, "The Revolution in Black Life," in Alfred F. Young, editor, *The American Revolution: Explorations in the History of American Radicalism* (DeKalb: Northern Illinois University Press, 1976), pp. 349-82, and Peter H. Wood, "Taking Care of Business in Revolutionary South Carolina: Republicanism and the Slave Society," in Jeffrey J. Crow and Larry Tise, editors, *The Southern Experience in the American Revolution* (Chapel Hill: University of North Carolina Press, 1978), pp. 268-93. In the same volume, pp. 235-67, Michael Mullin puts the issue in perspective: "British Caribbean and North American Slaves in an Era of War and Revolution, 1775-1807." Important for showing the dimension of black involvement in the Revolution are two articles by Sylvia R. Frey, "The British and the Black: A New Perspective," *Historian* 38 (February 1976): 225-38, and "Between Slavery and Freedom: Virginia Blacks in the American Revolution," *Journal of Southern History*, forthcoming in 1983. For the beginning of emancipation in the northern states the standard work is Arthur Zilversmit, *The First Emancipation: The Abolition of Slavery in the North* (Chicago: University of Chicago Press, 1967), and Thomas Jefferson's struggle with the issue is best presented by William W. Freehling, "The Founding Fathers and Slavery," *American Historical Review* 77 (February 1972): 81-93.

Every student of southern agriculture should begin with Lewis C.

Gray's monumental *History of Agriculture in the Southern United States to 1860*, 2 volumes (Washington, D.C.: Carnegie Institution, 1933), which is wide-ranging topically, geographically, and chronologically. Of the several valuable state studies, two stand out: John H. Moore, *Agriculture in Ante-Bellum Mississippi* (New York: Bookman Associates, 1958), and James C. Bonner, *A History of Georgia Agriculture, 1732-1860* (Athens: University of Georgia Press, 1964). In addition to Gray, I used Constance McL. Green, *Eli Whitney and the Birth of American Technology* (Boston: Little, Brown, 1956) for the story of the cotton gin. For Etienne de Boré and the development of sugar, see J. Carlyle Sitterson, *Sugar Country: The Cane Sugar Industry in the South, 1753-1950* (Lexington: University of Kentucky Press, 1953).

On the rise of the plantation system and its effect on southern life, politics, and economics, there is an enormous literature. After Gray one should turn to two classic volumes by Ulrich B. Phillips, which, despite their condescending tone toward blacks, contain marvelous information about the daily operation of plantations: *American Negro Slavery: A Survey of the Supply, Employment and Control of Negro Labor as Determined by the Plantation System* (New York: D. Appleton and Company, 1918), and *Life & Labor in the Old South* (Boston: Little, Brown, 1929). But Phillips must be complemented with Eugene D. Genovese, *The Political Economy of Slavery: Studies in the Economy and Society of the Slave South* (New York: Pantheon Books, 1965) and especially Gavin Wright, *The Political Economy of the Cotton South: Households, Markets, and Wealth in the Nineteenth Century* (New York: W. W. Norton, 1978). Wright's book represents the outstanding contribution of the "cliometricians" and builds on the pioneering article by Alfred H. Conrad and John R. Meyer, "The Economics of Slavery in the Antebellum South," *Journal of Political Economy* 66 (April 1958): 95-130. Eugene D. Genovese, *The World the Slaveholders Made: Two Essays in Interpretation* (New York: Pantheon Books, 1969) argues that the Old South was precapitalistic; Gavin Wright suggests otherwise and, I think, has the better argument. There is some useful data in Robert W. Fogel and Stanley L. Engerman, *Time on the Cross: The Economics of American Negro Slavery* (Boston: Little, Brown, 1974), but the book is riddled with errors and arrogance. It should be read with Paul A. David, Herbert G. Gutman, Richard Sutch, Peter Temin, and Gavin Wright, *Reckoning with Slavery: A Critical Study in the Quantitative History of American Negro Slavery* (New York: Oxford University Press, 1976), and Thomas L. Haskell, "The True and Tragical History of 'Time on the Cross'," *New York Review of Books* 22 (October 2, 1975): 33-39. Fred Bateman and Thomas Weiss, in *A Deplorable Scarcity: The Failure of Industrialization in the Slave*

Economy (Chapel Hill: University of North Carolina Press, 1981) dispute Genovese's claim in *Political Economy* that slavery itself retarded industrialization; they argue that inadequate transportation was the culprit. Two helpful books on plantation management are William K. Scarborough, *The Overseer: Plantation Management in the Old South* (Baton Rouge: Louisiana State University Press, 1966) and James O. Breeden, editor, *Advice Among Masters: The Ideal in Slave Management in the Old South* (Westport, Conn.: Greenwood Press, 1980). For the slave and the law in the Old South, see Daniel J. Flanigan, "Criminal Procedure in Slave Trials in the Antebellum South," *Journal of Southern History* 40 (November 1974): 537-64, and "The Criminal Law of Slavery and Freedom, 1800-1868," (Ph.D. dissertation, Rice University, 1973). The role of the slave woman is suggested by Jacqueline Jones, " 'My Mother Was Much of a Woman': Black Women, Work, and the Family Under Slavery," *Feminist Studies* 8 (Summer 1982): 235-69. For the controversial issue of the size and nature of the interstate slave trade, there is the classic study by Frederic Bancroft, *Slave-Trading in the Old South* (Baltimore, Md.: J. H. Furst, 1931), which supports the thesis of purposeful breeding of slaves. Several recent scholars concur, notably Richard C. Sutch, "The Breeding of Slaves for Sale and the Westward Expansion of Slavery, 1850-1860," in Stanley L. Engerman and Eugene D. Genovese, editors, *Race and Slavery in the Western Hemisphere: Quantitative Studies* (Princeton, N.J.: Princeton University Press, 1975), pp. 173-210. I have been persuaded otherwise by William Calderhead, "How Extensive Was the Border State Slave Trade? A New Look," *Civil War History* 18 (March 1972): 42-55; William L. Miller, "A Note on the Importance of the Interstate Slave Trade of the Ante Bellum South," *Journal of Political Economy* 73 (April 1965): 181-87; Stanley Engerman's critique of Sutch's article in Engerman and Genovese, editors, *Race and Slavery*, pp. 512-14; and especially Richard G. Lowe and Randolph B. Campbell, "The Slave-Breeding Hypothesis: A Demographic Comment on the 'Buying' and 'Selling' States," *Journal of Southern History* 42 (August 1976): 401-12. One should not overlook Wendell Holmes Stephenson, *Isaac Franklin: Slave Trader and Planter of the Old South* (Baton Rouge: Louisiana State University Press, 1938).

My brief treatment of food production on plantations is drawn from Gavin Wright's previously cited *Political Economy of the Cotton South*; Sam B. Hilliard, *Hog Meat and Hoe Cake: Food Supply in the Old South, 1840-1860* (Carbondale, Ill.: Southern Illinois University Press, 1972); Robert E. Gallman, "Self-Sufficiency in the Cotton Economy of the Antebellum South," *Agricultural History* 44 (January 1970): 5-24; and Forrest McDonald and Grady McWhiney, "The Antebellum Southern Herdsman: A Reinterpretation," *Journal of Southern History* 41 (May 1975): 147-66.

More generally, for most aspects of agriculture and plantation management see two valuable special issues of *Agricultural History*, 44 (January 1970) and 49 (April 1975), each of which contains numerous indispensable articles. Several historiographical or review essays contain preceptive information. I have found particularly valuable the following: Bennett H. Wall, "An Epitaph for Slavery," *Louisiana History* 16 (Summer 1975): 229-56; James C. Bonner, "Plantation and Farm: The Agricultural South," in Arthur S. Link and Rembert W. Patrick, editors, *Writing Southern History: Essays in Historiography in Honor of Fletcher M. Green* (Baton Rouge: Louisiana State University Press, 1965), pp. 147-74; and Harold D. Woodman, "The Profitability of Slavery: A Historical Perennial," *Journal of Southern History* 29 (August 1963): 303-25. A broadly interpretative book on many aspects of plantation life is Edgar Thompson's collection of essays, *Plantation Societies, Race Relations, and the South: The Regimentation of Populations* (Durham, N.C.: Duke University Press, 1975).

4: Life and Death in the Old South

Eugene D. Genovese's *Roll, Jordan, Roll: The World the Slaves Made* (New York: Pantheon Books, 1974) is an impressive storehouse of information on nearly every aspect of slave culture; I have drawn on it and on Leslie Howard Owens, *This Species of Property: Slave Life and Culture in the Old South* (New York: Oxford University Press, 1976) for information on food, clothes, and houses. In addition, for slave housing I have found useful Carl Anthony, "The Big House and Slave Quarters: Part II, African Contributions to the New World," *Landscape* 21 (Autumn 1976): 9-15; Robert Ascher and Charles H. Fairbanks, "Excavation of a Slave Cabin: Georgia, U.S.A.," *Historical Archaeology* 5 (1971): 3-17; and George W. McDaniel, *Hearth & Home: Preserving a People's Culture* (Philadelphia: Temple University Press, 1982). Since historians have been less concerned with detailed analyses of clothing, housing, and methods of food production, one must rely on impressions garnered from reading slave interviews, memoirs, antebellum travel accounts, brief discussions in most of the general histories of slavery, and the state histories. An important study of slave food is Tyson Gibbs, Kathleen Gargill, Leslie Sue Lieberman, and Elizabeth Reitz, "Nutrition in a Slave Population: An Anthropological Examination," *Medical Anthropology* 4 (Spring 1980): 175-262. Many of the studies of slave health care also contain information on food, clothing, and housing. Of these, the single most valuable book for this chapter is Todd L. Savitt's *Medicine and Slavery: The Diseases and Health Care of Blacks in Antebellum Virginia* (Urbana: University of Illinois Press, 1978). For the Indian contributions to southern cooking, see Charles Hudson, *The*

Southeastern Indians (Knoxville: University of Tennessee, 1976). The controversy surrounding Robert W. Fogel and Stanley L. Engerman, *Time on the Cross: The Economics of American Negro Slavery* (Boston: Little, Brown, 1974), also produced much valuable information on slave living conditions, including food.

In addition to Todd Savitt's study, which is essential reading, there are many valuable works, either older or more specific. Of the older ones I found the following very useful: St. Julien R. Childs, "Kitchen Physick: Medical and Surgical Care of Slaves on an Eighteenth Century Rice Plantation," *Mississippi Valley Historical Review* 20 (December 1934): 549-54; Bennett H. Wall, "Medical Care of Ebenezer Pettigrew's Slaves," *ibid.* 37 (December 1950): 451-70; and William Dosite Postell, *The Health of Slaves on Southern Plantations* (Baton Rouge: Louisiana State University Press, 1951). Among the recent articles in what has become an important subfield of medical history are the following: David O. Whitten, "Medical Care of Slaves: Louisiana Sugar Region and South Carolina Rice District," *Southern Studies* 16 (Summer 1977): 153-80; a series of articles by Kenneth F. and Virginia H. Kiple, "Slave Child Mortality: Some Nutritional Answers to a Perennial Puzzle," *Journal of Social History* 10 (March 1977): 284-309; "Black Tongue and Black Men: Pellagra and Slavery in the Antebellum South," *Journal of Southern History* 43 (August 1977): 411-28; "Black Yellow Fever Immunities, Innate and Acquired, as Revealed in the American South," *Social Science History* 4 (Fall 1977): 419-36; and "Slave Nutrition and Disease during the Nineteenth Century: The United States and the Caribbean," paper presented at the Organization of American Historians meeting, April 12, 1979; Yuet Wai Kan and Andrée M. Dozy, "Evolution of the Hemoglobin S and C Genes in World Populations," *Science* 209 (July 18, 1980): 388-90; Todd L. Savitt, "Smothering and Overlaying of Virginia Slave Children: A Suggested Explanation," *Bulletin of the History of Medicine* 49 (Fall 1975): 400-4; Michael P. Johnson's refinement of Savitt's idea, "Smothered Slave Infants: Were Slave Mothers at Fault?" *Journal of Southern History* 47 (November 1981): 493-520; Robert W. Twyman, "The Clay Eater: A New Look at an Old Southern Enigma," *ibid.* 37 (August 1971): 439-48; Nicholas S. Cardell and Mark M. Hopkins, "The Effect of Milk Intolerance on the Consumption of Milk by Slaves in 1860," *Journal of Interdisciplinary History* 8 (Winter 1978): 507-13; Todd L. Savitt, "The Use of Blacks for Medical Experimentation and Demonstration in the Old South," *Journal of Southern History* 48 (August 1982): 331-48; and Savitt, "The Invisible Malady: Sickle Cell Anemia in America, 1910-1970," *Journal of the National Medical Association* 73 (1981): 739-46, which has a discussion of the disease for the period before 1910. An impressive book that appeared too late to shape my discussion of slave health is Kenneth F. Kiple and Virginia Himmelsteib King, *Another Dimension to the Black Diaspora: Diet, Disease, and Racism* (Cambridge: Cambridge University Press, 1981), which is more critical of the quality of the slave diet than I am. William H. McNeill's wide-ranging *Plagues and Peoples* (Garden City, N.Y.: Doubleday, 1976) influenced my general understanding of disease and history.

5: Black Diversity in a Slave Society

Most of the general textbooks on the South and on slavery contain a discussion of the distribution of slaves among slaveholders. As usual, one should consult Ulrich B. Phillips, *American Negro Slavery: A Survey of the Supply, Employment and Control of Negro Labor as Determined by the Plantation Regime* (New York: D. Appleton and Company, 1918); Kenneth M. Stampp, *The Peculiar Institution: Slavery in the Ante-Bellum South* (New York: Alfred A. Knopf, 1956); and Lewis C. Gray, *History of Agriculture in the Southern United States*, 2 volumes (Washington, D.C.: Carnegie Institution, 1933), especially vol. 2. Of particular value is Chapter 2 of Gavin Wright, *The Political Economy of the Cotton South: Households, Markets, and Wealth in the Nineteenth Century* (New York: W. W. Norton, 1978), and Otto H. Olsen, "Historians and the Extent of Slave Ownership in the Southern United States," *Civil War History* 18 (June 1972): 101-16, although I think Olsen exaggerates the significance of the extent of ownership.

Behind the issue of slave distribution are questions about the nature of southern white society and its commitment to slavery as a social and economic institution. This is implicit in most of the titles cited above but is addressed more specifically by Morton Rothstein, "The Antebellum South as a Dual Economy: A Tentative Hypothesis," *Agricultural History* 41 (October 1967): 373-83; Gavin Wright, " 'Economic Democracy' and the Concentration of Agricultural Wealth in the Cotton South, 1850-1860," *Agricultural History* 44 (January 1970): 63-94; Frank L. Owsley's classic *Plain Folk of the Old South* (Baton Rouge: Louisiana State University Press, 1949); Fabian Linden's spirited critique of Owsley's earlier articles, "Economic Democracy in the Slave South: An Appraisal of Some Recent Views," *Journal of Negro History* 31 (April 1946): 140-89; Randolph B. Campbell, "Planters and Plain Folk: Harrison County, Texas, as a Test Case, 1850-1860," *Journal of Southern History* 40 (August 1974): 369-98; Eugene D. Genovese, "Yeomen Farmers in a Slaveholders' Democracy," *Agricultural History* 49 (April 1975): 331-42; and Randolph B. Campbell and Richard G. Lowe, *Wealth and Power in Antebellum Texas* (College Station: Texas A & M University Press, 1977).

The best descriptions of house-servants, field hands, and slave over-seers and drivers is in Eugene D. Genovese, *Roll, Jordan, Roll: The World the Slaves Made* (New York: Pantheon Books, 1974); Leslie Howard Owens, *This Species of Property: Slave Life and Culture in the Old South* (New York: Oxford University Press, 1976), chapters 5 and 6; John W. Blassingame, *The Slave Community: Plantation Life in the Ante-Bellum South* (New York: Oxford University Press, 1979), chapters 5 and 6; Blassingame, "Status and Social Structure in the Slave Community: Evidence from New Sources," in Harry P. Owens, editor, *Perspectives and Irony in American Slavery* (Jackson: University Press of Mississippi, 1976), pp. 137-51; Herbert G. Gutman and Richard Sutch, "Sambo Makes Good, or Were Slaves Imbued with the Protestant Work Ethic?," in Paul A. David, Herbert G. Gutman, Richard Sutch, Peter Temin, and Gavin Wright, *Reckoning with Slavery: A Critical Study in the Quantitative History of American Negro Slavery* (New York: Oxford University Press, 1976), pp. 55-93; Robert S. Starobin, "Privileged Bondsmen and the Process of Ac-commodation: The Role of Houseservants and Drivers as Seen in Their Own Letters," *Journal of Social History* 5 (Fall 1971): 46-70; William L. Van Deburg, "Slave Drivers and Slave Narratives: A New Look at the 'De-humanized Elite,'" *Historian* 39 (August 1977): 717-32, supplemented with his book, *The Slave Drivers: Black Agricultural Labor Supervisors in the Antebellum South* (Westport, Conn.: Greenwood Press, 1979); and William K. Scarborough, *The Overseer: Plantation Management in the Old South* (Baton Rouge: Louisiana State University Press, 1966), which, though primarily about white overseers, contains information also about black drivers.

An extensive literature has arisen on industrial slavery; the place to begin is with Robert S. Starobin, *Industrial Slavery in the Old South* (New York: Oxford University Press, 1970). This should be supplemented by a series of articles and monographs on specific industries or occupations: John H. Moore, "Simon Gray, Riverman: A Slave Who Was Almost Free," *Mississippi Valley Historical Review* 49 (December 1962): 472-84; Moore, *Andrew Brown and Cypress Lumbering in the Old Southwest* (Baton Rouge: Louisiana State University Press, 1967); Percival Perry, "The Naval Stores Industry in the Old South," *Journal of Southern History* 34 (November 1968): 509-26; Ernest M. Lander, *The Textile Industry in Ante-bellum South Carolina* (Baton Rouge: Louisiana State University Press, 1969); Lander, "Slave Labor in the South Carolina Cotton Mills," *Journal of Negro History* 38 (April 1953): 161-73; Richard W. Griffin, "Cotton Manufacture in Alabama to 1860," *Alabama Historical Quarterly* 18 (Fall 1956): 289-307; Norris W. Preyer, "The Historian, the Slave, and the Ante-bellum Textile Industry," *Journal of Negro History* 46 (April 1961):

67-82; for tobacco workers, John T. O'Brien, "Factory, Church, and Community: Blacks in Ante-bellum Richmond," *Journal of Southern History* 44 (November 1978): 509-36.

Much has been written on black coal miners and ironworkers. I have drawn primarily on the three essays by Charles B. Dew, "Disciplining Slave Ironworkers in the Antebellum South: Coercion, Conciliation, and Accommodation," *American Historical Review* 79 (April 1974): 393-418; "David Ross and the Oxford Iron Works: A Study of Industrial Slavery in the Early Nineteenth-Century South," *William and Mary Quarterly*, 3d series 31 (April 1974): 189-224; and "Sam Williams, Forgeman: The Life of an Industrial Slave in the Old South," in James M. McPherson and J. Morgan Kousser, editors, *Race, Region, and Reconstruction: Essays in Honor of C. Vann Woodward* (New York: Oxford University Press, 1982), 199-239; Robert H. McKenzie, "The Shelby Iron Company: A Note on Slave Personality after the Civil War," *Journal of Negro History* 58 (July 1973): 341-48; Ronald Lewis synthesizes his many relevant articles in *Coal, Iron, and Slaves: Industrial Slavery in Maryland and Virginia, 1715-1865* (Westport, Conn.: Greenwood Press, 1979); Marcus Christian, *Negro Ironworkers of Louisiana, 1718-1900* (Gretna, La.: Pelikan Publishing, 1972); for gold mining, see Fletcher M. Green's pioneering articles, "Georgia's Forgotten Industry: Gold Mining," Parts 1 and 2, *Georgia Historical Quarterly* 19 (June, September 1935): 91-111, 210-28; "Gold Mining in Ante-Bellum Virginia," Parts 1 and 2, *Virginia Magazine of History and Biography* 45 (July, October 1937): 227-35, 357-66; and "Gold Mining: A Forgotten Industry of Ante-Bellum North Carolina," Parts 1 and 2, *North Carolina Historical Review* 14 (January, April 1937): 1-19, 135-55; for salt mining, John Edmund Stealey, III, "Slavery and the Western Virginia Salt Industry," *Journal of Negro History* 59 (April 1976): 105-31.

The starting point for urban slavery is Richard C. Wade, *Slavery in the Cities: The South, 1820-1860* (New York: Oxford University Press, 1964), supplemented by Claudia Goldin, *Urban Slavery in the American South, 1820-1860* (Chicago: University of Chicago Press, 1976). Useful articles include Robert C. Reinders, "Slavery in New Orleans in the Decade before the Civil War," *Mid-America* 44 (October 1962): 211-21; Alan Dowty, "Urban Slavery in Pro-Southern Fiction of the 1850s," *Journal of Southern History* 32 (February 1966): 25-41; O'Brien's previously cited article, *ibid.* 44 (November 1978): 509-36; Marianne Buroff Sheldon, "Black-White Relations in Richmond, Virginia, 1782-1820," *ibid.* 45 (February 1979): 27-44; and Judith Kelleher Schafer, "New Orleans Slavery in 1850 as Seen in Advertisements," *ibid.* 47 (February 1981): 33-56. There is also relevant material in the beginning sections of Howard N. Rabinowitz, *Race Rela-*

tions in the *Urban South, 1865-1890* (New York: Oxford University Press, 1978), and in John W. Blassingame, *Black New Orleans, 1860-1880* (Chicago: University of Chicago Press, 1973). The practice of slave hiring is discussed in these works, but the pioneering article of Clement Eaton is still worth reading, "Slave-Hiring in the Upper South: A Step Toward Freedom," *Mississippi Valley Historical Review* 46 (March 1960): 663-79. On a related issue see Todd L. Savitt, "Slave Life Insurance in Virginia and North Carolina," *Journal of Southern History* 48 (November 1977): 583-600.

In between the status of the urban slave and the free black was the category Loren Schweninger has labeled "the free-slave." See Schweninger, "The Free-Slave Phenomenon: James P. Thomas and the Black Community in Ante-Bellum Nashville," *Civil War History* 22 (December 1976): 293-307, and Chapter 2 of his *James T. Rapier and Reconstruction* (Chicago: University of Chicago Press, 1978).

A rich literature has also arisen on the topic of the free Negro, beginning with two books written early in this century: John H. Russell, *The Free Negro in Virginia, 1619-1865* (Baltimore, Md.: Johns Hopkins University Press, 1913) and James M. Wright, *The Free Negro in Maryland, 1634-1860* (New York: Columbia University Press, 1921). The modern study of the subject began with Charles S. Sydnor, "The Free Negro in Mississippi Before the Civil War," *American Historical Review* 32 (July 1927): 769-88; Luther P. Jackson, *Free Negro Labor and Property Holding in Virginia, 1830-1860* (New York: D. Appleton-Century, 1942), and John Hope Franklin, *The Free Negro in North Carolina, 1790-1860* (Chapel Hill: University of North Carolina Press, 1943). Two good recent monographs are Letitia Woods Brown, *Free Negroes in the District of Columbia, 1790-1846* (New York: Oxford University Press, 1972), and Marina Wikramanoyake, *A World in Shadow: The Free Black in Antebellum South Carolina* (Columbia: University of South Carolina Press, 1973). To place free blacks in perspective, see David W. Cohen and Jack P. Greene, editors, *Neither Slave Nor Free: The Freedmen of African Descent in the Slave Societies of the New World* (Baltimore, Md.: Johns Hopkins University Press, 1972). Two indispensable general studies are Ira Berlin, *Slaves Without Masters: The Free Negro in the Antebellum South* (New York: Pantheon Books, 1974) and Leonard P. Curry, *The Free Black in Urban America, 1800-1850: The Shadow of the Dream* (Chicago: University of Chicago Press, 1981). Edwin Adams Davis and William Ransom Hogan present a wonderful account of the free black William Johnson in *The Barber of Natchez* (Baton Rouge: Louisiana State University Press, 1954). See also Suzanne Lebsock, "Free Black Women and the Question of Matriarchy: Petersburg, Virginia, 1784-1820," *Feminist Studies* 8 (Summer 1982): 271-92.

6: Community, Culture, and Rebellion

Although most early students of slavery argued that the African cultural background was insignificant in the United States, that viewpoint receives its most emphatic statement in the work of the black sociologist E. Franklin Frazier: *The Negro in the United States* (rev. ed. New York: Macmillan, 1957); *The Negro Church in America* (New York: Schocken Books, 1964), and *The Negro Family in the United States* (Chicago: University of Chicago Press, 1966). Melville J. Herskovits, an anthropologist, wrote the classic refutation of this position: *The Myth of the Negro Past* (New York: Harper & Brothers, 1941). Most recent scholarship—Blassingame, Rawick, Genovese, Gutman, Levine—follows in the footsteps of Herskovits. On the issue of the survival of African cultural traits I have found useful Daniel J. Crowley, *African Folklore in the New World* (Austin: University of Texas Press, 1977); Roger Bastide, *African Civilization in the New World*, translated by Peter Green (New York: Harper & Row, 1971); Norman E. Whitten, Jr., and John F. Szwed, *Afro-American Anthropology: Contemporary Perspectives* (New York: Free Press, 1970); Vera Rubin, editor, *Caribbean Studies: A Symposium* (Seattle: University of Washington, 1957); Sidney W. Mintz, "Creating Culture in the Americas," *Columbia University Forum* 13 (1970): 4-11; and especially Sidney W. Mintz and Richard Price, *An Anthropological Approach to the Afro-American Past: A Caribbean Perspective*, ISHI Occasional Papers in Social Change, No. 2 (Philadelphia: Institute for the Study of Human Issues, 1976).

For the material culture of slaves I have depended heavily upon John Michael Vlach, *The Afro-American Tradition in Decorative Arts* (Cleveland, Ohio: Cleveland Museum of Art, 1978), and Robert Farris Thompson, "African Influence on the Art of the United States," in Armstead L. Robinson, Craig C. Foster, and Donald H. Ogilvie, editors, *Black Studies in the University: A Symposium* (New Haven, Conn.: Yale University Press, 1969), pp. 128-77. See also Carl Anthony, "The Big House and the Slave Quarters," Parts 1 and 2, *Landscape* 20 (Spring 1976): 8-19 and 21 (Autumn 1976): 9-15; Gary B. Mills, *The Forgotten People: Cane River's Creoles of Color* (Baton Rouge: Louisiana State University Press, 1977); and Richard Price, "Saramaka Woodcarving: The Development of an Afro-American Art," *Man* 5 (September 1970): 363-78.

There are perceptive discussions of slave music in Eugene D. Genovese, *Roll, Jordan, Roll: The World the Slaves Made* (New York: Pantheon Books, 1974); John W. Blassingame, *The Slave Community: Plantation Life in the Ante-Bellum South* (New York: Oxford University Press, 1979); and especially Lawrence W. Levine, *Black Culture and Black Consciousness: Afro-American Folk Thought from Slavery to Freedom* (New York:

Oxford University Press, 1977). Levine's earlier essay, "Slave Songs and Slave Consciousness: An Exploration in Neglected Sources," in Tamara K. Hareven, editor, *Anonymous Americans: Explorations in Nineteenth-Century Social History* (Englewood Cliffs, N.J.: Prentice-Hall, 1971), pp. 99-130, is still invaluable. Dena J. Epstein's *Sinful Tunes and Spirituals: Black Folk Music to the Civil War* (Urbana: University of Illinois Press, 1977) is extremely helpful, particularly in her rich quotes from original sources. Paul A. Cimbala has written on the slave musician as performer: "Fortunate Bondsmen: Black 'Musicianers' and Their Role as an Antebellum Southern Plantation Slave Elite," *Southern Studies* 18 (Fall 1979): 291-303. A good selection of source materials, along with earlier interpretative essays, is in Bernard Katz, *The Social Implications of Early Negro Music in the United States* (New York: Arno Press, 1969). Two wideranging interpretative books useful for placing Afro-American music in a larger context are Eileen Southern, *The Music of Black Americans* (New York: W. W. Norton, 1971), and Bill C. Malone, *Southern Music/American Music* (Lexington: University Press of Kentucky, 1979).

The best analysis of black folktales and beliefs is in the previously cited book by Levine, *Black Culture and Black Consciousness*, though one can still find useful material in Newbell Niles Puckett, *Folk Beliefs of the Southern Negro* (Chapel Hill, N.C.: University of North Carolina Press, 1926). Lyle Saxon, Edward Dreyer, and Robert Tallant, compilers, *Gumbo Ya-Ya* (Cambridge, Mass.: Houghton Mifflin, 1945), should be used with caution. There is much information on American folk beliefs in J. Leitch Wright, Jr., *The Only Land They Knew: The Tragic Story of the American Indian in the Old South* (New York: The Free Press, 1981). Much exaggeration exists regarding voodoo. A useful corrective is Blake Touchstone, "Voodoo in New Orleans," *Louisiana History* 13 (Fall 1972): 371-86. And, as with practically every topic dealing with slavery, much can be learned from John Blassingame's *Slave Community* and Eugene D. Genovese's *Roll, Jordan, Roll*, both previously cited. On the socialization of slaves, see Thomas L. Webber, *Deep Like the Rivers: Education in the Slave Quarter Community, 1831-1865* (New York: W. W. Norton, 1978).

There is an increasingly sophisticated literature on the African religious background of American slaves. I have relied upon the following: Geoffrey Parrinder, *African Traditional Religion* (London: Hutchinson's University Library, 1954); M. Fortes and G. Dieterlen, editors, *African Systems of Thought* (London: Oxford University Press, 1965); John S. Mbiti, *African Religions and Philosophy* (Garden City, N.Y.: Doubleday, 1970); E. Bolaji Idowu, *African Traditional Religion* (Maryknoll, N.Y.: Orbis Books, 1973); Benjamin Ray, *African Religions: Symbols, Ritual, and Community* (Englewood Cliffs, N.J.: Prentice-Hall, 1976); and Dominique Zahan, *The Religion, Spirituality, and Thought of Traditional Africa*, translated by

Kate Ezra Martin and Lawrence M. Martin (Chicago: University of Chicago Press, 1979).

The older scholarship on Afro-American Christianity viewed it simply as an escape mechanism. This interpretation is represented by E. Franklin Frazier's previously cited *Negro Church in America* and Benjamin E. Mays's *The Negro's God as Reflected in His Literature* (Boston: Chapman and Grimes, 1938). More recent studies emphasize how religion gave meaning and purpose to slaves' lives. Eugene D. Genovese has a long and important treatment of slave religious faith in his *Roll, Jordan, Roll*, as do Blassingame in *The Slave Community* and especially Levine, *Black Culture and Black Consciousness*. See also Chapter 5 of Donald G. Mathews, *Religion in the Old South* (Chicago: University of Chicago Press, 1977); Mechal Sobel, *Trabelin' On: The Slave Journey to an Afro-Baptist Faith* (Westport, Conn.: Greenwood Press, 1979); Erskine Clarke, *Wrestlin' Jacob: A Portrait of Religion in the Old South* (Atlanta, Ga.: John Knox Press, 1979). My special emphasis on the biracial aspects of religion in the Old South, suggested in Chapter 5 of John B. Boles, *Religion in Antebellum Kentucky* (Lexington: University Press of Kentucky, 1976), is based on research in manuscript church records and is confirmed by such recent students as David Thomas Bailey, "Slavery and the Churches: The Old Southwest," (Ph.D. dissertation, University of California, Berkeley, 1978), the papers presented by Bailey, Larry James, and Clarence L. Mohr at the Southern Historical Association session entitled "Slaves and 'White' Churches in the Antebellum South," November 13, 1981; and Kenneth K. Bailey's pioneering article, "Protestantism and Afro-Americans in the Old South: Another Look," *Journal of Southern History* 41 (November 1975): 451-72. The best general account of slave religion, though it exaggerates the underground nature of slave worship, is Albert J. Raboteau, *Slave Religion: The 'Invisible Institution' in the Antebellum South* (New York: Oxford University Press, 1978). For the mission to the slaves one should consult Donald Blake Touchstone, "Planters and Slave Religion in the Deep South," (Ph.D. dissertation, Tulane University, 1973) and Donald G. Mathews, "Charles Colcock Jones and the Southern Evangelical Crusade to Form a Biracial Community," *Journal of Southern History* 41 (August 1975): 299-320. I have also been influenced by Timothy L. Smith's important article, "Slavery and Theology: The Emergence of Black Christian Consciousness in Nineteenth-Century America," *Church History* 41 (December 1972): 497-512; and Vincent Harding's "Religion and Resistance Among Antebellum Negroes, 1800-1860," in August Meier and Elliot Rudwick, editors, *The Making of Black America: Essays in Negro Life and History*, 2 volumes (New York: Atheneum, 1969), 1: 179-97. For the role of the slave preacher, see Eugene D. Genovese, "Black Plantation

Preachers in the Slave South," *Louisiana Studies* 11 (Fall 1972): 188-214. Even more than slave religion, the issue of slave rebellion has generated an enormous amount of scholarship, much of it outstanding. Perhaps one should begin with Eugene D. Genovese's *From Rebellion to Revolution: Afro-American Slave Revolts in the Making of the Modern World* (Baton Rouge: Louisiana State University Press, 1979), though Genovese tries too hard to link slave rebellion to European democratic struggles. His book also has an extensive bibliographical essay. My interpretation draws on Genovese and many other accounts, especially Marion Kilson's attempt to classify revolts, "Towards Freedom: An Analysis of Slave Revolts in the United States," *Phylon* 25 (Summer 1964): 175-87; William S. Willis, "Divide and Rule: Red, White, and Black in the Southeast," *Journal of Negro History* 48 (July 1963): 157-76; Edwin A. Miles, "The Mississippi Slave Insurrection Scare of 1835," *Journal of Negro History* 42 (January 1957): 48-60; Jeffrey J. Crow, "Slave Rebelliousness and Social Conflict in North Carolina, 1775 to 1802," *William and Mary Quarterly*, 3d series 37 (January 1980): 79-102; Michael P. Johnson, "Runaway Slaves and the Slave Communities in South Carolina, 1799 to 1830," *ibid.* 38 (July 1981): 418-41; Philip J. Schwarz, "Slave Criminality and the Slave Community: Patterns of Slave Assertiveness in Eighteenth-Century Virginia," paper presented at the Southern Historical Association meeting, November 10, 1978; Dan T. Carter, "The Anatomy of Fear: The Christmas Day Insurrection Scare of 1865," *Journal of Southern History* 42 (August 1976): 345-64; Charles B. Dew, "Black Ironworkers and the Slave Insurrection Panic of 1856," *ibid.* 41 (August 1975): 321-38; and Kenneth M. Stampp's influential essay, "Rebels and Sambos: The Search for the Negro's Personality in Slavery," *ibid.* 37 (August 1975): 367-92.

The best account of the Stono revolt of 1739 is in Peter H. Wood, *Black Majority: Negroes in Colonial South Carolina from 1670 through the Stono Rebellion* (New York: Alfred A. Knopf, 1974); on Gabriel's Revolt of 1800, and general slave resistance, see Gerald W. Mullin's innovative *Flight and Rebellion: Slave Resistance in Eighteenth-Century Virginia* (New York: Oxford University Press, 1972). Richard Wade in "The Vesey Plot: A Reconsideration," *Journal of Southern History* 30 (May 1964): 143-61, minimizes the conspiracy of 1822, but William W. Freehling, *Prelude to Civil War: The Nullification Controversy in South Carolina, 1816-1836* (New York: Harper & Row, 1966) argues, persuasively I think, for the existence of the plot. The most satisfactory account of Nat Turner's rebellion is Stephen B. Oates, *The Fires of Jubilee: Nat Turner's Fierce Rebellion* (New York: Harper & Row, 1975). Richard Price, editor, *Maroon Societies: Rebel Slave Communities in the Americas* (Garden City, N.Y.: Doubleday, 1973), is invaluable. Much of the recent work on slave rebellion is a commentary on the failings of Stanley M. Elkins's provocative analysis in *Slavery: A Problem in American Institutional and Intellectual Life* (Chicago: University of Chicago Press, 1959), wherein he argues that slaves in the United States became infantilized, docile Sambos. See the effective critiques in John W. Blassingame's *Slave Community*, Eugene D. Genovese's *Roll, Jordan, Roll*, and Genovese's essay, "Rebelliousness and Docility in the Negro Slave: A Critique of Elkins' Thesis," *Civil War History* 13 (December 1966): 293-314. Herbert Aptheker, *American Negro Slave Revolts* (New York: Columbia University Press, 1943), goes to the opposite extreme from Elkins but nevertheless contains useful information. Terrence Des Pres, *The Survivor: An Anatomy of Life in the Death Camps* (New York: Oxford University Press, 1976), even though it is not about Negro slavery in the Americas, has informed my understanding of slave culture and rebellion and has shaped my discussion of the slave as a creative agent, not a helpless victim.

7: An Unfinished Ending

For general background to the era of the Civil War there still is no substitute for J. G. Randall and David Donald, *The Civil War and Reconstruction* (Lexington, Mass.: D. C. Heath, 1969), though James M. McPherson's new *Ordeal by Fire: The Civil War and Reconstruction* (New York: Alfred A. Knopf, 1982) is also excellent. The best general history of the Confederacy is Emory M. Thomas, *The Confederate Nation, 1861-1865* (New York: Harper & Row, 1979). There is a definite beginning and ending for the story of blacks in the Civil War. Bell Irvin Wiley's pioneering *Southern Negroes, 1861-1865* (New Haven, Conn.: Yale University Press, 1938) has stood the passage of time extremely well, but it should be supplemented with Leon F. Litwack, *Been in the Storm So Long: The Aftermath of Slavery* (New York: Alfred A. Knopf, 1979), a richly documented book. These two volumes present a vivid portrait of the various ways blacks reacted to war, change, and freedom. This topic has elicited a series of other outstanding studies. For the black military participation, see Benjamin M. Quarles, *The Negro in the Civil War* (Boston: Little, Brown and Company, 1953) and Dudley T. Cornish, *The Sable Arm: Negro Troops in the Union Army, 1861-1865* (New York: W. W. Norton, 1966); for a marvelous account of black life and culture being transformed by freedom, see Willie Lee Rose, *Rehearsal for Reconstruction: The Port Royal Experiment* (Indianapolis, Ind.: Bobbs-Merrill, 1964); for blacks in Confederate Georgia, see Clarence L. Mohr, "Georgia Blacks During Secession and Civil War, 1859-1865," (Ph.D. dissertation, University of Georgia, 1974). Other useful books include Peter Kolchin, *First Freedom: The Response of*

Alabama's Blacks to Emancipation and Reconstruction (Westport, Conn.: Greenwood, 1972); Joel Williamson, *After Slavery: The Negro in South Carolina during Reconstruction, 1861-1877* (Chapel Hill: University of North Carolina Press, 1965); James M. McPherson, *The Negro's Civil War: How American Negroes Felt and Acted during the War for the Union* (New York: Random House, 1965); C. Peter Ripley, *Slaves and Freedmen in Civil War Louisiana* (Baton Rouge: Louisiana State University Press, 1976); and Victor B. Howard, *Black Liberation in Kentucky: Emancipation and Freedom, 1861-1884* (Lexington: University Press of Kentucky, 1983). Two articles and one section of a larger book were particularly useful to me: Leon F. Litwack, "Free at Last," in Tamara K. Hareven, editor, *Anonymous Americans: Explorations in the Nineteenth-Century Social History* (Englewood Cliffs, N.J.: Prentice-Hall, 1971), pp. 131-71; Clarence L. Mohr, "Before Sherman: Georgia Blacks and the Union War Effort, 1861-1864," *Journal of Southern History* 45 (August 1979): 331-52; and Eugene D. Genovese's brilliant section entitled "The Moment of Truth," in his *Roll, Jordan, Roll: The World the Slaves Made* (New York: Pantheon Books, 1974), pp. 97-112. I have also benefited from Robert C. Morris, *Reading, 'Riting, and Reconstruction* (Chicago: University of Chicago Press, 1981).

Of books on Abraham Lincoln there seems to be no end; I have relied on Stephen B. Oates, *With Malice Toward None: The Life of Abraham Lincoln* (New York: Harper & Row, 1977) and especially LaWanda Cox, *Lincoln and Black Freedom: A Study in Presidential Leadership* (Columbia, S.C.: University of South Carolina Press, 1981). Cox's argument should be moderated slightly by George M. Fredrickson, "A Man but Not a Brother: Abraham Lincoln and Racial Equality," *Journal of Southern History* 41 (February 1975): 39-58. The evolution of federal policy toward blacks can be traced in Randall and Donald, *Civil War and Reconstruction* and McPherson, *Ordeal by Fire*, cited earlier, and the following: Herman Belz, *Emancipation and Equal Rights: Politics and Constitutionalism in the Civil War Era* (New York: W. W. Norton, 1978); John Hope Franklin, *The Emancipation Proclamation* (Garden City, N.Y.: Doubleday, 1963); Benjamin M. Quarles, *Lincoln and The Negro* (New York: Oxford University Press, 1962) and especially Louis S. Gerteis, *From Contraband to Freedman: Federal Policy toward Southern Blacks, 1861-1865* (Westport, Conn.: Greenwood, 1973). For perspective George M. Fredrickson's *White Supremacy: A Comparative Study in American and South African History* (New York: Oxford University Press, 1981), is unrivaled.

In many ways the South was unprepared for the changes wrought by the Civil War. This theme is sketched out by Emory M. Thomas in *The Confederacy as a Revolutionary Experience* (Englewood Cliffs, N.J.:

Prentice-Hall, 1971), and made vivid by James L. Roarke, *Masters Without Slaves: Southern Planters in the Civil War and Reconstruction* (New York: W. W. Norton, 1977). Roarke shows how slavery began to crumble in the crucible of wartime pressure; see also Bell Irvin Wiley, "The Movement to Humanize the Institution of Slavery during the Confederacy," *Emory University Quarterly* 5 (1949): 207-220; Clarence L. Mohr, "Race, Religion, and Reform: Slave and White Churches in Late Antebellum and Confederate Georgia," paper presented at the Southern Historical Association meeting, November 13, 1981; and the invaluable work on the South's decision to arm the slaves and free them, Robert F. Durden, *The Gray and the Black: The Confederate Debate on Emancipation* (Baton Rouge: Louisiana State University Press, 1972). Charles P. Roland's *Louisiana Sugar Plantations During the American Civil War* (Leiden: E. J. Brill, 1957) portrays how in one state military necessity and wartime destruction virtually destroyed the slave society. The best depiction of how the war changed the South, the freedmen, and the involved northerners is Lawrence N. Powell's *New Masters: Northern Planters during the Civil War and Reconstruction* (New Haven, Conn.: Yale University Press, 1980); see Janet Sharp Hermann's engaging story of the Davis brothers and Benjamin Montgomery, their former slave overseer: *The Pursuit of a Dream* (New York: Oxford University Press, 1981).

The general histories of Reconstruction all discuss the issue of land redistribution; I have also benefited from Martin Abbott, "Free Land, Free Labor, and the Freedmen's Bureau," *Agricultural History* 30 (October 1956): 150-56; LaWanda Cox, "The Promise of Land for the Freedmen," *Mississippi Valley Historical Review* 45 (December 1958): 413-40; Carol Bleser, *The Promised Land: The History of the South Carolina Land Commission* (Columbia: University of South Carolina Press, 1969); and Claude F. Oubre, *Forty Acres and a Mule: The Freedmen's Bureau and Black Land Ownership* (Baton Rouge: Louisiana University Press, 1978). The material on the Christmas 1865 insurrection panic is drawn from Dan T. Carter, "The Anatomy of Fear: The Christmas Day Insurrection Scare of 1865," *Journal of Southern History* 42 (August 1976): 345-64. For black politicians, see Howard N. Rabinowitz, editor, *Southern Black Leaders of the Reconstruction Era* (Urbana: University of Illinois Press, 1982). The literature on the economic consequences of the Civil War and the emergence of sharecropping is rapidly increasing in size, sophistication, and economic complexity. The best guide to the recent scholarship is Harold D. Woodman, "Sequel to Slavery: The New History Views the Postbellum South," *Journal of Southern History* 43 (November 1977): 523-54. Among the new works I have found useful are Robert Higgs, *Competition and Coercion: Blacks in the American Economy, 1865-1954* (Cam-

bridge: Cambridge University Press, 1977); William Cohen, "Negro In-
voluntary Servitude in the South, 1865-1940: A Preliminary Analysis,"
Journal of Southern History 42 (February 1976): 31-60; Gavin Wright,
"Cotton Competition and the Post-Bellum Recovery of the American
South," *Journal of Economic History* 34 (September 1974): 610-35; Daniel
A. Novak, *The Wheel of Servitude: Black Forced Labor After Slavery*
(Lexington: University Press of Kentucky, 1978); and especially Roger L.
Ransom and Richard Sutch, *One Kind of Freedom: The Economic Conse-
quences of Emancipation* (Cambridge: Cambridge University Press, 1977).
The changes affecting the marketing and credit system are best portrayed
in Harold D. Woodman, *King Cotton and His Retainers: Financing and
Marketing the Cotton Crop of the South, 1800-1925* (Lexington: University
Press of Kentucky, 1968). For many aspects of these topics, see the special
issue, "Agriculture since the Civil War: A Symposium," of *Agricultural
History* 53 (January 1979). The classic work on the post-Reconstruction
South remains of course C. Vann Woodward's *Origins of the New South,
1877-1913* (Baton Rouge: Louisiana State University Press, 1951). His
discussion of the Populist rebellion should be supplemented by Lawrence
Goodwyn, *Democratic Promise: The Populist Moment in America* (New
York: Oxford University Press, 1976).

Index